Studies in Economic Theory

Editors

Charalambos D. Aliprantis
Purdue University
Department of Economics
West Lafayette, IN 47907-1310
USA

Nicholas C. Yannelis
Department of Economics
University of Illinois
Champaign, IL 61820
USA

Springer
Berlin
Heidelberg
New York
Barcelona
Hong Kong
London
Milan
Paris
Singapore
Tokyo

Titles in the Series

M. Ali Khan and Nicholas C. Yannelis (Eds.)
Equilibrium Theory in Infinite Dimensional Spaces

Charalambos D. Aliprantis, Kim C. Border and
Wilhelmus A.J. Luxemburg (Eds.)
Positive Operators, Riesz Spaces, and Economics

Donald G. Saari
Geometry of Voting

Charalambos D. Aliprantis and Kim C. Border
Infinite Dimensional Analysis

Jean-Pierre Aubin
Dynamic Economic Theory

Mordecai Kurz (Ed.)
Endogenous Economic Fluctuations

Jean-François Laslier
Tournament Solutions and Majority Voting

Ahmet Alkan, Charalambos D. Aliprantis and
Nicholas C. Yannelis (Eds.)
Theory and Applications

James C. Moore
Mathematical Methods for Economic Theory 1

James C. Moore
Mathematical Methods for Economic Theory 2

Mukul Majumdar, Tapan Mitra and Kazuo Nishimura
Optimization and Chaos

Katri K. Sieberg
Criminal Dilemmas

Katri K. Sieberg

Criminal Dilemmas
Understanding and Preventing Crime

With 24 Figures

 Springer

Assistant Professor Katri K. Sieberg
The College of William & Mary
Department of Economics
P.O. Box 8795
Williamsburg, VA 23187-8795
USA

ISBN 3-540-67804-2 Springer-Verlag Berlin Heidelberg New York

Library of Congress Cataloging-in-Publication Data applied for
Die Deutsche Bibliothek – CIP-Einheitsaufnahme
Sieberg, Katri K.: Criminal Dilemmas: Understanding and Preventing Crime / Katri K. Sieberg. – Berlin; Heidelberg; New York; Barcelona; Hong Kong; London; Milan; Paris; Singapore; Tokyo: Springer, 2001
  (Studies in Economic Theory; 12)
  ISBN 3-540-67804-2

This work is subject to copyright. All rights are reserved, whether the whole or part of the material is concerned, specifically the rights of translation, reprinting, reuse of illustrations, recitation, broadcasting, reproduction on microfilm or in any other way, and storage in data banks. Duplication of this publication or parts thereof is permitted only under the provisions of the German Copyright Law of September 9, 1965, in its current version, and permission for use must always be obtained from Springer-Verlag. Violations are liable for prosecution under the German Copyright Law.

Springer-Verlag Berlin Heidelberg New York
a member of BertelsmannSpringer Science+Business Media GmbH
http://www.springer.de

© Springer-Verlag Berlin · Heidelberg 2001
Printed in Germany

The use of general descriptive names, registered names, trademarks, etc. in this publication does not imply, even in the absence of a specific statement, that such names are exempt from the relevant protective laws and regulations and therefore free for general use.

Hardcover-Design: Erich Kirchner, Heidelberg

SPIN 10775770   42/2202-5 4 3 2 1 0 – Printed on acid-free paper

Dedicated to Erik Sieberg

Preface

Crime. This single, simple word can invoke a wide spectrum of emotions, opinions, suggestions, and proposals for action. The importance of this one word is highlighted by the prominence politicians devote to crime fighting policies during elections. The public cannot seem to get enough information about crime. This notion is underscored by the fact that, despite the recent widespread decrease in crime, the public's interest and passion in the topic remains high.

Why does such contradictory behavior in society exist? Why do we see an increase in fear over a phenomenon that is reported to be diminishing? Part of the answer lies in the very individual aspect of crime and victimization; *it could happen to you*. The possibility of becoming a victim sharpens our sense of vulnerability. The barrage of stories about heinous crimes committed in supposedly safe communities can cause people to feel less secure in their own. People lock their doors when they never had to before; and even children's' television programs warn, "never talk to strangers."

Adding to the complexity and fear of the issue is the fact that crime is a particularly personal experience. Even something as trivial as pickpocketing or a bicycle stolen from a garage creates a sense of violation. A mugging can leave, with the physical damage, a sense of insecurity. And it is almost impossible to comprehend the toll and mental anguish accompanying a rape or the sexual abuse of one's child. Accounting for the intense damage that can be inflicted upon the victim, it becomes understandable why even a remote possibility of finding oneself in such circumstances can send people crying for tougher laws, harsher penalties, and more visible action.

But is such response productive? As is the case for most situations charged with panic or high emotion, the initial reactions may not be ideal. The notion that crime is a problem is indisputable, but calls to "lock em up and throw away the key" are not necessarily the most prudent and cost effective proposals, and, furthermore, may not serve as a solution at all. This is a principal problem with our approach to crime. Since the issue is so emotional, it is critical to address the problem logically, in the abstract, with as few appeals to sentiments as possible. Unfortunately, what happens is that politicians, with an eye on popularity, may whip up or manipulate already existent public hysteria to win support for their particular policy proposals. Legislative decisions are not necessarily made on what laws will be more efficient in reducing crime, but, rather, in favor of which laws are tougher on criminals.

Tougher versus more efficient - much of the public tends to equate the two tactics, yet it is worthwhile to take the time to investigate whether or not the tougher laws really are more efficient. Initially, this equation seems intuitive; the existence of a criminal population, despite our laws, indicates that current penalties are insufficient to deter crime. For most of us, the threat of the penalty is more than sufficient to discourage criminal behavior. If some citizens are not deterred, then a natural public reaction is to demand an increase in the penalty. Yet, I show that, surprisingly, in many cases this strategy is counterproductive.

Rather than examining these issues from the perspective of a criminologist, politician, or law enforcement agency, the purpose of this book is to consider selective topics associated with crime and punishment from the perspective of basic concepts found in economics, game theory and political science. Since before Gary Becker's 1968 seminal paper, applying economic analysis to crime, economists have argued that their tools are essential in understanding criminal behavior and in evaluating policy. Nonetheless, prescriptions from economics are followed less frequently than are those from other fields. Indeed, as late as 1996, John DiIulio Jr, protested that "criminal justice is a field that needs to be conquered by economists"[1] but that, so far, insufficient contributions by economists had been made and even fewer had been instituted. This absence is unfortunate because economic analysis contributes significantly to the study of crime and criminal behavior. Some arguments explaining this phenomenon state that while potentially useful, the theory can be so complex that the suggestions arising from economics can be difficult to explain and sell to the public. Taking this problem into account, the concepts employed in this text are simple enough so they can be expressed in terms of common sense.

In particular, economics may be used to examine crime, the prevention of crime, and the effectiveness of punishments. This analysis is done in terms of incentives. In the absence of gains to be made from criminal activity, we would expect to see fewer criminals. Once we recognize that criminals stand to benefit from crime, we can attempt to identify means of reducing this gain, or, similarly, of adding to the cost of committing the crime.

The problem may be approached from the perspective of a businessman. This suggestion may sound absurd, but the analogy is appropriate. A businessman bases his or her decisions on the relative costs and gains associated with different lines of action. If a particular activity is likely to produce high costs with lower revenues, then it will probably be abandoned in favor of a more attractive option. It is fair to assume that many criminals use similar reasoning in their decisions to commit crime and in their choices among criminal actions. If we can devise a means of decreasing the gains to be made from a particular criminal activity relative to the costs involved, then we might be able to divert many potential criminals from this line of action. As a similar consideration, if we know that certain tactics can dissuade criminals from specific crimes, then we might wish to determine what would be the appropriate incentives to force a criminal into less violent actions.

Unfortunately, due to the existence of those who, due to some physical or mental inabilities, cannot avoid criminal activity, we know that an ideal world without crime is impossible. Even the best designed incentives will not affect these people, and, unfortunately, such people are not easily identifiable as being prone to criminal activity until *after* they have committed an act. Facing these circumstances, our task is to understand how we might minimize crime in a cost effective way, so that we can maintain some of our social income for expenses such as health, education, roads, and national defense.

---

[1] DiIulio, 1996, 3.

The designated task proposes solving some problem within a budget constraint. This very problem suggests the use of economics. However, as stated, economics results are often ignored in favor of suggestions arising from other fields. Let me elaborate. A serious mistake often made in analyzing the criminal is to treat him or her as sick or irrational. Without question, many criminals do fit into these categories. But, any generalization that applies this criterion to all, or even most, criminals is misleading in two important ways. First, the assumption that offenders are somehow unable to make rational decisions regarding criminal behavior unreasonably limits our proposals to combat crime and can make them counterproductive. If we do not believe that individuals willfully choose to commit crimes, then we are less likely to devise policies that provide disincentives for crime. Instead, policies tend to be reactive - focusing on efforts to arrest and punish the criminal *after* he or she has committed the crime.

This reactive, rather than predictive or deterrent, nature of criminal legislation is exacerbated by a second problem with current criminal analysis. The assumption that all or even most criminal behavior tends to arise due to an illness, social circumstances, poverty, or mental instability creates difficulties in developing predictive policy. Certainly, any of these factors can contribute towards, or even cause, criminal behavior, but we cannot assume that all individuals facing one, or even all, of these problems will commit crimes. Such assumptions would malign a large group of honest, law-abiding people. More seriously, in doing so, our predictive ability is weakened because we cannot predetermine when, where, or by whom, crimes will take place. Instead, we must rely on plans to apprehend criminals in the act or after the fact.

Economic analysis in no way serves as a substitute for established criminological study. Programs that identify and isolate factors that contribute to criminal dispositions are essential in creating policies which can decrease the impact of these factors. Social programs that help the unemployed find work, and efforts to recognize and treat individuals with mental health problems are just two of many projects that help reduce crime in society. However, the contribution of economic and political science teachings are equally as important in developing policy and should not be ignored.

Criminal behavior can be rational economic behavior. I do not commit crimes, and, to my knowledge, people with whom I associate do not do so either. However, we cannot ignore the fact that crime can be a lucrative profession. Consider the decision faced by an inner city youth who can make roughly $6 an hour in a fast food restaurant or who can make $800 a week selling drugs. As needs and wants accumulate, the latter prospect can become more and more attractive. Additionally, as our youth sees friends and family selling drugs to make a living, his or her reluctance to commit crimes may diminish. Clearly, the choices made by the youth are rational cost and benefit calculations, and not the uncontrolled reaction of a sick or irrational being. If this concept is accepted, then we can attempt to devise policies that will alter the costs and benefits such that crime becomes less attractive.

Why use economics, game theory, and political science to analyze crime? These fields correspond closely with the decisions made and the situations confronted by criminals. Economics studies the actions of individuals who are faced with costs, benefits, and risks. Every decision, whether to buy a new TV or to look for a new job, entails some conscious or subconscious calculation of the expected costs and benefits of the action versus those of the status quo. Many criminals make similar evaluations. Since, through economics, we are able to analyze, and sometimes predict, economic behavior, the extension of this methodology to the study of crime could yield insight and answers where previously we had few.

To understand how political science can contribute to our analysis, one area of the field describes an international arena of anarchy, where - due to the lack of a credible international court or police - appropriately designed power and force are essential resources in enforcing agreements and trade contracts. Compare this with the criminal world - also is a lawless world of anarchy in which the police cannot be used for protection or to enforce agreements. There are distinct differences; but the similarities of the situation allow us to borrow techniques through which we can gain insight into criminal activity.

In particular, appealing to concepts and intuition from political science, we can gain an understanding of why the use of force may be so common among criminals as well as insight into what strategies and mechanisms individual, and groups of, criminals develop to cope with the circumstances they face. Knowledge regarding the framework necessary to support criminal activity can be used in attempts to dismantle that framework and undermine the criminals.

By borrowing concepts from fields such as economics and political science, we can draw analogies between criminal behavior, which we do not understand and for which there is little reliable data and analysis, and phenomena in those fields that have been studied and analyzed. If the analogies are appropriate, then we gain a new perspective on the criminal problem, which can be applied to develop solutions.

Game theory adds additional perspective to the criminal dilemma. Through game theory, we learn that if more than one player is involved in a given decision, the outcome will depend on the interaction of *all players'* strategies. Thus, game theoretic analysis allows us to analyze situations in which a player's ideal is unobtainable and to identify "next-best" outcomes. The following two-player game is an example of this situation.

	A	B
A	-1,5	55, -1
B	3,7	0,0

Fig. 0.1

Players' payoffs depend on a combination of each players' strategies, A or B with those of the other player. The payoffs in each cell represent (the row player)

player 1's payoff, to the left of the comma, and (the column player) player 2's payoff to the right. A glance at the payoffs shows that player 1 would prefer the outcome (A,B) in which he obtains his highest payoff, 55. Unfortunately for player 1, player 2 will never play strategy B if 1 plays A, because doing so would give her her lowest payoff, -1. Player 2 would be much better off playing A if player 1 plays A, because she would then receive a payoff of 5. Thus, the outcome (A,B) is not an equilibrium, because player 2 would deviate from it. However, note that if player 1 blindly plays A in hopes of obtaining the payoff of 55, then player 2 will also play A and player 1 will get his *lowest* payoff, -1.

Once player 1 understands that his payoffs depend on player 2's moves, and vice versa, he can find an equilibrium, an outcome from which neither player would deviate unilaterally. This outcome is (B,A) in which player 1 obtains a payoff of 3 and 2 obtains a payoff of 7. For player 1, this payoff is significantly less than the ideal payoff of 55, however it is better than the payoff of –1 that he would obtain if he played A.

This type of understanding is crucial in creating criminal policy. We seek to eliminate problems, such as illicit drug use and prostitution, by making them illegal. Unfortunately, however, in doing so, we may overlook potential strategies of other players (drug dealers or prostitutes) involved. By doing so, we may find ourselves faced with our worst outcome, as depicted in the example above.

To Commit or not to Commit

The advantage to using concepts such as costs and benefits is that we do not have to isolate the individual likely to commit the crime in order to suggest preventative policies. Instead, the emphasis now is placed on determining what factors can discourage crime in society, *in general*. Once these components are highlighted, attempts can be made to institute them in a manner that criminal activity becomes less attractive.

The use of cost/benefit analysis suggests that one potential for deterring this activity is to raise the expected costs of committing a crime. This tactic can be accomplished in numerous ways. We can increase the probability of arrest and conviction, and we can increase the penalty imposed if arrested. Similarly, we, the general public, can make crime more difficult or expensive to commit by using more security measures: locking doors, using burglar alarms and lights, etc.

This economic form of reasoning has been fruitful in understanding and deterring criminal behavior; however, in some cases even our best efforts have failed to stop crime. Rather than accept these failures as an indication that economics is inappropriate, I contend that, in our evaluation of criminal behavior, we probably overlook certain factors that can influence a criminal's decision.

For example, despite increased police presence and recent increases in mandatory sentences for crime, we continue to see gang members committing serious offenses. Does this behavior indicate that these people are irrational or unaffected by deterrent efforts? Not necessarily; this assumption ignores crucial factors that affect gang members.

What are these factors? The police and the courts insist upon obedience to certain rules. But the gangs do likewise. Frequently the two sets of rules are in conflict with one another. A member's decision regarding the costs and benefits to criminal activity must include not only the probability of arrest and punishment if caught committing a crime, but also the probability of detection and penalty from the gang if caught avoiding the assigned crime.[2] If the drawbacks to the latter are greater, then the member would be better off fulfilling his or her duties and committing the crime. Thus, by taking a fuller account of the factors that influence decisions, we realize that what may appear to be irrational behavior could, instead, be rational, calculating activity.

Economic, political science, and game theoretic tools can incorporate these factors into an analysis. Ironically, one of the tools used frequently in this book is known as the Prisoner's Dilemma. The game is aptly named, for it is useful in combating, as well as analyzing, criminal activity. Most of us have seen the tactics involved in the game used in television shows or movies. Two criminals are apprehended for a crime that they have committed together. The police separate them so that they cannot communicate and give each of them the same proposal: If both refuse to confess, they will be charged with a petty crime and will serve 3 years in prison. If one confesses while the other does not, then the confessor is free and the other receives a sentence of 10 years. If both confess, they both receive 5 years in prison. Each offender ranks the outcomes as follows:

I confess/he doesn't: 0 years in prison = **4** Best option
Neither of us confess: 3 years in prison = **3**
Both of us confess: 5 years in prison = **2**
He confesses/I don't: 10 years in prison = **1** Worst option

Both players know their best options, and both are aware that they have to consider not only their own decisions, but also those of the other player. A convenient way to capture all of this information is to represent the decision problem in a matrix:

	Confess	Don't Confess
Confess	2,2	4,1
Don't Confess	1,4	3,3

Fig. 0.2

For simplicity, I refer to the players as Row and Column. The cells represent the terms of the offer given above. For instance, if both Row and Column confess, then this outcome is found in the cell on the table corresponding with Confess/Confess. In this cell, Row's payoff, to the left of the comma, is 2 and Column's payoff, to the right, is also 2. So if both players confess, they both receive their second lowest

---

[2] The issue of membership duties is addressed in Chapter 5.

payoff. Moving along the same line in the table, if Row confesses but Column does not then Row receives 4, his best outcome, while Column receives 1, his worst. On the next line of the table, if Row does not confess, but Column does, then Row receives a payoff of 1, his worst payoff, while Column receives his best, 4. If neither confesses, they both receive their second highest payoff, 3.

Comparing payoffs between the strategies, it becomes clear that because they cannot coordinate strategies, each player is always better off confessing, regardless of what the other player does. To demonstrate this assertion, compare the payoffs for the Row player. If Column confesses, then Row has two choices, either to confess or not. The strategy of confess will yield a payoff of rank 2 (or 5 years in prison), whereas not doing so will yield rank 1 (or 10 years in prison) for Row, the worst payoff. So if the Column player chooses to confess, then Row would be better off doing so also.

Now if Column chooses not to confess, compare Row's payoffs from the two strategies again. If Row confesses, then he receives a payoff rank of 4 (no prison time). If he does not do so, then he receives 3 (3 years in prison). No time in prison is preferable to 3 years behind bars, so, once again, Row is better off confessing. Since Column's payoffs are symmetrical, both players have an incentive to confess, which is what the police want, and both receive their second worst payoff. Despite the fact that both players *together* would be better off cooperating with one another by refusing to confess (receiving 3 years in prison), the incentives built into the system are such that each is better off *individually* confessing, and earning 5 years behind bars.

The game creates a negative message - cooperation is impossible. However, if the game is repeated, then other possibilities besides the "trap" emerge. To develop intuition, consider a cheapskate who is considering whether or not to tip his waitress. If he does not intend to return to the restaurant, then he can leave without giving a tip, and he will not have to worry about encountering her in the future. But if he does intend to return, then his decision regarding the tip becomes more important. If he neglects to tip the waitress and she serves him again, then he risks lousy service in the future (at best!) If he does tip her, then she may be more likely to provide him with good, or even improved service. The waitress faces similar concerns. If she provides a customer with slow or otherwise undesirable service, then the customer has the option of retaliating by withholding her tip. Thus, repeated interaction can affect strategies. If people are aware that there is some possibility that they might interact with one another in the future, then they might be more reluctant to betray one another, for fear of retaliation. Thus, cooperation with one another can be achieved.

With this knowledge, it becomes clear that the Prisoner's Dilemma game can used for more purposes than outsmarting felons. The logic found in the model is appropriate to apply to a wide range of concerns, ranging from pollution control, or cooperation in business deals, to international arms reduction treaties. In each case, mutual cooperation is necessary, but monitoring of one another's activities can range from difficult to impossible. Players risk the trap, but can avoid it with repeated interaction.

This same intuition and analysis can be applied to criminal activity. In many crimes, such as drug dealing and prostitution, cooperation between the criminal and the customer is necessary. However, because the activities are criminal, neither party (criminal nor customer) can appeal to the authorities in situations where he or she has met the terms of an agreement but the other has cheated (refused payment, refused goods, or refused services). In this case, the players may find themselves in a Prisoner's Dilemma. This type of reasoning plays an important role in my analysis of prostitution, drug dealing, and gang activity.

Appealing to the intuition from the model, an understanding emerges of the likely actions of the players. More specifically, predictions can be made as to when we should expect to see cooperation, and what alternative mechanisms may be developed in cases when cooperation is unlikely in the absence of enforcement. So, by the use of this simple tool, a large amount of information emerges about problems that were previously difficult to understand.

In fact, one of the surprises in this analysis is how these tools apply to a variety of topics. The reader will find that the same models have applications in subjects as diverse as prostitution, drug dealing, and extortion. The abstract power of this analysis is manifested by the way the same tools illuminate issues in different problems and allow us to develop similar insights. Thus, the field of crime develops from a collection of subjects that appeared only weakly related to a more coherent, cohesive topic in which intuition from one section can be applied to analyze another.

This brief summary of contributions from economics, political science, and game theory demonstrates that these fields do, indeed, provide tools that are critical in any analysis of crime. These are the kinds of models I use in the book. In the first chapter, cost benefit analyses, combined with evaluation of incentives behind criminal activity are used to compare prison sentencing to the use of alternative sentencing for nonviolent criminals. In the second chapter, similar tools are applied to understand drawbacks to the private prison industry. The third and fourth chapters address the difficult issues of prostitution and drugs. These chapters employ a combination of economics, game theory, and political science to explore situations, similar to the game in figure 0.1, in which the social ideal may be impossible to obtain. Chapter 5 explores the strategies, goals, and constraints of gangs and of their members. In Chapter 6, the emotional subject of gun control is analyzed. Arguments regarding the potential problems and benefits to open and concealed weapons laws are considered through an economic and game theoretic framework. The common theme in each of these chapters is that the tools of economics, game theory, and political science extend our understanding, and thereby our means of contending with, criminal dilemmas.

The analysis was done in the abstract, with little appeal to emotion. Subsequently, some of the proposals offered here may be unappealing, or even unacceptable to some people. I found this personally to be the case. Yet, having scrutinized the competing strategies, the proposals given in this book are the ones which appear theoretically most likely to minimize the total cost of crime.

The social cost of crime is overwhelming. The price includes the loss, pain, and suffering of the victims; funding for the police, court costs, and the cost of incarceration. To reduce this loss, we cannot afford to yield to emotions; we need straightforward and logical policy. The fields of economics, political science, and game theory can contribute significantly towards the development of this type of policy.

I would like to thank Professor Åke Andersson and the Institutet fur Framtiddstudier in Stockholm, Sweden for their encouragement and financial support for this research. I am grateful to the departments of Government and Economics at the College of William and Mary for giving me the opportunity to teach this subject as a seminar. I am also grateful to the participants in these seminars in 2000 and 2001 for their enthusiasm, comments and suggestions. Thanks also go to Roko Aliprantis for his interest and encouragement, to Carl Moody for his suggestions, and to Jonathan Kajeckas for his technical assistance. I would like to express my profound gratitude to my family for their support, tolerance, and encouragement during the research, writing, and rewriting of this book!

Katri Sieberg
College of William and Mary
Williamsburg, VA 23187
April, 2001

Contents

Chapter 1 Alternative Sentencing 1
   1.1 Prisons 8
      1.1.1 Retribution 8
      1.1.2 Rehabilitation 10
      1.1.3 Deterrence 13
   1.2 Protection of the Public 14
      1.2.1 Violent Crime and Sex Predators 15
         1.2.1.1 Recidivism and Violence 15
         1.2.1.2 Sex Offenders 16
         1.2.1.3 Incapacitation 19
      1.2.2 Criticisms 20
         1.2.2.1 Three Strikes 21
         1.2.2.2 Alternative Sentencing 25
      1.2.3 Victim Compensation 25
         1.2.3.1 Victim Model 27
         1.2.3.2 Benefits 29
         1.2.3.3 Compensation 30
         1.2.3.4 Pain and Suffering 31
      1.2.4 Alternative Sentencing - Fitting the Crime 32
   1.3 Conclusion 33

Chapter 2 Private Prisons 35
   2.1 Privatization Vs Public Service 35
      2.1.1 Positive Side 36
      2.1.2 Drawbacks 38
   2.2 Power and Money: Expanding Imprisonment and Profit 43
   2.3 Conclusion 45

Chapter 3 Prostitution 47
   3.1 Victimless Crime 47
      3.1.1 Why is Prostitution Illegal? 47
         3.1.1.1 Prostitutes 49
      3.1.2 Disease 50
      3.1.3 Drugs 53
      3.1.4 Crime and Violence 53
   3.2 The Economics of Prostitution 54
      3.2.1 Results 59
   3.3 Consequences and Costs of Hiding 59
   3.4 Pimps for Illegal Prostitution 61
      3.4.1 Anti-Pimping Laws 63
      3.4.2 Pimp Model 63
   3.5 Unilateral Legalization 68
   3.6 Conclusion 68
      3.6.1 Policy 69
         3.6.1.1 Limited Control 70

  3.6.2 Regulation 71
Chapter 4 Drugs 73
 4.1 Introduction 73
  4.1.1 The Ailment 73
  4.1.2 The Cure 74
 4.2 Illegal Versus Legal Drugs 75
  4.2.1 Illegal 75
   4.2.1.1 Hidden but Available 76
  4.2.2 Legal 78
 4.3 Supply Versus Demand 79
  4.3.1 Demand 79
  4.3.2 Supply 81
  4.3.3 Illegal Drugs - Negative Effects 82
   4.3.3.1 Quality 83
   4.3.3.2 Youth 84
 4.4 Violence 85
  4.4.1 Anti-Competitive Strategies 86
   4.4.1.1 Legal Behavior 87
   4.4.1.2 Criminal Behavior 89
   4.4.1.3 Organization 90
  4.4.2 Anarchy 92
   4.4.2.1 Contracts 93
   4.4.2.2 Informal Mechanisms 94
   4.4.2.3 Employee Relations 94
   4.4.2.4 The Cure? 95
 4.5 Legalization 96
  4.5.1 Undercutting the Black Market 96
  4.5.2 Experimentation 96
  4.5.3 Addiction Control 97
   4.5.3.1 Inelastic Demand 97
  4.5.4 Control 99
  4.5.5 Resources 101
 4.6 Legal -The Zurich Problem 102
  4.6.1 Voting With One's Feet 103
  4.6.2 International Prisoners' Dilemma 104
 4.7 Conclusion 105
Chapter 5 Gangs 107
 5.1 Motivations for Membership 108
  5.1.1 Structure 109
  5.1.2 Protection in Numbers 110
  5.1.3 Economics 115
 5.2 Extortion Model 115
 5.3 Job Search and the Market for Crime 121
 5.4 Conclusion 122

Chapter 6 Gun Control 125
    6.1 Introduction 125
    6.2 Gun Control 126
    6.3 The Right to Bear Arms 129
        6.3.1 The Criminals Have Guns 129
        6.3.2 Guns for Self Defense 130
        6.3.3 Firearm Accidents 134
        6.3.4 Information 134
        6.3.5 Black Market 135
            6.3.5.1 Buyers 136
    6.4 Deterrence 138
        6.4.1 Rural Versus Urban Characteristics 138
        6.4.2 Deterrence - the Fear of Armed Victims 141
        6.4.3 Open and Concealed Weapons 142
    6.5 Model 144
        6.5.1 Reputation: The Chain Store Paradox 146
        6.5.2 Massacres 149
    6.6 Statistics 150
        6.6.1 Accidental Deaths 153
        6.6.2 Gun Control 154
        6.6.3 Summary and Problems 154
    6.7 Implications and Suggestions 155
        6.7.1 Training 155
        6.7.2 Waiting Periods 157
        6.7.3 Safeguards 158
        6.7.4 Penalties 159
        6.7.5 Caveat 160
    6.8 Conclusion 161
Chapter 7 Bibliography 163
Chapter 8 Index 179

Chapter 1

Alternative Sentencing

The existence of the prison system is such a familiar part of society, that its use as a primary form of punishment is largely taken for granted. Indeed, recent efforts to "get tough on crime" have lead to a massive expansion of the corrections system. Mandatory sentencing policies have been imposed as a means of avoiding leniency or potential inconsistencies in judges' rulings. These policies dictate sentence lengths for all crimes, from that of drug possession to homicide. This no-nonsense approach, coupled with an increase in severity is meant to send the message to criminals that crime does not pay!

However, the criminals do not appear to receive the message as intended. Despite the lauded decrease in crime, an overwhelming number of offenses are committed in the U.S. (11.6 million crime index offenses reported in 1999 alone.) These figures suggest that the deterrent effect of prison sentencing is largely a failure.[3]

One of the themes in this book is that prisons should *not* be used to punish all crimes. Instead, I argue that there are a number of reasons why alternative sentences should be used to punish non-violent criminals.[4] For a preview, recall the well-documented fact that prisons are overcrowded and their resources could be put to better use in other areas of society. Prisons tend to serve as training grounds for criminals and have been relatively ineffective in terms of rehabilitation. On the other hand, having to face the victim and make repayments and/or reparations can make the criminal more accountable for his crime. In other words, the notion explored here is that the punishment should fit the crime - more serious crimes should receive more severe penalties, and the penalties should be distinct from one another.

Appealing to concepts from economics, I examine the choices that face criminals and depict how differential forms of sentencing may alter these choices. As we do with our personal decisions, most criminals make decisions based on what line of action appears most promising. Unfortunately, for some, the costs and risks of criminal activity are insufficient to outweigh the potential gains. Even more unfortunately, some criminals perceive the use of violence as a tool both for obtaining their goals and for avoiding penalty. Our task, then is not only to increase

---

[3] (U.S Dept of Justice, Uniform Crime Report, 2000). In theory, an increase in prison population should decrease crime, however, critics, such as John DiIulio Jr. have attributed the recent decrease in crime to factors other than the corrections system. There is a smaller population in the age cohort that generally commits the majority of crimes; the price of illegal drugs has decreased; and many of the wars over drug territory have been resolved. These are just some of the factors perceived as responsible for the decrease in crime.

[4] The proposal to use alternative sentences for nonviolent crimes is not new. The National Council on Crime and Delinquency recommended expanded use of these options in order to reserve prison space for violent offenders, repeat offenders, and felons who had substantially violated the public trust. (Wolf and Weissman, 1996, 193).

the costs to the criminal associated with all crimes, but also to provide a deterrent to the use of violence. Using simple cost/benefit analysis, I argue that a hybrid policy of incarceration of violent criminals and alternative sentencing for nonviolent criminals is a reasonable means of meeting this task.

To begin, it is helpful to explore the economic background for deterrence. Economists start with the basic assumption that criminals make rational decisions regarding whether or not to commit a given crime. In each case, a criminal weighs the potential gains from the crime against possible costs (typically probability of arrest and severity of punishment) to derive an expected value of committing the crime.

$$EV(C) = p(X-A) + (1-p)X \qquad (1)$$

To explain these terms, in this very simple model, the criminal must calculate her expected value, (EV(C)) of committing a crime, C. To make this calculation, she would evaluate the lottery over the expected gains from the crime, X, given a probability of arrest, p, and a punishment if arrested, A.

This decision may be illustrated with an example of a choice commonly faced by most of us. Frequently, we must decide whether or not to put money – say a quarter - in a parking meter. The gain from not paying is $0.25 if you get away with it, but the risk involves a possible penalty of $10 if you are caught. Using this equation, your expected value of the crime of not paying for parking would be:

$$EV(C) = p(.25-10) + (1-p)(.25)$$

In contrast, the expected value of paying for the parking (EV(NC)) would be:

$$EV(NC) = -.25$$

In order for you to be willing to take this risk, the expected value of not paying must exceed that of paying. For this to occur, it must be the case that

$$p(.25-10) + (1-p)(.25) > -.25$$

or that the probability of getting a ticket must be less than .05. Thus, if you suspect that there is at least a 5% chance of the meter being checked before you return to your car, you will be unwilling to take the risk.

Now, return to the criminal. If the expected value – given the risk – exceeds what the individual would obtain by not committing the crime (here we could say EV(NC)= w, where w represents the legal wage obtainable by the criminal), then she will commit the crime. In other words, there is an economic incentive to commit the crime if:

$$EV(C) = p(X-A) + (1-p)X > EV(NC) = w \qquad (2)$$

The model is overly simplistic,[5] however, it does highlight variables of interest in terms of deterrence. These variables are the probability of arrest, p, and the severity of punishment, A. It is easy to see that if the probability of arrest and/or the severity of punishment were to increase, then, at a certain point, the inequality would reverse and the criminal would be better off avoiding crime. For instance, returning to the parking meter example, if the area is swamped with enforcement, so that the probability of a ticket is roughly 50%, then the expected value of the decision to avoid paying for parking would be a loss equal to:

$$EV(C) = .5(.25-10) + .5(.25) = -4.75.$$

Similarly, if the penalty were increased to $30, rather than $10, then the only way in which not paying for parking would be more profitable would be if the probability of getting a ticket were less than .017.

These results have obvious policy implications. Indeed, there has been a significant amount of research investigating the question of which variable, the probability of arrest or the severity of punishment, has a greater deterrent impact on the criminal's decision.[6]

For our purposes, however, the above model ignores our concern with violence. The model yields a "one size fits all" approach to the issue of crime, in which all crimes are fought with the same set of tools. All crimes are not equal, however. Statistics show that people fear violent crime more than other types.[7] If this is the case, then perhaps we should reassess our criminal policies to determine whether different techniques would be more appropriate in terms of fighting and deterring violent crime in particular.

To explore these concerns, consider the following simple model that demonstrates the argument for the use of alternative sentencing. The idea is to extend our intuition about how a criminal might make decisions into more than two dimensions. For example, consistent with the above equation, criminology tells us that at a certain probability of arrest, a given number of people will choose to commit a crime. This means that if the probability of arrest, P(arrest), is fixed at a value p*, then some number of people, N, will find it profitable to commit a crime. This suggestion is graphically represented as follows.

---

[5] The model does not take into account allocation between legal and illegal activity, labor costs, risk of injury, or other factors. For examples of more realistic extensions of the model, (see Becker, 1974, Heineke, 1978, and Stigler, 1988.)

[6] See, for example, Becker, 1968, Mendes and McDonald, 1999.

[7] See Rubin, 1998.

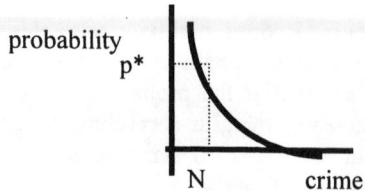

Fig. 1.1

Roughly, the above curve represents the sense that as the probability of arrest increases, more people will be deterred from crime, whereas as the probability decreases, fewer people will be deterred, and more crimes will be committed. Most approaches start with these assumptions and manipulate p (and severity of punishment) to achieve a point along the curve that is socially acceptable.[8]

To differentiate between violent and nonviolent crimes, extend this argument into three dimensions by dividing the number, N, of crimes, into those people who will commit a violent crime and those who will commit a non-violent crime. (This approach can be compared to the example that, at any given income level, a fixed number of people will vote, but some will vote Democrat and some Republican.) There can be more than two possibilities; a criminal, for instance, could choose among infinite levels of violence in order to achieve his gains, but for the sake of simplicity, here we narrow it down to two.

Fig. 1.2

The notion we want to pursue is whether a policy that targets violent criminals for a harsher punishment than non-violent ones (i.e. prison time with work[9] versus an enforced work program with probation) might sway some of those

---

[8] Of course, we would prefer to have as little crime as possible, but crime fighting and punishment are costly. Joan Petersilia notes that current prison and enforcement expenditures in California are so high that they have significantly reduced the number of funds available for education. (Petersilia, 1999) In order to achieve a balance between crime fighting and other social expenditures, a society must select a level of crime that is "acceptable."

[9] The inclusion of work in the prison sentence is crucial. In order to be a deterrent, prison time must not be easier than the alternative sentence; otherwise we risk obtaining a result that is opposite to the one intended - offenders committing violent crimes in order to avoid the labor involved in the alternative sentence.

who will commit these heinous crimes towards non-violent ones. We would, of course, prefer a crime-free environment, but in the spirit of realism, let's examine incentives and policies that might lead toward the more acceptable of two evils. The important aspect of this analysis is that the criminal has an element of control in his own differentiation.

For simplicity, fix both the probability of arrest and the number of people willing to commit a crime at this level. Again, consider a criminal making a decision based on potential gains. If the expected gains from a certain criminal activity outweigh the possible losses, then the criminal will take the risk. This decision making process can be modeled as follows. The criminal has a choice between the following outcomes: at a probability p*, he or she will be arrested and either punished with jail time, J, or with an alternative sentence, A. At this preliminary stage of the analysis, we will not be concerned with the particulars of the alternative sentence. Instead, it suffices to imagine that we will create circumstances such that that jail time is worse than an alternative sentence, J<A.

In order to create a deterrent, the government must ensure that most criminals are not enamored with violence, but rather they are interested in personal gain. This means they would prefer to commit a non-violent crime and possibly pay the consequences than to risk doing jail time, regardless of the satisfaction, S, or payoff allotted to the different types of crime. In economic terms we want:

$$p^*(A) + (1-p^*)(S_{NV}) > p^*(J) + (1-p^*)(S_V) \qquad (3)$$

where S_{NV} is the payoff from a non-violent crime, and S_V is the payoff from a violent crime.

This equation is a simple extension of the previous model; however, it makes an interesting contribution. This new model makes a careful distinction between two types of crime, and punishes the criminal for these types accordingly. The equation specifies two types of punishment, one for nonviolent crime and one for violent crime, and it creates a situation in which the punishment for violent crime is worse than for that of a nonviolent crime. The selection in levels of punishment is chosen so that, for the criminal, the likelihood of getting caught and serving an alternative sentence for a nonviolent crime, $p^*(A)$, plus the chance of avoiding apprehension and enjoying the fruits of the nonviolent crime, $(1-p^*)(S_{NV})$, are preferred to the tradeoff between possibly serving a jail sentence - that includes work - for violent crime $p^*(J)$, and the chance of freely enjoying the presumably greater rewards from a violent crime $(1-p^*)(S_V)$.

Now that we understand what the equation means, let's examine some consequences. First, if we have a blind "let them rot in jail" attitude about all types of crimes, then the punishment level, A and J are essentially the same. If there is not much difference between the levels A and J, then a criminal may be better off seeking the rewards from a violent crime.

For example, consider the decision faced by a robber who has encountered a witness to his crime. The robber knows that he could receive a sentence of 10 years for his crime and one of roughly an additional 5.9 years for murder. The robber also knows that if he allows the witness to live, then there is a high probability that he will be apprehended. If the robber is contemplating the potential benefits of killing the witness to his crime in an attempt to silence him and avoid the original sentence, then the threat of an additional 5.9 years in prison for murder may not be a large enough deterrent. In economic terms, the robber's decision is as follows:

$$EU(M) = p(X - 15.9Y) + (1-p)X$$

$$EU(NM) = q(X - 10Y) + (1-q)X$$

In this case, the expected utility[10] of murdering the witness, M, takes into account the probability of arrest, p, the gains from the robbery, X, and the amount of time in jail multiplied by a variable, Y, that accounts for the utility of serving time in jail. The expected utility of not murdering the witness, NM, uses the same variables, where q is the probability of arrest. Given that there is a witness to the crime, we can assume that q is much larger than p. If the robber believes that q is close to 1 and that p is relatively low, then he may choose to murder the witness in order to achieve the higher expected utility. So we see that if we keep the levels of punishment for the two types of crime similar, then we are not discouraging criminals from committing violent crimes. In fact, we may be doing the opposite.

The above analogy gives us the sense that appropriately setting the different levels of punishment can be a valuable tool. The following examples demonstrate the effect that these variables can attain.

1. **A=J**: Imagine the likelihood of a criminal's arrest is 60 %, (.6). Further imagine that a criminal can earn $700 in one day from nonviolent drug dealing, but that she can earn $1,000 if she were to kill one or two of her competitors. The decision she faces is, given the chance of being arrested and paying a penalty, should she engage in violence or not?
The expected payoffs for the various types of crime are:

Nonviolent = .6(A) + .4(700)
Violent = .6(J) + .4(1,000)

Since A=J, the difference becomes:

.6(A) + 280 < .6(A) + 400,

and the criminal will choose to take the risks involved with violent crime.

---

[10] This equation assumes that the criminal is risk neutral. Becker (1968), among others, has argued that criminals are risk preferring. Others (Mendes and McDonald, 2000) have claimed that this assumption is unwarranted. For simplicity, I will assume risk neutrality.

2. A < J: If our criminal faces the same circumstances as above except for the fact that the penalty for a violent crime is now 10 times worse than for a nonviolent crime, $J = 10A$, the decision may be altered:

Nonviolent = $.6A + 280$
Violent = $.6(10A) + 400$

It can be difficult to find a monetary equivalent for a sentence such as community work or jail time with labor, but for simplicity, we can assume that A is roughly equivalent to a fine of $100 and, correspondingly, J is equal to a fine of $1,000. If this is the case, then the choice is:

Nonviolent = $-60 + 280 = 220$
Violent = $-600 + 400 = -200$

The payoff to violent crime is not only significantly lower than that for nonviolent crime, but by being negative, it is counterproductive. Our criminal will be better off abstaining from violence.[11]

There are several conceptual advantages to this approach. One of the functions of law enforcement and prison/punishment is for protection of the public. If we understand that we cannot eliminate all of crime, then we should attempt to minimize its cost. By using the above model, we can attempt to create policy so that we can at least influence the criminals' actions in a more desirable direction.

Current policy, perhaps in a sensitive reaction to expressions from the general public, does little to differentiate between violent and non-violent crimes.[12] Additionally, alternative sentencing, if proposed, is suggested most often as a relief for the overcrowding of prisons, and is as likely to include violent criminals as non-violent ones. Due to this inclusion, the public is exposed to violent criminals through the use of alternative sentencing, and the system does not accomplish its role of protecting the public. The following section examines current corrections policy. The analysis scrutinizes perceived goals and objectives to determine whether these goals are met, or if other policies would be superior.

---

[11] It is also possible to show that if we change the probabilities of arrest for the various types of crime, we can have a similar effect. Because much of law enforcement and arrest is reactive, rather than predictive, however, this type of policy is more difficult to implement.

[12] Wolf and Weissman (1996, 202) criticize the system by stating that "In light of the obvious fiscal benefits, the barriers to enacting [alternative sentencing] reforms are in essence political: proposing expanded alternative options implies leniency in a system that focuses on punishment and views imprisonment as the primary means of achieving social control."

1.1 Prisons

The role of prisons has been given various purposes. Among the goals, prisons are ideally intended to provide: retribution, rehabilitation, deterrence, and protection of the public. Arguably, and unfortunately, most prisons have not met these objectives.

1.1.1 Retribution

The goal of retribution may be contrasted with that of revenge in that retribution is also an attempt to make the criminal *accountable* for the crime. Many critiques of the prison system argue that a prison sentence does little to make the criminal accountable for his or her crime. Consider what happens: the average prisoner spends 23 hours a day, locked in a cell. The person is not forced to come into any contact with the victim of the crime, nor to compensate that victim. A typical prison sentence does not involve labor. The punishment is a restriction of freedom for a limited time. Arguably, this type of sentence does little in the form of retribution. Instead, by the defective sense of punishment replacing a forced revaluation of why the criminal is in prison, we can easily imagine how such a jail term ends up contradicting societal goals. We can envision bitterness rather than reflection, and thoughts of revenge rather than reform.

How could we improve this situation? An alternative sentence, in contrast, in which a criminal is forced to confront his or her victim and repay or make repairs for the crime committed more readily fulfils the goal of retribution. Not only must the criminal provide restitution for the crime, but he or she must also face the person who has been wronged. One can imagine that, if done properly, this sort of confrontation can make a criminal more accountable for his or her acts.

It is not difficult to construct a counter-argument; namely that the loss of freedom associated with a prison sentence is a harsher form of punishment than is some alternative sentence. Moreover, the latter allows the criminal to "get off easy." If this is indeed the case, then why should we coddle the wrong-doer? Evidence from recent studies, however, shows that this tradeoff, this "leniency" towards nonviolent criminals, is not borne out. Instead the surprising fact is that given a choice between prison and community sentencing, 7 out of 10 offenders chose prison. Why? Because it was easier.[13]

Many readers might find this assertion to be absurd. How could a prison term be easier? But consider the fact that, for many of the convicted, prison is less onerous than the force of dealing with the victim who, formerly, might have been anonymous.[14] When we additionally consider the fact that most prison sentences do not involve labor, then the prison sentence begins to appear more lenient.

---

[13] *The Economist*, 1/20/96, 55.

[14] As a very simple analogy, a typical punishment imposed upon a child who has been caught stealing is to force that child to return the goods and to admit his or her misdeed to the victim. The humiliation this punishment entails frequently serves as a deterrent against any future crimes of this type.

It is this kind of evidence about attitudes that leads many to refer, either correctly or wrongly, to prisons as country clubs. Critics claim that the leisure of prison, combined with privileges such as access to weights and unlimited phone use, as well as cable television, compact disc players, stereos, and computers in a prisoner's cell,[15] have diminished the punitive effect of prison, and have hampered officials in bringing about retribution.

> "...[W]e want to make prisons a place you don't want to go to,"[Mississippi State Representative] Smith said.
> "It used to be you'd pick cotton, and people weren't too crazy about going to prison. Nowadays, if you want to lead a life of luxury, sit around and watch TV, you can go to prison."[16]

Given the differential effects of the two forms of punishment in the case of retribution alone, it is hard to argue that a prison sentence is more effective or worthwhile. Now, factor in our personal costs as taxpayers. When we do so, we realize that, when the costs of prison versus that of community sentencing are compared, a prison sentence, particularly in the case of a nonviolent criminal, becomes even more difficult to support. In 1996, it cost on average $25,000 a year to house one offender in a state prison. In contrast, state governments spent only $200 a year per probationer.[17] We are forced to a natural conclusion: If prison sentences are not meeting the prescribed goals, then they are not arguably worth the additional expense.

The issue of social cost yields an economic argument for the use of alternative sentencing. All crimes impose a cost upon society. The levels of the cost vary with the crime and may include harm, fear, and destruction of property among other elements. Our current tactic to reduce these costs is to increase enforcement (to increase probability of arrest) and to increase prison time (to increase severity of punishment). Both of these tools are extremely costly to society. The overall effect is that crime and crime fighting, combined, involve a net loss to society. The argument supporting this activity is that if we reduce expenditures on crime fighting, we will suffer higher costs due to crime. In effect, social policy involves an attempt to find a balance.

$$\text{Min } p \; SC(p,N) = C(p,A,N) + E(p,N) + P(A,N)$$

We seek to minimize social cost of crime, SC. This cost is computed by combining the following costs. The first costs entails the loss due to crime, C, which is affected by the number of crimes, N and inversely affected by the probability of arrest, p, and the severity of punishment. The next cost, A; is the expense due to enforcement, E, which increases with any increase in the probability of arrest, p, or in the number of crimes, N. Finally, the cost of

---

[15] Gavzer, 1995, 6.
[16] Nossiter, 1994, 11.
[17] Butterfield, 1995, 6.

punishment, P, increases with any increase in the probability of arrest, p, or in the severity of punishment, A. In economic terms, we seek to find the point where the marginal cost of crime fighting equals the marginal utility of crime reduction.

An alternative sentencing policy offers a reduction in social cost. The logic is simple. Every crime imposes a cost on society. Every nonviolent criminal who serves an alternative sentence must repair damages to the victim. Although part of the cost of crime cannot be repaid (fear and anger may remain), alternative sentencing serves to reduce part of the net cost of crime to society. Furthermore, as stated above, alternative sentencing is less expensive than are prison sentences. Thus, alternative sentencing reduces the cost of crime and crime fighting to society.

1.1.2 Rehabilitation

If prisons fail in terms of retribution, they do even worse in terms of rehabilitation. Instead of providing incentives for offenders to stay away from crime, prisons are better known as a training ground for criminals.

> There is not enough prison-industry work to keep all inmates busy...
> The chief activity, then, is talk. I heard long discussions about whether it is better to be a burglar (usually you never see your victim) or a robber (it only takes a few minutes at most). There are tips about how to get a new identity, where to find fences for stolen goods, where to buy guns. An inmate named Virgil told me, "I'll never be here again." I thought he had vowed to go straight, but then he added, "I'll never be caught."[18]

In this type of a community of criminals, with the wrong type of career reinforcement, there is an understandable increase in recidivism. Indeed, by 1991, forty-five percent of inmates in the United States had been in prison at least three times.[19] Studies have shown that "a period of time in prison/jail actually *increases* the risk of subsequent offending once these individuals are released to the community."[20]

The negative influence - the criminal career counseling and anti-social attitude - of the other inmates is not countered, but possibly increased by the unwillingness of the prison industry to spend money on rehabilitative programs. Cuts are frequently made in the more expensive programs: education, training, and therapy for sex offenders are often eliminated in response to budget cuts. In other words, by eliminating those programs that are intended to adjust a criminal to an acceptable societal role, we achieve false economic savings. These cuts are made regardless of the fact that, as recent studies suggest, these programs tend to be most effective in reducing rates of recidivism.[21]

---

[18] Gavzer, 1995, 5.
[19] Ibid
[20] Byrne. and Brewster, 1993, 6.
[21] *The Economist*, 1/ 20/96, 55.

What compounds the problem is that the lack of rehabilitation in the prison system is continued after the sentence is filled. Because money for crime fighting funds is diverted mainly into the prisons themselves, probation programs find themselves with insufficient funds. Probation officers are overloaded with clients to the extent that their time with and effect on an individual probationer is insufficient.[22] In most cases, probationers are not required to meet with their officer more than once a month. In the meetings, the officer is generally so pressed for time that he or she is merely satisfied if the client has not been charged with a new offence. The officer does not offer many incentives for the client to become rehabilitated nor encouragement to the client to find or hold a job.[23] Much of the inherent difficulty is captured by the comments of Lois Forer, a former judge, who claims that unless an offender is self-motivated to avoid crime and to find legal employment, chances are that he or she will face the criminal justice system again.[24]

The prison system fails to encourage rehabilitation in another important way. It fails to discourage others from committing the same crime. For instance, many crimes committed by lower income individuals are economically motivated. Offenders may, for example, sell drugs to support a family.[25] Drug dealing can be lucrative, and the problem is that the gains to be made often appear greater than the risks of being caught. Recall the equation used above. Many drug dealers consider that even with the risks, the amount they can gain outweighs their potential losses if caught. They believe that:

$$p^*(A) < (1-p^*)(S_{NV}).$$

In other words, they think that what they could earn from dealing drugs is greater than the potential losses due to the possibility of arrest and penalty. Given these beliefs, it is rational for a person to sell drugs.

But if a member of a family is locked in jail for dealing drugs, then, instead of deterring other members from committing the same crime, they may be prompted to sell drugs themselves in order to make up for the lost income. Consider the continuum cycle. With the loss of family income, the younger the remaining members are, the fewer legal alternatives they may have to earn sufficient money to support themselves and their family.

> Ask Jovan Rogers why he got into the drug business and he will tell you about the three younger sisters he has to take care of, about his mother...[who] had trouble making ends meet, about her boyfriend who went to prison for selling drugs, about the family refrigerator that did not have enough food in it and an apartment with no electricity because his mother lacked money to pay the light bill... "I was the only man in

---

[22] Chanoff, 1994, 47.
[23] Forer, 1994, 133.
[24] Ibid
[25] Wilkerson, [B], 12/13/94, B12.

the house, and they had to eat. They knew I was out there hustling for us."[26]

Instead of discouraging crime, the prison system can indirectly provide very strong economic incentives for children to enter the market of crime.

Thus, instead of an arena of rehabilitation, basic economic analysis suggests that the prison system fosters, maybe even encourages, an environment of recidivism. It takes little responsibility for the prisoner when he or she has completed the sentence. Even worse, prisons can create a vicious cycle in which others are given incentives (instead of disincentives) to commit similar crimes.

Would alternative sentencing for nonviolent criminals provide a better aspect of rehabilitation? It would: If done correctly, community sentencing forces the offender to work off his or her crime. The busier the offender is, the less opportunity that person has to compare notes on criminal activity with other offenders. Furthermore, by putting the offenders into the legal community, where they will interact with law-abiding citizens instead of only with other offenders, the organization of criminals is weakened. There is mounting evidence that alternative sentencing programs achieve a higher degree of success, in terms of rehabilitation, than do other forms of punishment.[27] But, right up front, let us be clear. For any of this form of alternative sentencing to work, to be accepted by society, strong assurances, that are backed by accountability of officials, must be made that all actions of offenders in these programs are monitored.[28]

Alternative sentencing would aid attempts at rehabilitation in another way. By releasing nonviolent criminals from prison into alternative sentencing programs, much of the expensive funding that had been spent on housing, feeding, and otherwise providing for these offenders would be freed for other programs. More money could be directed towards rehabilitation programs and also for probation and alternative sentencing programs, so that these could work more efficiently.

Finally, alternative sentencing could help break the vicious cycle in which the offspring of criminals follow in their parents' footsteps. If a nonviolent offender is placed in a program in which he or she is allowed to remain in the home, but must work off the sentence (while presumably collecting a legal wage at the same time), then that person can serve as a more positive role model than an absent, jailed parent. The offspring will have the benefit of the parent's presence, will see the parent work to make amends for the crime, and will presumably have some income

---

[26] Ibid

[27] Byrne and Brewster, 1993, 4, and Wolf and Weissman, 1996, 201.

[28] Although, ideally, this type of statement should not be necessary when discussing the important security aspects involved in handling offenders, critics of alternative sentencing programs, which include video and electronic bracelet monitoring, have complained that officials do not have the proper work ethic. Maintenance of offenders is a 24 hour responsibility, yet many officials tend to provide a 9 to 5 service, leaving the offenders unmonitored the majority of the time!

from the legal employment of the parent. Thus, the destructive scenario seen above could be avoided.

1.1.3 Deterrence

Arguably, the prison system has not served as a strong deterrent against crime. The United States houses more inmates than any other country,[29] but continues to have a large crime rate. Cultural differences aside, these figures provide evidence that the prison system is not an effective deterrent.

> Bulging prisons have not led to the expected drop in the crime rate nationally or, in some unspecified way, dampened it...Some might argue that...the observed rise in age-adjusted violent crime rates would have been even greater had it not been for the would-be deterrent or incapacitative effects of rising prison populations. But there is nothing in the prison or crime statistics themselves that suggests such an interpretation.[30]

In fact, far from eliminating crime, many prisons house criminals who continue to take an active role in, and even profit from criminal activity. Most notably, from his prison cell, Larry Hoover, the leader of the Chicago street gang, the Gangster Disciples, allegedly continued to control gang activities and even collect taxes from the profits of non-member drug dealers.[31]

Taking the gains to be made from crime and comparing them with the losses associated with a current prison sentence, it might make sense to take the risk. As early as 1975, the journalist Thomas Plate learned from criminal contacts that jail time was an expected part of a criminal's life.

> ...[A] prison sentence is really just part of the overhead cost of doing business. The theme one hears over and over again in this connection is, "If you can't do the time, don't do the crime"[32]

Looking at the situation from the perspective of an economist, we understand that the criminal could either choose to be employed legally or in the field of crime. Legal employment will guarantee a set wage that will be taxed and that will restrict certain hours for work. The wage is risk free. In crime, the criminal could earn large, but risky wages, tax free, and choose her own hours. She faces a period of unemployment if she happens to be arrested, but she also does not have to provide for herself (meals, medical bills...) during that time. Prison time could

---

[29] In 1999, the United States housed the most inmates, 1.85m, followed by China, 1.4m, and Russia, 1.05m. (Walmsley, 2000).
[30] Steffensmeier, and Harer, 1993, 9.
[31] O'Connor, 1/4/96, 17.
[32] Plate, 1975, 19.

entail a loss, due to the unpleasantness of the situation. After prison, the criminal can choose again if she wishes to be employed legally or in crime.

Given these options, the person can choose a field. If the wages from crime, minus the costs associated with crime (moral costs as well as risk associated costs and danger of injury and death, depending on the type of crime), are greater than the constant wages of legal employment, then our offender will choose criminal activity.

A rough mathematical representation for this decision-making process can be shown as follows:

$$\max \{w, \frac{1}{1-\delta} \int F(c)dc \}. \tag{4}$$

To explain these terms, w is the legal wage. The variable δ is the discount factor, in other words, δ represents how much an individual values the future. If the person is merely concerned with the present, then δ will be very low (close to zero) and if the person values the future then δ will be close to one. The variable F(c) represents some distribution of wages from crime in which in some circumstances the payoff could be high and in others it could be very low – even negative. The integral indicates that all possible distributions, and the probabilities under which they occur, are added together. The individual will select the option that offers the highest wages. If crime is far more profitable than legal work, then a period of no wages, representing prison time, will be insufficient to deter potential criminals.[33]

Alternative sentencing, in contrast, forces offenders to make repairs for their crimes (through community sentencing, repayment for theft, etc.) These actions add to the cost of crime. In this way, these programs can have a deterrent effect on the criminal's activity. From an economic analysis, the goal should be to increase the costs of crime, so that the criminal has a material incentive to avoid crime. For instance, if a criminal seeks to rob a victim in search of an economic gain, the possibility of having to repay that amount, plus a fine, to the victim could be a deterrent. Instead, a natural response is the old standby reaction of more prison time. The intent of alternative sentencing is to remove the profits from criminal activity. A more in depth discussion of this effect will be given further in the chapter.

1.2 Protection of the Public

If the prisons are unable to meet the goals listed above, then do they serve any purpose? It is important to note that the objectives are better met by alternative sentencing programs *in the case of nonviolent offenders*. Even in the case of repeat

---

[33] To gain a perspective of how legal wages could be lower than the wages of crime, consider the legal employment opportunities for a high school dropout, and compare those potential wages (probably minimum wage) to those of selling drugs. Not all, or even most, people in this income bracket will choose to commit crimes, because, for many, the risks involved with crime pose a sufficient cost on criminal activity to deter them from this type of action. If the costs do not appear that large, however, criminal activity could be tempting.

offenders, alternative sentences provide a means by which the social cost of crime is – at least partially – repaid. A repeat offender, if caught and punished, will have to repeatedly work to repay his or her debt to society. When we take violent offenders into account, protection of the public is clearly better met by the prison system than by any alternative sentencing program. So long as they are incapacitated by being locked in a prison, violent criminals do not serve as a threat to the general community. By providing this security, the prison fills a crucial role in society.

1.2.1 Violent Crime and Sex Predators

1.2.1.1 Recidivism and Violence

As previously stated, it is arguable that recent policy has erred by failing to distinguish between violent and nonviolent criminals when selecting participants for alternative sentencing programs. Through this mistake, as already argued, we must expect the general public to be exposed to the threat of violent recidivists. This is no small threat.

With the recent crackdown on crime, particularly on drug dealing, prisons have become overcrowded.[34] So what is the solution? The current response is possibly the worst from the perspective of the general public. Namely, to relieve pressure on the prisons, many prisoners are released before they have served their full sentence. Instead of taking the severity of the crime into account, prisoners are frequently released because of "good behavior." Admittedly, this type of system does provide appropriate incentives for the prisoners to cooperate in prison, in the hopes of cutting short a prison term. However, it seriously fails to take into account that good behavior in prison does not necessarily promise good behavior outside. It is not clear, in any manner, whether appropriate behavior in a highly controlled, but negative culture will translate into desirable behavior once the constraints are removed and the temptations are reinstated.

Because the system provides the incentives for all of the inmates, many violent criminals have the same opportunity as nonviolent criminals to become eligible for early release.[35] In fact, due to the mandatory sentencing laws for drug related crimes, violent criminals may find themselves with an even greater chance of decreasing their terms than will drug dealers. "The average murderer released in 1992 from a state prison had served only 5.9 years in jail."[36]

Statistics show that the good behavior responsible for a violent criminal's early release from prison has little correlation with his or her activities when

---

[34] In 1996, 60.8% (50,754 out of a total population of 83,515) of the federal prison population were drug dealers. In contrast, drug dealers constituted only 16.3% of the federal prison population in 1970. (Federal Bureau of Prisons, "Quick Facts", May, 1997.)

[35] Few states sentence convicted murderers to a life sentence without parole. Among these few, it is still possible to obtain early release by applying to the Board of Pardons for a commutation. (Berger, 4/4/95, B1-2.)

[36] *The Economist*, 1/27/96, 28.

released. According to the report made by the Council on Crime in America, in 1990, among those accused of violent crimes, 12% were awaiting trial for earlier offences when they allegedly committed rape, murder, assault, or robbery. The case could be made that, had these people been detained in prison while waiting for their trials, then a large part of this crime would not have occurred. The report further states that 23% of defendants of violent crimes are on probation or parole. Since 1977, people who were supposedly "supervised" in parole or probation have committed 13,200 murders and 11,600 rapes.[37] According to the Bureau of Justice Statistics, in the 1980's, 59.6% of released violent offenders were rearrested within 3 years of release, most often for another violent crime. Released rapist were ten times more likely to be rearrested for rape than were non-rapists, and released murderers were five times more likely to be rearrested for homicide than were other offenders.[38]

Stories of the misdeeds of released violent offenders are numerous. In one case, a work-release inmate, Clarence Prude, who was serving a four-year sentence for armed robbery, was charged with killing a 20-year-old woman while supposedly under the supervision of a work-release program.[39] Because of such occurrences, in 1995, Pataki, the Governor of New York, signed an executive order prohibiting violent criminals from participating in prison work-release programs.[40] The order was criticized because it increased the number of inmates who would have to remain in New York's overcrowded prisons. However, the critics fail to take into account that a crucial function of the prisons *is to protect the public*. If overcrowded prisons must be relieved in some manner, this relief should be done in a way that poses the *minimum* threat to the public. The following section explores some of the crimes against which we must be protected.

1.2.1.2 Sex Offenders

Violent crime includes sexual offences. The tendency for sex offenders to repeat their crimes when released from prison has been a controversial issue in recent years. The problem is complex. Communities have a natural urge to protect their residents and desire to be informed if a sex predator (as they are called in the press) will be taking up residence in the area. Armed with this knowledge, the people can take steps to protect their children and themselves from any further offence attempts by the predator. The people's right to know contrasts with the rights of the ex-convict to privacy and to avoid double jeopardy - being punished twice for the same crime.

The problem with this situation, is that the focus, in sentencing, is placed on the *punishment*. In prison, an offender spends a certain number of years that are deemed appropriate punishment for the crime that he or she has committed, and then that person is released into the community once more. Rehabilitation, if

---

[37] *The Economist*, 1/27/96, 28.
[38] Beck, 2/19/97.
[39] Sack, 1/25/95, A1.
[40] Sack, 1/25/95, A1&B5.

rehabilitation is even possible, is rarely attempted. Furthermore, the issue that is the most important, that of protection of the public, is only raised upon the prospect of the offender's release.

How much time in prison constitutes an appropriate punishment for a sexual offence? The question is not easy to answer. The answers can frequently be arbitrary. If a person can serve a mandatory 10-year sentence for selling a set amount of marijuana, then is 13 years sufficient punishment for a sexual offence, or should it be 20? At what point can we be satisfied that a sexual predator has served his debt to society? With this arbitrary amount of punishment filled, are we correct in releasing someone into the public, even if it is likely that that person will commit the same offence again and harm an innocent person? What we need to do, as a society, is to confront the twin issues of incarceration, for whatever reason, and the protection of society.

Under laws that were followed until very recently, the above options were the only ones. The problem can be seen vividly in the case of Leroy Hendricks. Hendricks had a three-decade record of pedophelia. The crimes for which he was arrested included: exposing himself to girls in 1956, molesting two boys in 1960, molesting a 7-year-old boy in 1963, taking indecent liberties with two children in 1965, and attempting to molest two 13-year-old boys in 1984.[41] Between each of these crimes, Hendricks served prison terms. Upon release, he committed another crime.

When his last sentence had ended, the state of Kansas refused to release him, sending him to a state mental health facility instead.[42] This case provoked a great deal of dispute. Opponents of Hendricks' continued containment argued that the state had essentially committed double jeopardy, and was unconstitutionally violating Hendricks' rights. Others said that the only way to stop Hendricks from committing another crime would be to keep him out of society. They claimed that it was the duty of the criminal justice system to protect the public.

> The attorney general of Kansas counters that Hendricks must be locked up to protect the community. Hendricks has said that he won't stop molesting children until he dies. We know he's likely to do it again. We've got to stop him.[43]

Under the laws, however, it was unconstitutional to detain Hendricks, even though he himself admitted that he would commit the same act.

> "Well," asked Chief Justice William H. Rehnquist at oral arguments, "is the state of Kansas required to wait until he does it again before locking him up?" The answer, unfortunately, is yes.[44]

---

[41] Associated Press, 12/9/96, 17.
[42] Ibid.
[43] Krauthammer, 12/16/96, 21.
[44] Ibid.

The ensuing debate caused many to argue that sexual predators should be locked up for life.⁴⁵ Criminologists and psychologists have claimed that sexual predators cannot be rehabilitated.

> As a psychologist, I believe that people can change and should be given the opportunity to do so, but molesters are an exception. They rarely stop, even with therapy. Sexual abusers of children should be offered counselling, but it should take place during long prison sentences. And these sentences should never be reduced for "good behavior". These abusers should never be given the opportunity to find new victims.⁴⁶

Others argued that the courts should attempt to determine whether or not an offender poses a threat to the public. If the person is a threat, that person should not be released into the public, in order to protect society.

> We already use civil commitment to protect the public from the criminally insane. Anyone who is deemed to be both mentally ill and dangerous to himself or others may be placed indefinitely in a mental institution.⁴⁷

On June 23, 1997, the Supreme Court upheld the constitutionality of these ideas by stating that states may confine violent sex offenders in mental hospitals after they have served their sentences in prison. An important point is that states may do so even if the offenders are not considered mentally ill to the extent that generally qualifies for civil commitment of an individual against his or her will.⁴⁸ The actions of the Supreme Court were taken for reasons consistent with the arguments of this chapter.

> Commitment under the act does not implicate either of the two primary objectives of criminal punishment: retribution or deterrence.⁴⁹

> Rather, [Justice Thomas] continued, "incapacitation may be a legitimate end of the civil law," even if no treatment is available. Justice Thomas cited a 1902 Supreme Court case permitting the involuntary quarantine of people suffering from communicable diseases.⁵⁰

---

⁴⁵ Ibid, and Chapman, 12/22/96, 19.
⁴⁶ Landers, 6/25/97, 3.
⁴⁷ Chapman, 12/22/96, 19.
⁴⁸ Supreme Court of the United States, 6/23/97.
⁴⁹ Ibid
⁵⁰ Greenhouse, 6/24/97, A10.

1.2.1.3 Incapacitation

The actions taken by the Supreme Court in this case represent a key argument in this chapter. In consideration of sentencing for sexual offenders or other violent criminals, protection of the public should be the primary concern. Rather than address issues of retribution and deterrence, the courts should attempt to ensure that, if an individual poses a risk to society, that person should be incapacitated so that he or she is unable to commit the same or similar crimes in the future. This same objective was the intent of the "Three Strikes" legislation discussed later. Here, it suffices to recall that this law imposes a mandatory life sentence without parole for a third felony conviction. The problem with this legislation, however, is that it does not differentiate between violent and nonviolent felonies. Furthermore, a recent RAND study concludes that a policy that guarantees a full term sentence for first time serious and violent offenders can achieve the same reduction in crime at a lower cost to the tax payer.[51] This result is consistent with the above economic analysis.

As stated above, the courts have previously erred in focusing on prison as a form of *punishment* for a violent offender. What court or judge is qualified to accurately determine the appropriate punishment for a violent crime? In the case of abuse, rape or molestation, the effects on the victim can be devastating, and can last a lifetime. In the case of a murder, the effects are even more thorough. What amount of punishment can adequately repay society, or the victims, for these losses?

The focus should lie instead on *incapacitation* of the offender. If an offender commits a violent crime, then he or she should be kept out of society, in prison or in some sort of institution, until he or she no longer serves as a threat to society - for life, if necessary. Indeed, this purpose is explicitly stated in the Supreme Court ruling.

> The Act does not establish criminal proceedings, and involuntary confinement under it is not punishment...
> The confinement's potentially indefinite duration is linked, not to any punitive objective, but to the purpose of holding a person until his mental abnormality no longer causes him to be a threat to others.[52]

Using this concept, the idea of a mandatory sentence length has no meaning. If prison sentences are not meant for punishment, so much as they are meant for incapacitation, then violent criminals will not be released once they have "paid their debt to society." The emphasis changes from "debt to society" - which is not fulfilled without some form of retribution - to "protection of society."

If, for certain crimes, the prime purpose of prison is not intended for punishment, then the issue of a person's having served his debt to society will not arise. The prisoners are not repaying a debt; they are merely kept away from

---

[51] Greenwood, Rydell, Abrahamse, Caulkins, Chiesa, Model, and Klein,. 1997.
[52] Supreme Court of the United States, 1997.

society so that they cannot harm anyone else. In a manner similar to the quarantine analogy used by Justice Thomas, these individuals pose a threat and the criminal justice system is serving a function by removing them from society. If the stress is placed on this aim, rather than on that of punishment, then a person can be incarcerated as long as is necessary.

This idea is consistent with the model above. To see this consistency, imagine two types of offenders: one who is capable of making a decision regarding whether or not to commit a violent act and one who is not. In this case, both individuals face the circumstances described in the model. Additionally, they are aware that if they commit a violent crime, they will be kept out of society, and thus lose their freedom, until they are considered safe (possibly for the rest of their lives).

Arguably, the individual who is incapable of avoiding violent crime will eventually commit one, and, with probability p*, that person will be arrested and kept in prison. If this is the case, society bears the loss associated with the crime, but may avoid future crimes by that offender. In this circumstance, the laws found in the model provide no deterrence. They merely serve to protect the public as well as they can.[53]

The deterrence in the model is provided in the case of the other individual - the one who can choose whether or not to commit a violent crime. As described above, if, by including work with the sentence,[54] jail time is made less attractive than some alternative sentence, then the offender should be deterred from using violence. If, additionally, the person is aware that he or she could be deemed a threat to society and be committed for life, then the prison sentence would be even less attractive, and the deterrent effect would be even stronger.

This effect can be demonstrated with the simple equations given previously.

$$EU(NV) = p^*(A) + (1-p^*)(S_{NV}) > EU(V) = p^*(J) + (1-p^*)(S_V) \qquad (3)$$

Assuming that the penalty of a life sentence with work (S_V) is more distasteful than an alternative sentence (S_{NV}) a criminal will be more likely to opt for the nonviolent crime.

1.2.2 Criticisms

The suggestions above, as is the case with most policy proposals, are sure to face criticisms. Some potential critiques will be addressed here.

---

[53] Similarly, the Kansas v. Hendricks ruling makes no claims to be a deterrent, "since persons with a mental abnormality or personality disorder are unlikely to be deterred by the threat of confinement." Supreme Court of the United States, "Kansas v. Hendricks" No. 95-1649.

[54] When we recall that most offenders prefer prison time to work, the inclusion of labor in a prison sentence becomes important. In other words, we do not want to provide an incentive to commit a violent crime, instead of a nonviolent one, in order to obtain the more leisurely prison sentence over the enforced work of an alternative sentence.

The idea of incapacitation includes the troubling possibility that the violent criminal will be placed in prison for life. The question may be raised as to who is capable of determining what characteristics a person must possess in order to state that he or she represents a threat to society. Does the ability to make this judgment confer a great deal of power on the judge who decides? Isn't there a great potential for abuse? Will we slide towards serious abuse, such as where "undesirables" such as people labeled "communists" are arrested as potential "threats to society?" This is a real concern, as underscored by the documented abuses of mental laws in the former Soviet Union being directed towards dissidents, as well as the political incarceration of dissidents in other totalitarian societies.

Addressing the last issue first, in the United States, the First Amendment to the Constitution ensures that people have the freedom of speech. There have been unfortunate governmental abuses of this right during our history. Vigilance is always crucial. But, as ideology or beliefs do not, in any streak of imagination, qualify as "violent crimes," individuals are no more likely to be imprisoned for their beliefs under the laws suggested here than under current laws. Furthermore, under this type of policy, the likelihood of imprisonment for ideology is even somewhat decreased, because, unlike our current system, in order to be imprisoned, a person must commit a violent crime.[55]

The issue of who can decide whether or not a person is a threat is a delicate, tricky question. But one potential answer comes by appealing to our democratic tradition of trust in peers. Thus, the question should be determined in the same manner as it is today, with a judge and jury. The United States is one of the few nations that has a death penalty. If judges and juries can be considered thoughtful and reliable enough to decide whether or not a person will live or die, then these same people ought to be able to make a decision as to whether or not a person poses a threat to society. Again, importantly, the issue is *not* deciding an appropriate *punishment* for a criminal. If a person has committed a violent crime, then that person should be removed from society until he or she is no longer a threat. Here it should be noted that cases should be judged individually. If someone has committed a violent crime for some reason such as self-defense then that person does not represent a threat.

1.2.2.1 Three Strikes

Another potential problem with the sentencing proposal is associated with the difficulties facing the "Three Strikes You're Out" sentencing laws. The "Three Strikes" laws are aimed at the similar goal of deterring felonies. More precisely, the law states that if a person is convicted of three felonies, then he or she receives a life sentence without parole. The law was designed to reduce the number of

---

[55] The Federal Bureau of Investigations classifies violent crimes as including: murder, forcible rape, robbery, and aggravated assault. U.S. Department of Justice, Federal Bureau of Investigation, "Uniform Crime Reporting Program Press Release -- 10/13/96." An extended list includes: kidnapping/hostage, sexual abuse, extortion, and firearms use. Wolf and Weissman, 1996, fn. 11., 203.

repeat offenders, with the belief that if a person is aware that he or she faces a life sentence, then, even if two felonies have already been committed, the person will not risk a third.

Unfortunately, where this law has been enacted, the police encountered some surprises. Instead of necessarily deterring criminals, third time offenders tended to *increase* the violence in order to avoid capture. For example,

> An ex-convict surrendered Monday to face charges that he masterminded bombings at a courthouse and a bank to thwart a drug trial that would imprison him for life under California's "three strikes" law.[56]

Thus, the police faced an escalation in violence for crimes that normally would have shown a criminal offering little resistance to arrest.

The reason behind this escalation is simple. When the laws were created, the planners made the error of assuming that the criminals thought on only two dimensions, i.e., the decision was either to commit a crime or not. If this assumption were true, then it was reasoned that as the probability of arrest increased, the criminal would be less likely to commit a (third) crime.

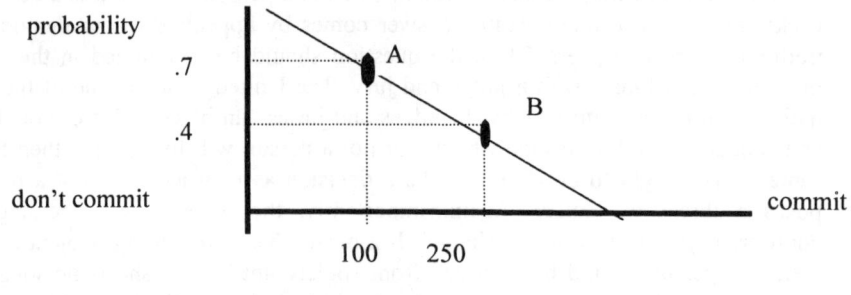

Fig. 1.3

For example, we might imagine a situation similar to point B in the graph above in which the probability of arrest was 40% (.4). In this case, the number of people willing to commit a crime would be 250. If, in this fictitious society, the probability of arrest were increased to 70%, then the number of people willing to commit a crime would drop to 100, seen in point A.

The error in this judgment lies in ignoring that the criminal has other options. For instance, suppose the criminal decides to commit the crime despite the law, because he believes there is only minimal risk. If he risks arrest, the personal cost now becomes much greater. The criminal faces a life sentence, which is equivalent to (or even greater than) the sentence for murder in some states. Faced with this penalty, the criminal can do no worse by committing murder in an attempt to escape. If he succeeds in escape, he can do better. Therefore, the law inadvertently

---

[56] Associated Press, 2/4/97, 11.

provides an incentive for the criminal to try to shoot his way out. Since arrest is not certain for any given crime, this option may appear to be optimal.

Again the analysis involved in computing relative payoffs to violent versus nonviolent crime is applicable here. A simple economic representation of the decision is as follows: A person must decide whether to resist the temptation to commit a third felony or not. If he does not wish to resist, he must choose between violent and nonviolent activity.

$$EU(NC) = w - L_w$$

$$EU(C_{NV}) = (1-p^*)(S_{NV} - L_{NV}) - p^*(PP - L_{NV})$$

$$EU(C_V) = (1-p')(S_V - L_V) - p'(PP - L_V)$$

Here, the expected utility of not committing, NC, a third crime includes the wages that the ex-convict can earn, w, minus the cost of labor, L_w. The expected utility of committing a third felony, but meekly accepting arrest if it occurs, C_{NV} includes the gains to be made from the crime, S_{NV} minus the cost of committing the crime, L_{NV}. These gains also take into account the probability of arrest, p^* and punishment of life in prison, PP. The expected utility of committing a third felony, but using violence to resist arrest if it occurs, C_V, includes the gains to be made from the crime, S_V minus the cost of committing the crime, L_V. These gains also take into account the probability of arrest, p', which is presumed to be lower than p^*, and punishment of life in prison, PP.

Most people generally recognize that legal wages for an ex-convict are low and that the cost of this labor is high. However, the assumption is that the severity of punishment encapsulated in the life sentence should serve as a deterrent against the commission of a third strike. The analytical mistake commonly made is in ignoring the alternative of violence. If a criminal correctly or incorrectly believes that he can sufficiently decrease his or her probability of arrest through the use of violence – causing p' to fall below p^* - then the expected gains to be made from a third felony may lead the person to opt for the choice of crime.

In this case, the criminal is using three dimensions in making his decision. This means of modeling the criminal's decision is similar to the rough model used above for sentencing. The criminal has some idea of the probability of arrest, and correspondingly makes his or her decisions regarding the level of crime he or she wishes to commit and the level of violence to be used.

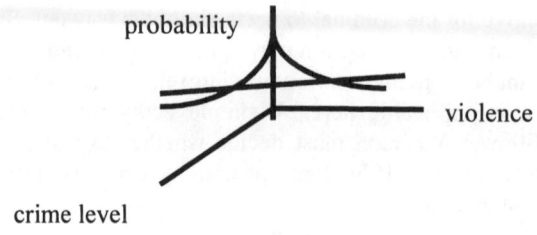

Fig. 1.4

By allowing for the possibility that a decision could involve three or more dimensions, we must accept that many of our ideas may not produce expected results. Because we have ignored the possibility that criminals could choose violence as a means of deterring arrest, we open the unfortunate chance that police officers are unprepared for attacks.

There is statistical evidence that supports the theoretical possibility that the use of three-strikes laws will provoke an increase in violence. Using state-level multiple time series analyses, Marvell and Moody find that three-strikes laws are associated with 10% to 12% more homicides in the short run and up to 29% more homicides in the long run. This effect is found in almost all of the 24 states that have three-strikes laws.[57]

The proposal to keep only violent criminals in prison, possibly for life, can have similar repercussions. If a criminal is aware that if arrested for a violent crime, he will stay in prison for life, then he can either avoid the use of violence, or he might choose not only to use violence but also increase the level of violence in an attempt to escape arrest.

The potential for increased violence in this case is disturbing. However, it should not be used as a reason to abandon the proposal. Consider the alternatives. By targeting only violent criminals, nonviolent criminals have an incentive to refrain from using violence. This notion has anecdotal support. Police in New York and Chicago found that in response to severe penalties for possession of handguns, the number of guns found on people they arrested dropped significantly.[58] This suggests that the prospect of stiff penalties, judiciously designed, can affect criminal behavior in the desired direction. Applying this logic to the choice between violent and nonviolent crime, the offenders with the strongest incentive to increase their violence are the violent ones. If left alone, these people are free to harm more innocent people. If subject to arrest, their resistance will most often be directed at police officers who are trained to cope with violent situations, rather than at the public that is not. Once arrested, the public will be protected.

---

[57] Marvell and Moody, 2000, p.2.
[58] Pooley, 1/15/96, 56.
[58] Lacayo, 1/15/96, 53

1.2.2.2 Alternative Sentencing

If prisons are to be used only for violent criminals, then the alternative sentencing programs for nonviolent criminals must be carefully designed in order to aid in the goals of retribution, rehabilitation, and deterrence. As argued earlier in the chapter, effective, carefully administered alternative sentencing programs can meet these goals. What follows is a discussion of what makes the programs effective.

Today's alternative sentencing programs are under-funded and ineffective. As previously stated, it cost, on average, $25,000 a year to house on inmate in 1996. At the same time, only $200, on average, was spent per probationer, per year.[59] If the proposal were followed, and nonviolent offenders were released into alternative sentencing, then millions of dollars would be freed to be spent on improving alternative sentencing programs. Although these programs are likely to be less expensive over time, in the short run, they may be more expensive. The reason is due to set-up costs; the current system must be re-organized and vastly improved.

It should be noted that although, in the long run, alternative sentencing programs are likely to be less expensive than prisons, in the short run, costs may appear to be high. Because the current system of probation and community sentencing is understaffed, inefficient, and underfunded, much of the savings from the prison budget would have to be invested into alternative programs to bring them to the desired level of effectiveness. The staff would have to be increased and trained, and more programs would have to be made available. In order for an alternative sentencing program to function, it will require on site supervision of the offenders. If necessary, this supervision could include escorting offenders to and from their place of service.

Recall that 7 out of 10 inmates preferred jail time to community sentencing. These people could be likely to resist work during their mandatory assignment. Unsupervised, an offender could choose to do little or nothing during his or her sentence. The result would be no rehabilitation for the offender and no retribution for the victim. Supervised, an offender would either have to work or would continue to return until the work was finished. A day without cooperating could have to be made up by an additional day added to the sentence. Provisions could be made that the offender earned a legal wage while working and that a portion of this wage went to pay off the offense.

In the next section, some alternative sentencing proposals will be examined in terms of their ability to meet the goals listed above.

1.2.3 Victim Compensation

Crime entails a loss to society. The loss is manifested in terms of loss of property; loss of resources that are devoted towards fighting and controlling crime which could otherwise have been invested in production; and loss of security;

---

[59] Butterfield, 1/6/96, 6.

among other costs. One of the key losers is the victim. And yet, as criticized by former judge, Lois Forer, and others, the victim receives little neither from the judicial system nor from the criminal, in form of compensation.

> Victims are treated simply as witnesses. They are compelled to appear in court and testify, often at great risk of physical danger, embarrassment, and emotional trauma. They are paid a witness fee...and then forgotten.[60]

Forer and others argue for victim compensation, an objective that is consistent with the goal of retribution. The belief is simply that the person who suffers from the crime should be repaid by his or her attacker.

The idea of compensation is not new. Some courts already use it to a limited extent. Additionally, federal law enforcement agencies allocate proportions of confiscations from criminals to the local police departments. Here, the amount received is in proportion to the amount that the department helped in fighting the particular criminal.[61] The "fairness problem," however, is that the *victim* does not receive compensation. It is important to question, however, is this compensation approach useful and effective in fighting crime, or is it simply a nice idea?

To face this question, it is informative to examine the argument using an economic model. The economist and Nobel Laureate, Gary Becker advocates the system of fining a criminal in order to deter him or her from criminal activity. Becker argues that if a fine were to be set sufficiently high, then the criminal would, in fact, choose not to commit the crime.

The difficulty with this analysis is that it does not answer who should receive the money from the fine.[62] Should it go to the police? Should it go to the victim? How much should each party receive? If the fine is sufficiently large, will people pose as victims, to collect payments? Similarly, if the fine is awarded to the police, will we find an increasing number of arrests (possibly of innocent people) to collect payments? The potential for abuse is great. The harmful incentives are increased when we recollect that Becker admitted that, because he was contrasting the effectiveness of punishment versus that of probability of arrest, the level of the fine must be very large to serve as a deterrent.

With this background, *is* there a mathematical justification for victim compensation? Using a simple model, based on ideas drawn from Becker's analysis and from basic economic theory, I argue in favor of victim compensation.

---

[60] Forer, 1994, 126-127.

[61] Interview with a Federal Law Enforcement Official, 9/95.

[62] In this analysis, Becker (1968) treats the problem of crime in a manner similar to the treatment of externalities in economics literature. In externalities studies, the problem can be eliminated with a fine, which is roughly equal to the damage that the polluter (or externality producer) inflicts, in order to deter the firm or individual from continuing the activity without a cost to themselves. The remaining problem is that the literature is indefinite as to where this money should go. In some cases, the money is simply set aside, or wasted, in order to avoid the question of who will get the money.

1.2.3.1 Victim Model

A victim bears a certain loss. Although this loss includes physical and psychological tolls, for the purposes of a simple model, assume that it is strictly economic.

Imagine that a criminal who steals the amount X from a victim is apprehended and convicted. The issue we must address is the amount of money needed to make the victim feel compensated. In other words, how much money would make the victim feel roughly equivalent to how he/she felt before the crime occurred?[63]

A related question is to determine how *little* money, in addition to full compensation for the loss, would leave a victim indifferent between being a victim and being reimbursed, and not being a victim at all. To understand the importance of this question, recall that awarding too much money to a victim creates an incentive to both overstate a loss, or to be careless and become a victim in order to obtain the extra money. To simplify the model, focus on the latter question.

We will give our victim an extra amount, E, which is determined in the following way:

Before the crime, the victim had X, with certainty. After the crime, the victim is compensated for the loss, on the condition that the criminal is arrested and sentenced. For these purposes, let the probability of arrest and conviction be denoted by p. To make our victim indifferent between the two options, the payment E should be enough to compensate for the loss of certainty of payment, and for the possibility that the victim will not be compensated. Expressed mathematically, this is:

$$X = p(X+E) + (1-p)0 \qquad (5)$$

Notice the interesting relationship. The higher the value of p, the lower the value of E. In other words, from this perspective, there is a relationship between the efficiency of the law enforcement establishment and the level of extra compensation.

To illustrate with numbers, if the victim originally had $100, and the probability of arrest is very low, roughly 20%, then the amount that he would need to be compensated for the possibility of not regaining that money is

$$100 = .2(100 + E)$$
$$E = \$400$$

So if the criminal is arrested, he will have to repay the hundred dollars, plus an additional fine of $400.

---

[63] Of course, because of the social loss, lack of security, etc...involved, the victim will never feel as secure, or equivalent, as he/she did before the crime.

If the probability of arrest is higher, say 70% likely, then the amount of compensation would be lower. Using the same example with the higher probability, the equation would be

$$100 = .7(100 + E)$$
$$E = 43$$

Now if the criminal were arrested, his fine would only be roughly $43, in addition to the repayment of $100.

To analyze the incentive problem facing the criminal, assume that the average criminal faces roughly the same probability of arrest, p. (Of course, factors which might change this include the skill of the criminal, location, etc. but it is reasonable to assume that the average criminal faces the average p.) The question is to determine how large the fine, F, must be so that the criminal does not wish to commit the crime, knowing that he/she will have to repay the full amount stolen plus the fine if arrested.

If X is the amount stolen, and F is the fine, the decision facing the criminal is captured with the equation computing costs and rewards:

$$0 = -p(X+F) + (1-p)X \qquad (6)$$

Where 0 represents the amount the criminal would have if he did not commit the crime. Here, the criminal compares the choice of no action with that of crime in which he faces the possibility of arrest and penalty (represented by the minus sign, indicating that the criminal will have to pay that amount) and also the possibility of successfully completing the crime.

Solving the two above equations, leads to the conclusion that:[64]

$$X(1-p)/p = E$$
$$X(1-2p)/p = F$$

The next step is to determine whether E or F is bigger. This knowledge is critical because if the fine needed to deter the criminal is larger than the amount necessary to compensate the victim, then we will need to impose a larger fine on the criminal. However, if the amount needed to compensate the victim, E, were larger than the deterrent fine level, F, then the victim compensation scheme would deter criminals. Setting $E \geq F$ we have, after cancellation, that:

$$X(1-p)/p \geq X(1-2p)/p$$
$$-p \geq -2p$$

---

[64]These results were obtained by the following calculations:
$X = pX + pE \qquad p(X+F) = (1-p)X$
$X - pX = pE \qquad pX + pF = X - pX$
$X(1-p) = pE \qquad 2pX + pF = X$
$\qquad\qquad X(1-2p) = pF$

2 > 1

We find that E is indeed larger than F. In other words, the amount that is necessary for a victim to be compensated for the loss of certainty of repayment is greater than the level of fine necessary to deter a criminal. Thus, the victim compensation program provides a penalty that is more than enough to deter a criminal from that particular crime.[65]

Returning to our example, should the probability of arrest be 20%, the amount needed to compensate the victim for the loss of $100 would be an additional $400. At this probability of arrest, the level of fine necessary to deter the criminal from the theft of that $100 would be

$$0 = -.2(100+F) + (1-.2)100$$
$$F = 300$$

So the level of fine necessary to deter the criminal from committing the crime and risking arrest and penalty is $300, which is lower than the amount necessary to compensate the victim.

1.2.3.2 Benefits

The above model suggests that, for a certain class of crimes, victim compensation is relevant and effective policy. Not only will part of the loss to society be filled, but the repayment also serves as a deterrent. While the model is simple, it provides insight to the question regarding the value of victim compensation. This rough model shows how an alternative sentencing policy can meet the goals of retribution and of deterrence.

Victim compensation policy can have other indirect benefits. For instance, the above computations showing that victim compensation is better for the individual victim and worse for the criminal, has accompanying consequences working to the advantage of the law enforcement officials. Namely, an obstacle in crime prevention is that many crimes go unreported. People do not report crimes for reasons, ranging from a lack of trust in the police, a belief that the police cannot help them, to the fact that they do not want to be bothered by the accompanying paperwork. But, since the police consequently have less information, they are less likely to find and arrest criminals. In turn, this failure on their part reinforces the citizens' belief that the police are not effective. The result is a vicious cycle, which is beneficial only to the criminals.

The lack of information also can create a divide between the people and the police and a lack of trust in the system. If people do not report crimes, the police are less aware of the extent of crime in the area, where it generally occurs, and the types of crime. Without this knowledge, their reputation for coming to the aid of

---

[65] This result is based on the assumption that a criminal is risk neutral. It can be shown that this result can also be applied for a risk seeking criminal with a utility function $u(x) = x^2$.

victims will suffer, and they may react with less speed to criminal reports (because of lack of familiarity with the area and with the crime there).[66] Again we encounter a vicious cycle, where the victims trust the police less and less, and the police are less and less able to function due to the lack of trust and information.

Now consider scenarios associated with the belief that the police are ineffective. Lack of trust on the part of the victims might lead these people to take the law into their own hands. This reaction can eventually lead to a disintegration of the justice system, if left unchecked. It can also cause an escalation of violence, in which people use force to gain retribution over one another. At worst, the situation can deteriorate into one of gang violence, or a Hobbesian "survival of the fittest," in which people join groups for their own self protection against others, because they do not or cannot trust the police to protect them.[67]

How can these cycles be avoided or broken? Quite clearly, this involves citizens reporting crimes. Now, if victims had a chance of being compensated for their losses, they would have a greater incentive to report crime to the police. The more crime is reported the more information would be available to the police, and thus, the more likely it is that the police will be able to find the criminals. Through this scenario, we could hope to replace the vicious cycle with a virtuous cycle. As the probability of arrest would increase, the people would be more likely to believe in the efficiency of the system.

1.2.3.3 Compensation

The first question, asking how much would be necessary to compensate a victim for the total loss due to crime, was not answered in this model. An easy answer to the question lies in a comparison of two schemes: one that provides victim compensation with one that does not. Through this comparison, we can determine which one leaves the victim better off.

The analysis for this comparison does not need numbers. Under the victim compensation scheme, the expected value for the victim (or potential victim) is precisely equal to the amount that the victim possessed prior to the crime. In other words, taking probability of arrest into account, the victim faces no monetary loss or gain.

Compare this argument with the standard scheme of no compensation. Here, the victim's expected value is his or her loss. With no monetary compensation, the

---

[66] This statement does not attempt an excuse for the police. Unfortunately, in several cases, police do not respond with speed in a given area because of racism or neglect on their part. Instead, the argument simply illustrates that the obvious consequence of not reporting crime is that the police become less aware of the crime occurring in a given area, so they are less able to control it.

[67] These comments sound extreme. This precise effect can be seen today in Russia where the police cannot be relied upon because they are either corrupt or ineffective or both. Many people have come to (or have been coerced into) reliance upon mafia groups for protection from other groups or criminals. In this case, the groups hold the power in the system, and create their own system of order. For more detail, see Saari-Sieberg, 1998.

only benefits from arrest and punishment of the criminal derive from a sense of satisfaction on the victim's part. Since, in addition to the monetary compensation that a victim stands to gain, the same satisfaction and sense of justice can arise from the compensation scheme it is fair to say that the compensation scheme has a greater expected value for the victim. Due to the fact that the victim's loss is decreased, a portion of the social loss due to crime is also decreased. Thus, the compensation plan is effective in its goal to decrease the personal and social loss due to crime.

1.2.3.4 Pain and Suffering

Why don't we institute a plan that completely compensates the victim for his/her loss as well as distress suffered? In other words, appealing to the first question, why don't we compensate a victim for the monetary loss *plus* pain, fear, and suffering? The complexity in responding to this question lies in the difficulty in measuring social loss. Any individual who wishes to be fully compensated for his/her loss due to crime, would need to estimate the total loss. This loss would extend beyond monetary value, to include: medical costs, fear, pain and suffering, etc... Not only are these costs difficult to estimate, but the system provides an unfortunate incentive for the victim to overstate them, especially if they are aware that the scheme provides a legal retribution to someone who has harmed or terrorized them. The victim becomes the oppressor. Schemes have been proposed in other areas, in order to attempt to induce honesty in cost evaluations, but even these are subject to error, and would be difficult to apply in this case.[68]

An additional problem with the prospect of awarding more money than the compensation scheme proposes, comes from the moral hazard problem mentioned above. The compensation scheme essentially makes the victim monetarily as well off as he/she would have been without the crime (in expected value terms). Any other compensation would yield the victim more, in order to compensate for suffering, than he/she had before the crime. This benefit could produce an incentive, in some, to become victims of crime (or, at least, to not avoid being the victim of a crime) in order to gain the additional benefit from the compensation.

A full answer is, to say the least, complex. Nevertheless, even taking the above problems into account, the victim compensation scheme is an attractive proposal. It decreases social and individual loss, and decreases the likelihood of creating a moral hazard problem. Also, as mentioned before, the scheme could aid in decreasing crime. The more incentive a victim has to report a crime, the more likely he/she will be to do so. Thus, the police will have more information and will be more likely to apprehend criminals.

---

[68] For example, schemes have been developed to calculate the amount necessary to compensate people for disruption or loss due to a governmental project, such as a road. However, Gibbard and Satterthwaite show that no institution is immune from the possibility that people will prefer to misrepresent their true preferences. (Ordeshook, 1986, 95-6.) Thus, even the best mechanisms are subject to the possibility that people will overstate the extent of their loss in order to receive more compensation.

1.2.4 Alternative Sentencing - Fitting the Crime

It is easy to envision how a victim compensation scheme could become part of a broader alternative sentence program. For instance, a valid criticism of the plan is that if the offender has insufficient money to compensate the victim, then he or she will either be forced to commit some other crime to obtain the funds, or will simply refuse to make the payment. This possibility suggests designing an alternative sentencing program where the offender works off the amount (either in direct service to the victim or through some form of community service) until the cost of the crime is repaid.

This type of policy would facilitate sentencing for a wide range of crimes from destruction of property to white-collar crimes such as embezzlement. It offers a means of molding the punishment to fit the crime. The current system of punishment treats all crimes in a relatively homogenous way; the majority of crimes are given a variation of the same penalty - time in prison. Attempts to "fit the crime" tend to result only in a difference in the length of the sentence.[69] This system is problematic because it can have little deterrent impact on the offender. For example, if a person can receive 10 years to life for dealing crack cocaine, then the prospect of an additional few years for some other crime, such as armed robbery, may be meaningless and may do little to dissuade the individual from undertaking the crime. It is easy to imagine that if an individual faces the probability of prison time for a minor crime, then he or she may have an incentive to commit a more serious crime as well, to make it worth the penalty.[70]

Allotting the same (or similar) punishments for most crimes can be detrimental to the deterrent goals of the state. If every crime receives a similar punishment, then the choices for a criminal are altered. The criminal may even be deterred from committing smaller crimes, in favor of bigger ones, because the payoffs minus the cost of the punishment are low, relative to what they could gain from a bigger crime.

In contrast, under alternative sentencing programs, the offender would repay, or work off, his or her debt to society and the victim. The larger the crime, the more the offender needs to do to compensate for the transgression. This system should discourage an escalation in crime, because the more crime an individual

---

[69] Wolf and Weissman find that in the federal sentencing guidelines, "There is no category of offense which, or offender who, is considered ineligible for prison." p. 194. In fact, despite the NCCD recommendations of decreased use of prisons, several studies have shown an increase in incarcerative sentences. (Wolf and Weissman, 1996, 194.) These prison terms are based on guideline requirements, rather than on judge's discretion. Judges have complained that due to the need for uniformity, a prison sentence is frequently required when some intermediate sanction would have been preferable. (Wolf and Weissman, 1996, 195.)

[70] This theme is captured by the popular film *Thelma and Louise* which depicts two women who inadvertently commit a crime. Realizing that they will probably face time in prison, the two subsequently commit a string of offenses. The inherent logic is that since they will be punished already, they have no further incentive to obey the law.

commits, the greater the amount he or she will be likely to have to repay.⁷¹ The system may also discourage the tendency to accept plea-bargaining, because the victim has an incentive to recapture the full loss. Finally, as previously stated, the system provides motivation for victims to report crimes to the authorities. This situation would provide more information to the police and would, correspondingly, improve their ability to combat crime.

1.3 Conclusion

Despite its persistence as the principal form of punishment, the prison system is an inappropriate means of addressing all types of crime. In meeting the goals of the corrections system: retribution, deterrence, rehabilitation, and incapacitation; prisons are inefficient in all but the last. When we take into account that this insufficient system comes at an annual cost of billions of dollars to the taxpayer, it becomes evident that some alternative form of sentencing is necessary.

This analysis indicates that a hybrid policy of imprisoning violent criminals and imposing alternative sentences on nonviolent criminals would be superior in terms of fulfilling society's goals. The maintenance of the prisons for violent offenders would provide protection of the public, both by incapacitation of those who are violent and by deterring others from the use of violence. Alternative sentencing could yield an improvement over the current system in terms of retribution, rehabilitation, and deterrence – but only if done seriously and carefully. Importantly, this more positive form of sentencing, involving some form of repayment, reduces the individual and social cost of crime.

---

[71] An important element of alternative sentencing should include the possibility for offenders to earn money while serving time, so that they can continue to provide for their families. Otherwise, if a working offender has no means of supporting herself and her family, she may be induced to commit other economic crimes.

Chapter 2

Private Prisons

Of the systems of punishment in current use, prisons are the best known. Prisons appear to be an unfortunate necessity, but are they efficient? Is our corrections system providing optimal service, or could we meet the same goals at a lower cost by contracting out some of the responsibilities to private enterprises. Given the fact that the prisons system costs the taxpayers billions of dollars each year, the prospect is enticing. This is not a new concept; already the government is experimenting with a small number of private prisons in order to determine if these savings can really be achieved.

The intent of this chapter is to demonstrate that the new surge in interest for private prisons is not necessarily motivated by the "right" reasons. The penal system was ideally created to deter, punish, and rehabilitate criminals and to protect the public. By appealing to concepts from economics and political science, this analysis explores the actual incentives for private and public firms. Through this evaluation, I demonstrate that private prisons meet few, if any of the above goals. Instead, it becomes arguable that the new popularity of private prisons stems largely from a combination of self-interested profiteers and the current political climate.

A significant drawback to transferring responsibilities is that prisons are becoming wealth-creating enterprises where individuals and companies stand to gain from their existence and expansion. If we examine prisons, in particular private prisons, from this perspective, we discover that prisons and prison sentences are advocated largely from a demand from prison lobbies and from the lobbies of groups who gain from their existence. In other words, where alternative crime fighting measures would be beneficial, they are frequently ignored *because influential groups have a moneyed interest in prison sentencing.*

This chapter explores some of the successes and failures of private prisons as well as the financial motivations that they provide. One of the conclusions is that instead of saving the taxpayer money, private prisons motivate those who manage and supply them to stress the use of prisons when other measures would be more effective and less costly.

2.1 Privatization Vs Public Service

Drawing from economic ideology, the move to privatize public services has become popular in recent years. The motivation is that, in theory, if a firm owns a company that provides a good or service, then that firm not only receives the profits, but also bears the costs of production and/or supply. In order to maximize profit, it will be in a firm's best interest to minimize costs and to reduce waste. Unlike the public sector, which spends public money, the private firm has an incentive to be efficient.

Lately, as prison budgets shrink and prisons become overcrowded, governments have been experimenting with the notion of contracting out prisons to private operations. Private prisons appear, on the surface, to be the ideal tool to balance the public's many and often contradictory wants. Part of the complexity reflects calls from the population demanding a tougher approach to crime fighting while also spouting the conflicting cry for lower taxes. Locking more criminals in prison increases prison costs; increases taxes. To meet both demands, a more efficient and less costly prison system seems to be the best option.

A problem that had to be addressed, in seeking a move to privatization, was how to make the prisons more accountable to avoid the exploitation of the prisoners. There are reasons for this concern; in the past, private prisons developed a reputation for cruelty to and exploitation of prisoners. No constraints had been placed on protecting the welfare of the prisoners. Inmates in private prisons "suffered malnourishment, frequent whippings, overwork and overcrowding."[72] To cut costs, the prisons ran a bare-bones organization. Profits were gained both from spending as little as possible of the state money on the prisoners and by selling the labor of the prisoners. By the 1950's, scandals of prisoner abuse at private prisons were so widespread that the government was compelled to take over the administration of prisons.[73]

To address these problems, regulations are imposed forcing private prisons to meet certain criteria. Private prisons must also show that they can run the prisons at a lower cost than that of state and federal prisons[74] while providing evidence that inmate treatment is at least equivalent to the conditions in non-private prisons. Most contracts specify that private prisons satisfy ACA (American Correctional Association) accreditation.[75] This requirement indicates that the prisons meet minimum standards over such aspects as: staffing levels, training requirements of the guards, levels of health care, food service, education, and other inmate programs. Private prisons are monitored by state officials to observe compliance with the conditions.[76]

2.1.1 Positive Side

A surface examination of private prisons indicates that these institutions are meeting the goals and even improving on the services provided by state and federal prisons. Some private prisons have been shown to run at a cost that is less than the costs in state and federal prisons. Others, however, have equivalent or greater

---

[72] Smith, 1993, 2.

[73] Ramirez, 8/14/94, 1&6.

[74] In Texas, private prisons must provide assurances that they will operate with savings of at least ten percent of the state's cost. (Report to the Subcommittee on Crime, House of Representatives, 8/96, 21). Florida, in contrast, does not prescribe a specific cost savings; the contracts require "substantial savings" in building and operations. Florida Corrections Commission *1996 Annual Report*.

[75] Report to the Subcommittee on Crime, 8/96.

[76] Ibid.

costs.[77] But, due to the paucity of systematic comparisons of the different levels of quality between private and government run prisons, researchers cannot accurately determine quality differences among the prison types.[78] Despite the lack of evidence, private prisons claim to provide superior inmate treatment. Many private prisons invest in prison programs and services such as education and vocational training; services which are frequently the targets of elimination, due to budget cuts, in non-private prisons.[79] One private company boasts that,

> The company assumes a greater responsibility for prisoners than just "housing" them. All Wackenhut Corrections facilities provide basic education, job and life skills training and rehabilitation programs. In every case and in all ways, Wackenhut Corrections adheres to standards equal or higher than government run facilities, while achieving ongoing cost savings of 10 to 20 percent.[80]

One way to analyze the prospective savings and quality concerns is to recall the organizational structure and to envision what incentives the structure may provide. Corporations claim that since prison owners and managers are shareholders in the institutions, they have an incentive to pursue policies that minimize unrest and damage.[81] It stands to reason that when prisoners are occupied, they are less likely to be violent or destructive. Thus, potentially quarrelsome prisoners are kept busy with the programs offered in the private prisons. Company officials admit that these programs add to prison costs at first, but they believe that they will save the private prisons money in the long run.[82] With these goals in mind, unlike state and federal prisons, private prisons are willing to bear the initial costs of these programs.

Some of these approaches have demonstrated their worth. Reducing the destructive tendencies of the prisoners can reduce the costs of replacing and repairing in the prison.

> "In this environment, little problems become big monsters real fast," said Jimmy Turner warden of Metro Davison.
> "In a state prison," Mr. Turner continued, "if a prisoner said, 'I'm going to tear this cell up if you don't talk to me,' Well, the attitude of the state employee was, 'Go ahead and tear it up. We'll repair that $1,000 commode, but you're not going to threaten us to talk to you.'"
> Mr. Turner paused. "I can tell you right now, as a shareholder in this company, if an inmate wants to talk to me, he can talk to me."[83]

---

[77] Report to the Subcommittee on Crime, 8/96.
[78] Ibid.
[79] Wackenhut Corrections, [A], 1998.
[80] Ibid.
[81] Wackenhut Corrections, [A], 1998.
[82] Ramirez, 8/14/94, 6.
[83] Ramirez, 8/14/94, 6.

In this aspect, the private prisons constitute an improvement over many non-private prisons. In state prisons, cuts are made all too frequently in the more expensive but more useful privileges. Education, training, time spent out of prison cells, substance abuse training, and therapy for violent criminals or sex offenders are often the targets for elimination.[84] However, as prior studies suggest, these programs are most effective in reducing recidivism rates.[85] Thus, although cutting these programs may bring short-run savings, in the long-run the costs may outweigh the benefits.

Private prison officials also claim that improved conditions for the inmates lead to better work conditions for the guards.[86] A positive environment for prison employees can, theoretically, decrease costs. If the occupied prisoners are less prone to violence, then guards face less stress in the workplace. With a reduction in stress, the guards may be less prone to the "blue flu"- taking sick days. Thus, officials believe that investing money into programs should decrease the costs associated with absenteeism and overtime.[87]

2.1.2 Drawbacks

With the above evidence, it appears difficult to understand why private prisons would have any negative aspects. Yet other issues must also be taken into account. A natural question that leaps to mind is, if private prisons are not cutting costs by eliminating programs or by reducing living standards, then where are the savings coming from?

In part, private prisons save money by cutting the benefits and pensions of the guards and by reducing their pay.[88] Because the companies are not unionized, they can hire and fire workers more easily than government agencies.[89] Several private prison officials claim that the cutback in benefits to the guards is balanced by the improved atmosphere and working conditions.[90]

We can use simple economics to evaluate this assertion. A theoretical argument to support their claim would, as in the previous chapter, assess the costs and benefits involved in employment as a prison guard. A significant cost of employment entails the dangers faced by guards who control dissatisfied inmates. This cost should not be understated. Between 1988 and 1994, assaults on guards, and other employees in state and federal prisons, rose from 1,695 a year to 13,379.[91] To compensate for these risks, guards are generally promised benefits in

---

[84] Florida Corrections Commission *1996 Annual Report*, 2&5.
[85] *The Economist*, 1/20/96, 55.
[86] Ramirez, 8/14/94, 6.
[87] Ibid. These costs can be significant. If one guard calls in sick, he is still paid for the day. However, since a post cannot be left unmanned, other guards must fill in and are paid salary plus overtime. (Marx, 3/19/95,)
[88] Marx, 3/19/95, 4.
[89] Ibid.
[90] Ramirez, 8/14/94, 6.
[91] Porter, 11/26/95, 44.

the form of high pay, medical insurance, and pensions. But, if improved standards of living for the inmates decrease the likelihood of unrest and assault, then this also decreases the costs of employment to the guards. Correspondingly, their compensation could also be decreased. Theoretically, the expected utility of employment as a guard in a state or private prison should be roughly equal.

Some critics disagree. In a *Chicago Tribune* editorial, Henry Bayer, executive director of the Illinois chapter of the American Federation of State, County, and Municipal Employees, which represents most state Department of Corrections employees, claims that private prisons face greater security lapses due to inadequate training and staffing levels. He believes that because private prisons profit at the expense of employee wages and benefits, it can become more difficult to keep experienced, motivated staff.[92] He cites an example in which a jail, run by the Wackenhut Corrections Corporation, in Florida had to use untrained part-time corrections officers because the wages the jail offered were insufficient to attract and maintain staff. This use, he says, caused a higher incidence of escapes from the jail.[93]

Bayer contrasts his examples with State prison records. The Illinois Department of Corrections had no escapes from its twenty-four adult facilities in 1994, despite being filled to nearly 170% of capacity and incarcerating over 35,000 inmates.[94]

> With the mixed record, at best, of private prisons, it's hard to imagine why anyone would consider gambling with public safety by entrusting them with the difficult and dangerous task now performed by an agency and employees with a proven track record.[95]

Due to the fact that the state and federal corrections facilities have been able to outperform private prisons in many ways, especially in the important area of security, Bayer does not feel that private prisons are worth the risk.

Other critics are also concerned that profit motives provide incentives for private prisons to cut corners and take some security risks. These savings for the company run the risk of unsafe conditions, threatening the safety of the public.[96] As a means of cutting costs, many private prisons use the minimum necessary number of guards. At least two private prisons have lost their contracts in the past five years because of disagreements with government agencies over staffing levels and prison conditions.[97] Another company, the Corrections Corporation of America, has clashed with the Tennessee Department of Corrections over the best way to discipline unruly inmates. At one of the company's centers, there have been several

---

[92] Bayer, 4/15/96.
[93] Ibid.
[94] Ibid.
[95] Ibid.
[96] Smith, 1993, 5.
[97] Marx 3/19/95, 4.

major confrontations between inmates and the staff, and a few inmates escaped from the facilities.[98]

Security is paramount in prison operation. If part of a prison's function is to protect society from criminals, then a prison that cannot control or minimize escapees is failing to fulfill its role. If any policies followed by a prison, private or otherwise, cause a lapse in security, then these policies must be seriously reconsidered. Savings gained by cutting costs in one area will not be sufficient to make up for the costs associated with escape, including: damage repair, pursuit, recapture, trial, and reconviction, to name a few, not to mention the psychological costs to the public, given the awareness that a felon has escaped prison.

Prison guards and corrections officers are crucial in maintaining prison security. Returning to the theoretical argument, any consideration regarding a decrease in their salaries or benefits should take into consideration that these people work in a dangerous and inhospitable environment.

> "You want to know what real intimidation is?" [Deputy Warden] Johnson asks. "It's dropping a piece of paper out of your cell when an officer walks by that has his address on it."[99]

Many people will take a job in a prison only when they have no other choice.[100] Attentive and motivated guards are crucial in prison control. In order to attract and retain these people, salaries must be sufficient. These salaries must, in some way, compensate the guards for the risks they take on a daily basis. The actual costs and benefits may be unknown to guards when they commence employment. If, despite the improved environment, the risks associated with guard work outweigh the (now decreased) benefits, the added costs offer the guards an incentive to seek employment elsewhere.

This policy of decreasing benefits to the employees is inefficient in several ways. First, a high turnover of guards increases the cost of prisons because new guards must be recruited and trained, and the remaining guards must be paid wages plus overtime to cover the abandoned posts. Secondly, if the guards are not motivated, then they will be less likely to deal adequately with problems, leading to possible violence and destruction of prison property. Thirdly, if a prison is staffed with unmotivated, poorly trained, and/or overworked guards, prison security may suffer. Taking these problems into account, the it follows that private prisons are not necessarily meeting either the goal of saving the taxpayer money, nor of providing secure prisons that incapacitate the inmates and protect the public. Unless the costs and benefits are calculated precisely, attempts to save money at the expense of prison employee compensation can be a hazardous gamble. For these reasons alone, private prisons do not appear to be the solution they claim to be.

---

[98] Ibid.
[99] Horowitz 10/10/94, 32.
[100] Porter, 11/26/95, 72.

These problems, however, are not the only drawbacks to private prisons. The unique features of private prisons can cause other, unanticipated problems. Some states, due to local prison overcrowding, send prisoners to private prisons in other states. While economically, this trade may be sensible, legally, the issue becomes complicated. The sensitivity of the issue is portrayed vividly in the case of private prison escapees in Texas. Two sex offenders, who had been convicted in Oregon and sent to a private prison near Houston, escaped. When they were apprehended, the state could do nothing to punish them for the escape because, under legal technicalities involving the status of private prisons and their employees, the men had not committed the offense of escape. The state of Oregon was also unable to prosecute the men for escape in Oregon, because the escape occurred in Texas.[101]

Adding to the frustrations that result from interstate exchange of prisoners into private facilities, state officials complain that they are not notified as to what types of offenders are housed in private prisons. Private prisons are only required to notify federal authorities.[102] State officials expressed further concerns over the lack of compensation received for tracking down escapees and quelling riots.[103] Solving the problems of a for-profit company at the public expense must be treated as an added subsidy for these companies and draws suspicion on any claims of savings that a private firm can offer.[104]

> "If you're keeping someone for profit...why should the public be charged with apprehending them?" [Texas State Senator] Whitman asked.[105]

In addition to retrieving private prisons' escapees and stopping their riots, state officials are obliged to assume other responsibilities for private prisons. State and federal prisons must be constantly prepared to take over a private prison in the case of an emergency. They must have contingency plans for assuming control of a private prison in case a private firm goes out of business, loses control of its inmates, or its staff walks out.[106] In this way, private prisons demonstrate that they are more dependent on state and federal prisons than they might appear.

An examination of the shortcomings highlights an important issue. From an economic standpoint, private prisons appear ideal because the profit motive provides incentives to reduce costs in order to increase the net gain of the firm. Under this same motive to cut costs, however, private prisons have incentives to decrease security to the minimum level necessary. This tendency may be exaggerated if private prisons can depend, cost-free, on the resources of state and

---

[101] Associated Press, 11/7/96, 34.
[102] Ibid.
[103] Ibid.
[104] This frustration is increased in the case of interstate prisoner exchange, because in these situations, taxpayers from one state are forced to bear the expense related to the misdeeds of residents of another state.
[105] Associated Press, 11/7/96, 34.
[106] Marx, 3/19/95, 4.

federal authorities to remedy their security failures. Thus, the very features which made private prisons appear attractive are responsible for making them inappropriate.

In recognition of these drawbacks, the Justice Department reversed its plans for using private contractors to operate facilities designated in the 1996 and 1997 budget proposals. To explain this decision,

> [T]he Justice Department noted that it was "unable contractually to reduce the risk of a strike or walk out" of correctional officers employed by private firms.[107]

The need for contingency plans also reveals that private prisons face certain problems as a direct result of being privatized that state and federal prisons do not. State and federal prisons do not "go out of business." Unlike private prisons, they do not have the financial incentives and pressures which would lead them to abandon the institution should it become unprofitable. Ironically, the very traits that tend to cause criticism of state and federal prisons may lend them greater stability. State and federal prisons are supposed to function within a certain budget, and may even face budget cuts, but, in an emergency, necessary funds are available. Independently, private prisons cannot guarantee that their funds will be sufficient. Functioning as a business, once the costs greatly surpass the profits, the private prison will be forced to shut down.

The possibility of a private prison going out of business destroys the potential to "save" private prisons by increasing contractual constraints. For instance, it would be possible to fine a prison a given amount for every expense incurred by state and federal prisons. By placing these requirements into a contract, the public would essentially allow the private prisons to maximize revenue subject to specified constraints.[108] Although this provision would not eliminate the problems associated with interstate escapees, it could increase the incentives of the private prison to increase security in order to avoid the costs associated with escapes. Unfortunately, as we have seen above, these incentives will function only as long as the business is profitable. If the costs become too large relative to the revenue, the private firm will go out of business.

This analysis does not ignore the very real criticism that state and federal prisons, because they have a potentially unlimited access to funding, may be prone to waste. If prison sentencing were the only available means of punishment and deterrence, then the choice is between the possibilities of a type of moral hazard, the risk that people will behave irresponsibly because they know that they will be rescued if things go wrong, or a breach of security. That difficult choice would depend greatly on whether society wished to lock criminals behind bars at any cost, or whether they were willing to tolerate a level of escapes and/or prison failures.

Fortunately, there are alternatives to tradeoff between private and public prisons. Community service, work release, probation, drug rehabilitation, and other

---

[107] Report to the Subcommittee on Crime, 8/96, 3.

[108] I am grateful to Jason Maga for making this point.

forms of alternative sentencing can be used as a form of punishment and deterrence for non-violent criminals.[109] This form of sentencing should help to solve the problem of prison overcrowding and, in the long-run, be a cost effective means of fighting crime. By using these forms of sentencing, the above choice becomes easier to make.

2.2 Power and Money: Expanding Imprisonment and Profit

The above summary demonstrates that, despite outward appearances, private prisons are not successful in providing adequate prison control at a lower cost to the taxpayer. In fact, because of the problems inherent in current private prison setup, these prisons could actually result in costing the taxpayer more than he would pay for non-private prisons. This reality makes it questionable why we should continue to support private prisons.

This question is recurrent in the study of government: why do inefficient structures persist? All issues regarding prisons, their use, management, and sentencing, are decided in government. In theory, the government consists of benevolent individuals who are placed in power by the people to make the best decisions possible. Unfortunately, legislators also have incentives that, at times, may run counter to the best interests of the people.

In creating and/or supporting policies, legislators must balance the myriad demands of their voters and lobbyists. To be able to keep their job and make future legislation, legislators must create or vote for policies that reflect the desires of those who elect them.

Support for private prisons appears to be sound legislation, particularly since, as stated above, the goals of private prisons are to run prisons at a savings to the taxpayer. This proposal is understandably attractive to voters. It appears to meet both their desires to decrease crime and to lower their taxes. Therefore, a proposal to increase use of private prisons should meet little resistance from the voters.

Some of the public will undoubtedly research the proposal, and even speak out against its implementation. Unfortunately, the political system provides disincentives to unorganized groups in terms of passing or preventing legislation. For an individual to bring attention to the flaws of certain policies, that person would have to research the issue, and bear the costs of publicizing (advertising, editorializing, campaigning, etc...) his or her opinion. Unless a person feels very strongly about a particular issue, he or she has little incentive to assume this personal expense, because his or her share in any gains made by changing the policies would be smaller than the individual costs entailed in effecting that change. Since each individual reaps small benefits or bears small costs from most policies, the cost of organization and action is not always seen to be worth the effort.

---

[109] See Chapter 1 for more details and for an argument regarding out of prison sentences for non-violent criminals.

On the other hand, private prison companies benefit from proposals to use or increase the use of private prisons. These groups already are organized; they have a large financial stake in the passage of these proposals, and thus they have an incentive to lobby and advertise in order to pressure legislators to act in their favor. Any lobbying costs for privatization of prisons are likely to be compensated by the gains to be made through private prison contracts.

Thus, a simple cost/benefit analysis indicates why all too frequently policies are decided *not* on what is in the best interest of the people, but on what is in the best interests of the lobbyists. By making a proposal appear attractive to the voters, it is likely to be passed. Individuals simply do not have the financial incentives of companies to organize and successfully push for their ideal legislation.

A natural question might be, do private prisons really present large financial incentives? The answer appears surprising. Prisons have become as a market of growth for large corporations. The federal and state governments have recently allocated billions of dollars to prison budgets.[110] Spending on the construction and operation of prisons is increasing twice as fast as the growth in overall state spending.[111]

In 1995, less than two percent of the nation's 1.5 million inmates were in private prisons.[112] However, President Clinton's 1996 budget included a proposal that would let private prisons manage most of the federal pretrial detention centers and also the minimum and medium-security prisons.[113] Some private prison facilities are built and operated by the private companies, but most are built with public money, and are run on contract by private firms.[114]

With low start-up costs, these companies can be very profitable. One company, for example, manages 27 facilities and has about 15,000 beds under contract. The company is paid approximately $40 a day per inmate, and earned about $4 million in profits in 1993.[115]

With so much money to be gained in prisons, many penologists are concerned that even if the public attitude towards prisons were to change (especially if the growth in prisons proves to be ineffective against crime) the emerging interests groups would move to prevent a change in policy.

> ...[T]he prison-building surge may create its own constituencies - architects, contractors, vendors, labor unions, whole communities - with a vested interest in maintaining the status quo.[116]

Even faced with the knowledge that the crime fighting policies in place were costly, ineffective, and wasteful, private prison companies and the companies that

---

[110] Kuntz, 11/6/94, 3.
[111] Holmes, 11/6/94, 3.
[112] Marx, 3/19/95, 4.
[113] Ibid.
[114] Report to the Subcommittee on Crime, 8/96, 21.
[115] Marx, 3/19/95, 4.
[116] Holmes, 11/6/94, 3.

did business with them would lobby actively to maintain and increase their activity. Although ideally, their role in society is to protect the public and punish criminals, realistically, their main goal is to make a profit. If representing the best interests of society were to cause a corporate loss, then these more lofty ideals would most often be abandoned.

These lobbies would not only oppose any decrease in the prison budgets, they would oppose any change, however beneficial it might be, if the change threatened their personal interests. Recall the previous section's assertion that the use of alternative sentencing policies helps avoid the choice between moral hazard and security problems. In Chapter 1, an argument is made that the use of alternative sentencing, instead of prison, for nonviolent criminals could provide many benefits. Some of these benefits include: relieving much of the current overcrowding conditions in prisons, protecting the public from violent criminals, providing a deterrent against violent crimes, making the punishment fit the crime, and attempting to break the vicious cycle of crime in families by keeping a nonviolent offender parent with his or her children instead of placing him in prison.

To make a profit, normal businesses need to attract customers. This is done through advertising and other marketing devices. To make a profit, a private prison needs a steady or increasing flow of prisoners. Thus, the incentives exist for private prisons to lobby for increased prison time, rather than alternative sentences, to punish crimes.

Private prisons incarcerate minimum and medium security inmates, many of whom have committed nonviolent offenses. The above policy would threaten their interests, or even their survival. Revised legislation and sentencing guidelines that would remove nonviolent criminals from prison would severely decrease their proportion of inmates. To private prisons, which are paid on a per prisoner per day basis, the loss of a large number of prisoners would decrease their revenue and profits. Examining this situation through the perspective of economics, if the revenue were to fall below the costs, then the private firm would eventually go out of business. Given this possibility, private firms have every incentive to lobby against alternative sentencing, as well as to use scare tactics to turn the public against the proposals as well.

2.3 Conclusion

From the above analysis, it becomes clear that private firms and their lobbies are not solving the crime problem as much as maintaining their market shares. Although on the surface they appear to be the answer to society's conflicting desires for better crime control at a lower cost, a closer look reveals that they may actually increase costs and decrease security. Additionally, once entrenched, private prisons will be difficult to eliminate without a struggle. Not only the companies themselves, but all companies who do business with them will lobby and advertise in order to secure the continuation of the private prisons industry. Instead of serving and protecting the public, private prisons are in the business of serving and protecting their own interests.

Chapter 3

Prostitution

Prostitution is rightfully known as the oldest profession, because, quite frankly, it has always existed. Arguments against it stem from morality, to fears of the spread of disease, to protection of the family, and to fears of the subordination of women. Many of these concerns are legitimate, but the criminalization of prostitution has not proved to be effective in eliminating the profession.

This is an interesting puzzle. Why haven't the threats of penalties uprooted this problem? Insight can be obtained by use of analytic tools from the social sciences where I show the counterintuitive assertion that criminalization can actually increase the problems associated with prostitution. I further argue that while legalization clearly fails to solve our moral issues, it could be the best solution to the mosaic of drawbacks that presently accompany prostitution.

3.1 Victimless Crime

One principal reason that prostitution is a difficult issue to address in an analysis of crime is that the identity of the victim is not clear. Is it the prostitute, the client, or the sensitivity of the community? To complicate the matter, there are places, such as Nevada and certain European countries, where prostitution is not illegal. This fact confounds the issue by making it more vague. Why is prostitution viewed as a crime in some places, and who are the victims?

In terms of child prostitution, the victim is easily identified; it is the child. Children, especially young ones, are neither old enough nor sufficiently mature to choose this line of work for themselves. But when the prostitute is a consenting adult, the identity of a victim becomes blurred. We cannot automatically consider a prostitute as a victim, if, in a realistic sense, that person has made a free decision to enter the profession. This is true no matter however degrading or unappealing the profession may appear. It is difficult to claim that the customer is a victim because he or she has sought and purchased the services of the prostitute. The spouse/significant other of the customer could be treated as a victim, but, arguably, it is not the purpose of legislation to enforce marital fidelity and moral codes. For that reason, prostitution cannot be treated as a crime against a client's partner. A vague argument can be made that society as a whole is a victim, but this idea needs more explanation.

3.1.1 Why is Prostitution Illegal?

To understand the issue of prostitution and its illegal status, the topic needs to be explored in more depth. For various reasons, some are obvious, prostitution and those who practice it have generally been stigmatized throughout history. According to Davis and Shaffer, even that portion of the general public who tolerate prostitution prefers to keep it invisible and somehow separate from the rest of society.[117]

The second class status forced on prostitutes has evolved for a number of reasons. As a sample, consider the moralists, who believe that prostitutes separate society from the goals for which we should strive; and the feminists, who frequently view that prostitution wrongfully increases men's power and position over women.[118] This negative attitude regarding the profession has persisted for several millennia; proof is found in the Bible. Without question, people are generally uncomfortable with prostitution.

> The presence of prostitution begs, however subliminally, the awkward question of who is using their services. Whose husband? Whose mate?[119]

Continuing our examination, if we view prostitutes as victims, then a case can be made to protect them. Prostitutes put themselves in danger. After all, customers have been known to steal from prostitutes,[120] and prostitutes are often the victims of rape or other types of assault.[121] In fact, the dangers are so extreme that in Canada the mortality rate for women prostitutes in the 1980s was estimated to be 40 times larger than the national average.[122] This is worrisome. Adding to the difficulties, pimps have created exploitative relationships with prostitutes where they offer protection and obtain clients in return for a coerced share in the prostitute's earnings.

No matter how we may try to finesse moral issues, there remain serious societal problems associated with prostitution. Prostitution has been blamed for the spread of venereal diseases and AIDS.[123] Members of the public complain that prostitution is followed by a rise of crime and violence.[124] As supported both by fact and by general public impressions, some prostitutes use illegal drugs,[125] while others steal from their customers.[126]

An initial reaction to this information could be to argue for tougher laws and sanctions in order to eliminate the problems and issues involved in prostitution. A long-term perspective, however, suggests that criminalizing the profession may only make matters worse.

---

[117] Davis, and Shaffer, 1997.
[118] Shrage, 1996, 41.
[119] Riddel, 1997, 7.
[120] Ottawa: Department of Supply and Services, 1985.
[121] Shrage, 1996, 42.
[122] Davis and Shaffer, 1997, 14.
[123] San Francisco Task Force on Prostitution Final Report, 1996.
[124] See all of the above.
[125] Ibid and Simon and Witte, 1982, 257-8.
[126] Simon and Witte, 1982, 257.

3.1.1.1 Prostitutes

Who is a prostitute? Simon and Witte define a prostitute as,

> [A]ny person who grants nonmarital sexual access to a number of clients by mutual agreement, and without emotional ties, for remuneration which provides part or all of that person's livelihood.[127]

Why do people chose prostitution? The many offered reasons range from tax free activity, to psychological reactions caused by having been abused in childhood, to a desire for independence. Most women, however, give economic reasons for their decision. This argument is supported by one source which claims that female prostitutes can earn anywhere from 4 - 10 times the median annual wages of legally employed women, and that these earnings are tax free.[128] In fact, a researcher quoted one prostitute as saying,

> I don't think you can ever eliminate the economic factor motivating women to prostitution. Even a call girl could never make as much in a straight job as she could at prostitution. All prostitutes are in it for the money...[T]he choice is not between starvation and life, but it is between $5,000 and $25,000 or between $10,000 and $50,000. That's a pretty big difference.[129]

So, simply from a standard "supply and demand" economic perspective, prostitution is unlikely to disappear. Due to basic human drives, there probably always will exist a demand for the services of prostitutes, and, as long as that demand exists, it will be profitable for others to supply those services. But, if the services cannot be provided legally, they will be offered illegally, at a somewhat higher cost, to include the risk of arrest.

The presence of higher costs follow from standard economic logic. If prostitution is a free market activity, then competition will drive prices down to the point at which the costs of labor are essentially equal to the profits. If prostitution is illegal, then the supply of prostitution will shift, or decrease. By making the services of a prostitute more difficult to obtain, the prostitute has greater leeway in charging higher prices. It is the prospect of these larger wages that creates an incentive to choose this profession - thus perpetuating the profession's existence. The remaining question is, if prostitution is unlikely to disappear on its own, then what effect do criminal laws have on the various problems prostitution entails?

---

[127] Simon and Witte, 1982, 243.
[128] Simon and Witte, 1982, 259.
[129] Millett, 1975, 34-5.

3.1.2 Disease

The issue of disease is crucial. In a world in which AIDS has become a large and continual growing concern, where the UN estimates that approximately 1% of all men are infected, the possibility that sex workers may spread the disease should cause alarm. But, in direct conflict with popular opinion, the U.S. Department of Health claims that only 3-5% of sexually transmitted disease in the U.S. is related to prostitution.[130] Additionally, studies have shown that prostitutes tend to be at a lower risk of carrying HIV than are their customers.

These results are surprising, but there is a simple explanation based on economics. Because of the risk posed by their livelihood, prostitutes tend to be more likely to require condoms and to use other safety precautions.[131] This makes economic sense. An expected value analysis similar to that in Chapter One dictates that the prostitute should decrease potential costs – here, the likelihood of disease – to increase expected earnings. In fact, one study has shown that prostitutes who do not use intravenous drugs are less likely to spread AIDS than are men who frequently change sexual partners.[132] Davis and Shaffer note that,

> It is men [customers] who generally refuse to use condoms; we have never heard of a woman [prostitute] holding a gun to a man's head and forcing him to have sex without a condom, but we have heard of the reverse.[133]

On the other hand, other studies have shown that the more economically dependent upon prostitution the person becomes, the more willing that prostitute will be to engage in unsafe sex.[134] Again, this is a natural economic reaction. If a prostitute needs a certain threshold income for basic needs, then he or she may be willing to accept a higher level of risk in order to obtain this income. If the prostitute refuses, he or she faces the possibilities that the customer will seek the services of a competitor.

The last finding sheds light on two important issues. The first regards the very notion of the prostitute as a transmitter of disease. Many studies view the prostitute as a "vector" of disease.[135] In other words, the prostitute is portrayed as one who takes the disease from one client and spreads it to others. The bias in this depiction is evident; it shows no concern for the health or safety of the prostitute. Additionally, it depicts the prostitute as one who is willingly spreading disease to "innocent" clients. The clients are portrayed as victims, rather than as co-actors in

---

[130] Prostitutes' Education Network, [A], 1997. (Statistics are based on studies made during the 1980's and reflect current trends.)
[131] Davis and Shaffer, 1997, 10.
[132] Jolin, 1993.
[133] Davis and Shaffer, 1997, fn 49, 57. (Material from Maggie's, the Toronto Prostitutes' Community Service Project.)
[134] Browne and Minichiello, 1996, 39.
[135] See Downe, 1997, and Browne and Minichiello, 1996.

unsafe sex. They are absolved of all responsibility for their actions.¹³⁶ In most cases, however, it is the clients who desire unprotected sex. If the prostitute needs the income, she or he may be willing to take the risk of disease in order to avoid losing the customer. Thus, the decision is made based on economic reasons, rather than out of a lack of morality or judgment.

> Despite their high level of knowledge about AIDS, clients of male sex workers frequently engage in non-condom sex with sex workers and rarely wear condoms with regular sex partners.¹³⁷

If we accept the fact that clients also are responsible for the spread of disease, then calls to abolish prostitution on the grounds of disease control are weakened. In fact, if prostitution were legalized and controlled, where an important aspect of legalization includes mandatory use of condoms and testing for disease, then the prostitute could be even less likely to be a vector or a victim, of disease.

If prostitution were legal and licensed, then health standards imposed upon the profession could require the prostitutes to engage in safe sex. This requirement would both improve the control of contagious disease, and it would protect the prostitutes themselves. If, as argued above, the prostitute in need of money and worrying about losing a customer to another prostitute tends to comply with the demands, then that prostitute may be willing to take risks that he or she otherwise would not. If prostitution were controlled, however, then the risk of losing the customer to another prostitute is diminished because no legal prostitutes will engage in unsafe sex.¹³⁸

As an economic analogy, consider the argument for minimum wage. Proponents of minimum wage claim that competition places workers at a disadvantage, because if one worker demands a higher (or fair) wage for his labor, then instead of meeting his demand, the employer can easily replace him with someone else who is willing to work for the lower wage. The same situation applies to the quest for minimum working conditions. Thus, due to the fact that other laborers are available, the ability of any one worker to make even minimal demands is weakened. Facing the threat of unemployment, laborers may have to accept insufficient wages or unsafe working conditions. Just as minimum wage/working conditions laws help workers to avoid this weakened bargaining position, legalization of prostitution, coupled with control, would protect the prostitute from having to take risks.

The problems described above can also be examined through the use of game theory. Using a game similar to the "divide the dollar" game, we can imagine a scenario in which two players may split a dollar between them if they are able to

---

¹³⁶ Browne and Minichiello, 1996, 35-6.

¹³⁷ Browne and Minichiello, 1996, 43.

¹³⁸ It is important to note here that some illegal prostitutes may arise to meet the demand for unsafe sex, but these people could be punished in the same way that other illegal enterprises are treated. Because legalization, under the description given below, should meet most demand, this number should be small.

come to an agreement. In this game, however, the rules change so that one of the two players to split the dollar must be John. If Mary proposes a 50-50 division of the dollar with john, Sue would be left out, but can counter with a 40-60 division, with the 60 cents going to John. Obviously, Mary can make a counter-proposal of 30-70 to avoid being eliminated from the game. Continuing this progression, John can earn up to the dollar minus the reservation level of Mary or Sue. Clearly, John has an established ability to exploit the other players. One way to counter this effect would be in Mary and Sue formed a coalition. Another way would occur if the rules were to change – requiring that each player received at least a certain amount. Changing the rules of the game – in terms of prostitution – would either entail violence, which is counter to society's needs, or by legalization and regulation.

Ironically, by taking the power to make this decision away from the prostitute, the government could give him or her more power. Thomas Schelling noted that if a person is prohibited from taking an action that he does not wish to take anyway, then others will not force him to do so.[139] As an analogy from political science, a president can frequently refuse to meet demands from foreign leaders if it is known that Congress will not ratify them. Thus, by having less power domestically, the president has more power internationally. Similarly, if both the prostitute and the client are aware that unsafe sex between a prostitute and client is forbidden, then the prostitute has a greater ability to deny such a request, should one even arise.

From the analysis, we see that although concerns of the spread of disease are legitimate, these concerns are better addressed through legalization than through criminalization. Of course, even with legalization, some illegal prostitution will persist. The size of this outlaw community would depend on what members would be excluded from, or, due to the restrictive structure, who would choose against participation in, the legal profession. This, in itself, underscores the importance of correctly designing the accompanying legislation.

But, for purposes of our discussion of transmitted diseases, suppose, first, that infected prostitutes are excluded from legal work, second, that this is widely known, and third, that there are a reasonable number of legal and disease-free prostitutes to handle natural demand. Now, by use of economic reasoning, consider the decision problem facing a client. In knowledge of the restrictions placed upon the services of legal prostitutes, the client can choose a legal or illegal prostitute. The rewards are sexual release and pleasure; the costs include the fee as well as the likelihood of incurring a serious disease. Given the very fact that legalization would offer clients the ability to make a decision between risk and safety, it is not hard to envision that the more positive decision is to use legal rather than illegal services.[140]

---

[139] Schelling, 1966.

[140] This analysis entails an explicit parallel to that found in Chapter 1 regarding the choice between a violent or nonviolent crime.

3.1.3 Drugs

Without question, a legitimate belief and concern is that some prostitutes will begin to use drugs, or to increase their drug intake, with the profession. If this is so, we are caught in a vicious cycle where many will continue to engage in prostitution in order to support their habit. The personal problems of a prostitute continue to escalate; by sinking money into the consumption of drugs instead of investing money into the future, the prostitute may find him or herself in a position in which the practice of prostitution is continued indefinitely.

Mixing drug use with prostitution is indeed a risk. Studies have shown that prostitutes who used illegal drugs were more likely than their counterparts to engage in unsafe sex and to thereby spread AIDS.[141] In addition to the economic argument advanced above, mind-altering substances may impact the prostitute's negotiating skills and can lead to an increased willingness to engage in unsafe sex.[142] Some studies show, in contrast, that the use of drugs or alcohol by a client can lead to a decreased risk because of impotence or of loss of interest in the prostitute.[143]

What means could we employ to side-step the potential difficulties? Part of this analysis is described in the Chapter 4. For now, it suffices to point out that the criminalization of prostitution has not solved this problem, just as criminalization has not helped in other areas. Consider, however, a potential benefit from legalization. By obtaining influence in how the profession is regulated, we can control some of the problems that accompany drugs, such as disease. As already argued, legalization should involve accountability. Drugs could be prohibited in the workplace to accommodate concerns over safety lapses. If drugs were to be used, then provisions would have to be made to ensure that compliance with health and safety standards would continue.

3.1.4 Crime and Violence

A very real reason that the public is resistant to the existence of prostitution is that it is frequently associated with public disturbance and with a rise of crime and of violence.

> The police cannot ignore residents in red-light districts who complain about condoms and needles littering the street, or about their wives being harassed by kerb-crawlers.[144]

To add an emotional but real tone, imagine your reactions if your young son or daughter is forced to traverse such districts on their way to a park or to school.

---

[141] Davis and Shaffer, 1997, 10 & fn 46, p. 57.
[142] Browne and Minichiello, 1996, 41.
[143] Ibid.
[144] *The Economist*, 11/12/94, 73.

This is not mere speculation or charged rhetoric; evidence does show that prostitutes are often found in the midst of such surroundings. However, Davis and Shaffer claim that the direction of causality that is generally perceived can be misguided. Instead of prostitution causing crime and violence, they argue that prostitution is generally found where these elements already exist.[145] The authors use the example of Holland to support their claim. They note that after Holland legalized prostitution, the problems of crime, violence, public disturbance, and drugs normally associated with prostitution were no longer as prevalent among Holland's prostitutes.

Why would prostitutes choose to work in unsafe, criminal areas? By increasing risk, doesn't this increase the prostitute's costs? For most of us, it is difficult to understand why anyone would willingly work in this type of surroundings. But, appealing to economics makes this phenomenon understandable. Recall that the economic decisions of a prostitute are not unrelated to those of a businessman. The income from customers must be balanced with daily costs. For a prostitute, some of the short-term costs involve the possibility of apprehension with an accompanying fine or prison time. We expect an efficient businessman to take actions to reduce the likelihood of higher costs. In the same way, prostitutes might decide to work in an area where they face a lower probability of apprehension. This action can lower their potential costs.

Using this economic line of reasoning, it becomes clear that because prostitution is a criminal act, the prostitutes must locate themselves in areas in which they are either unseen or tolerated by the police. Criminalization makes these safe, well-lit areas that would be preferable working conditions for prostitutes, out of reach. Instead, the prostitute is required to hide in darker, more dangerous places, in order to continue to work without hassles from the police.

3.2 The Economics of Prostitution

If a prostitute chooses to continue to work in a more dangerous location, in order to avoid police detection, then the decision can be described as essentially making an expected utility calculation. Again, this calculation is of the type used in the economic decisions of businesses. The decision is based upon the values and risks to be gained by hiding, H, by risking arrest in the open, O, or by "going straight," S.

To explain the following calculus facing the prostitute, start by examining what happens if she is working while hiding in an unsafe area. Here, she must compare her expected income, I, with the possibility of a cost, C, which could arise due to crimes committed against her, and the possibility of costs, A, arising from arrest. To make sense of her computations, the prostitute can reason that the likelihood of having a crime committed against her is some probability, denoted p_u. For example, if the probability of being a target of a crime in the unsafe area is

---

[145] Davis and Shaffer, 1997, 57.

roughly 40%, then the prostitute can expect that 40% of the time she would expect to lose, C. Additionally, the probability of arrest in the unsafe area is denoted Q_u.

The expected gains of hiding in an unsafe area include the likelihood of not being arrested $(1- Q_u)$, times the income) $[(1-p_u)I - p_uC]$, which includes the locale's dangers. The costs are the likelihood of being arrested times the cost, $Q_u(A)$. Therefore, the expected utility for Hiding is:

$$EU(H) = (1-Q_u)[(1-p_u)I - p_uC] - Q_u(A). \qquad (7)$$

Now consider the prostitute's "earnings versus cost" equation if she operates in the open. Here, the major expenses include the cost, A, due to arrest, which happens with probability Q_o, and the cost associated with harm which occurs with (the presumably lower) probability p_o. Using similar reasoning, this means that the prostitute's expected earnings in the safer Open area are:

$$EU(O) = (1-Q_o)[(1-p_o)I - p_oC] - Q_o(A). \qquad (8)$$

Finally, the prostitute can select the option of "going straight" and finding legal employment. This prospect offers the risk-free wage of w.

$$EU(S) = w \qquad (9)$$

The choice facing the prostitute involves all factors. If the expected legal wage, w, is very low for an individual, then that person may elect to take the risks of either open or hidden prostitution. In our simple analysis, this is true if w is less than the expected gains from either of the remaining options. (For simplicity of analysis, I have left out other cost factors, such as the stigma attached to prostitution. These factors, however, do not change the sense of the following analysis; they merely affect the income level.[146]) The decision between the remaining options is affected both by the respective probabilities and by the potential costs.

A great deal of criminal analysis assumes that if we increase the probability of arrest and/or amount of punishment, then the criminal will be deterred from crime.[147] The notion is that changing the factors can make crime costly for the criminal, relative to legal activity. In particular, this means that we chose the cost of arrest, A, and the probability of arrest, Q, to be high enough so that

$$(1-Q)[(1-p)I - pC] - Q(A) < w ,$$

---

[146] A change in the income level can produce a change in the decision made. If the cost due to stigmatization is very high, then people may not choose prostitution. However, the use of stigmas for policy matters would be imprecise at best. Consider the alternative: if the cost due to stigmatization is very high, then prostitutes may never be able to find legal work, and may be dependent on prostitution.

[147] See, for example, Becker, 1968.

then the legal employment becomes attractive. However, a crucial assumption in this analysis is that the criminal has only two choices: between legal and illegal activity. Anecdotal evidence informs us that prostitutes recognize that they have a third choice - continued but hidden activity. If this is the case, then police and criminologists must take into account the risks and rewards of underground employment and the comparisons that criminals will make with those of open activity. By this, I mean that if we increase the costs and likelihood of apprehension, we make the undesired, hidden activity, more attractive. Namely, if $EU(H) > EU(O)$, or if

$$(1-Q_u)[(1-p_u)I - p_uC] - Q_u(A) > (1-Q_o)[(1-p_o)I - p_oC] - Q_o(A).$$

or if the risks of the unsafe area are dominated as

$$p_u < [p_o(Q_o-1)/(Q_u-1)] + [(Q_u-Q_o)(I+A)/(I+C)(Q_u-1)], \qquad (10)$$

then the risks of working in an unsafe area become profitable. Thus, the hidden activity of doing business in an unsafe environment with all of its accompanying risks (as captured by p_u), is more profitable than open activity. Moreover, if the expected utility of hidden activity is larger than what a prostitute could earn by going straight, then the prostitute will continue to practice his or her trade.

It is easy to attack this analysis. After all, the safety and health problems accompanying work in unsafe surroundings, described by the cost, C, can be much more severe than the cost of arrest, A, of even a vindictive society. But what complicates this analysis is the likelihood of either cost occurring. Just as a businessman may assume a highly risky venture, if that risk is within bounds, the prostitute also instinctively compares not only A and C, but also the likelihood of either cost occurring.

Note that the above inequality takes into account both the respective probabilities of arrest in an unsafe and open location as well as the probabilities of being harmed in either location. It is possible to determine the effect of these variables, as well as the effect of a change in income, cost of injury, or cost of arrest on the prostitute's decision by the use of comparative statics. We can rename the equation, let:

$$p_u < p_o(Q_o-1)/(Q_u-1) + (Q_u-Q_o)(I+A)/(I+C)(Q_u-1) = F \qquad (11)$$

By use of calculus, we can determine the effects of a change in any particular variable on the prostitute's decision regarding working in hiding. If the sign of the derivative is negative, then an increase in the variable will lead to a decrease in the advantages of working in hiding. If the sign is positive, then an increase in the variable will lead to an increase in working in hiding.

Start by determining the effects of changing p_o, the likelihood of arrest in an open area. A direct computation shows that

$$\partial F/\partial Q_o - [(I+A) - p_o(I+C)]/(I+C)(1-Q_u)$$

The result of this equation is that an increase in the probability of arrest in the open may result in an increase in the prostitute's decision to operate in hiding. As the denominator is positive, because Q_u is less than one, the numerator determines whether or not the effect of an increase in the probability of arrest in the open will lead to an increase in hiding. This decision will be determined by the relative values of p_o, C and A. If

$$p_o < (I+A)/(I+C),$$

then the equation will be positive meaning that an increase in the probability of arrest in the open will lead to an increase in working in hiding. If, in contrast,

$$p_o > (I+A)/(I+C),$$

then we would see the opposite. As p_o is a probability, it is less than or equal to one. If the values for C and A are equal, then the right hand side will be equal to one, so an increase in Q_o will lead to an increase in those working in hiding.

Recall that C includes the cost of crimes committed against the prostitute. If the severity of crimes committed against the prostitute were to increase, then the cost, C, of these crimes might increase relative to that of arrest, A. In this case, the value of $(I+A)/(I+C)$ will be lower. Eventually, a point is reached where $p_o > (I+A)/(I+C)$. At this point, an increase in the level of Q_o, the likelihood of arrest in the open, would cause a decrease in the attractiveness of working in hiding. Would this lead to the counter-intuitive assertion that more law enforcement actually increases the activity of open prostitution? The economic analysis suggests this is the case if legal wages remain low.

Upon consideration, the result makes sense. We would expect that as the probability of arrest in the open increases, then a prostitute would be better off hiding. Furthermore, it makes sense that this decision would also be based on the relative costs of injury versus those of arrest. If the cost of injury becomes much larger than the cost of arrest, then we might expect that prostitutes would choose to work in the open. Although this option might entail a greater risk in terms of arrest, it might avoid some of the lower expected utility in the form of higher costs due to injury.

Now turn to the effects of increasing the likelihood of arrest in hiding. A computation shows that

$$\partial F/\partial Q_u = \{-1/(Q_u-1)^2\}\{p_o(Q_o-1)\} + (I+C)(I+A)(Q_o-1)/[(Q_u-1)(I+C)]^2$$

$$= (1-Q_o)[(I+C)p_o + (I+A)]/(I+C)(Q_u-1)^2$$

This equation shows the effect of an increase in the probability of arrest in hiding. All terms are positive. This means that an increase in the probability of arrest in hiding, Q_u will increase the decision to operate in hiding. This result may appear counterintuitive – it implies that an increase in the probability of arrest in unsafe locations will cause an increase in operating in unsafe locations. However, the result makes sense as an increase in the probability of arrest, even in an unsafe location, would realistically drive a criminal – prostitute or otherwise – even deeper into hiding, while continuing to engage in criminal activity.

To determine the effects of a change in income, I, the computations are

$$\partial F/\partial I = (Q_o - Q_u)(C+A)/(1-Q_u)(I+C)^2.$$

This equation shows the effect of an increase in income on the prostitute's decision regarding where to work. Because we know that $(1-Q_u)$ is positive, the denominator of the equation is positive. The sign of the comparative static depends on the relative values of Q_u and Q_o. If the probability of arrest in hiding, Q_u, is larger than the probability of arrest in the open, Q_o, then the equation will have a negative sign, and the prostitute will react to an increase in income by decreasing her work in hiding and by working in the open. If, in contrast, Q_u is smaller than Q_o, then an increase in income from prostitution will be followed by an increase in working in hiding. Again, the result is intuitive – it demonstrates that the effect of a change in income alone cannot determine the prostitute's decision. Rather, the decision is also dependent upon the relative probabilities of arrest in the open and in hiding.

To understand the effects of punishment, computations show that

$$\partial F/\partial A = (Q_o - Q_u)/(1-Q_u)(I+C)$$

This equation shows the effect of an increase in the cost of arrest on the prostitute's decision regarding where to work. Again, because $(1-Q_u)$ is positive, the denominator of the equation is positive. As in the last equation, the sign of the comparative static depends on the relative values of Q_u and Q_o. Intuitively, if Q_u, the probability of being arrested in hiding, is smaller than Q_o, then an increase in the cost of arrest from prostitution will be followed by an increase in working in hiding.

The equation

$$\partial F/\partial C = (Q_u - Q_o)(1-Q_u)(I+A)/(Q_u-1)^2(I+C)^2.$$

shows the effect of an increase in the cost of injury, C, on the prostitute's decision regarding where to work. Here, the denominator of the equation is positive. Thus, the sign of the comparative static depends on the relative values of Q_u and Q_o. If Q_u, the probability of being arrested in hiding, is greater than Q_o, then the equation will be positive. Thus, an increase in the cost of injury from prostitution will be followed by an increase in working in hiding.

This result may appear counterintuitive. While we would expect that a prostitute would increase work in hiding if the probability of arrest were lower there, we might also expect that a prostitute has a higher likelihood of being injured on the job when working in an unsafe location than she or he would in the open. If this is the case, then it seems odd that as the cost of injury increases, a prostitute may choose to subject him or herself to more potential injury in hiding. However, the dependence of this decision on the relative probabilities of arrest can serve as an explanation. A prostitute may be willing to risk even high levels of injury in order to avoid arrest. Indeed, there is evidence of this type of decision making in prostitution.

The equation

$$\partial F/\partial p_o = (1-Q_o)/(1-Q_u),$$

shows the effect of an increase in the probability of injury in the open, p_o, on the prostitute's decision regarding where to work. The sign of the equation is positive. The result follows intuitively by asserting that an increase in the probability of being injured in the open will lead to an increase in working in hiding.

3.2.1 Results

According to these expressions, comparing open versus hidden activity, we learn that even if the cost of arrest, A, is less than that due to crime, C; it can be in the prostitute's best interests to continue with prostitution in hiding. Of course, this will be true only so long as the benefits of prostitution exceed a legal wage:

$$(1-Q_u)[(1-p_u)I - p_u C] - Q_u(A) \geq w.$$

Our unfortunate conclusion, then, is that the results challenge the notion that the strategy of increasing the probability of arrest or the level of punishment can decrease crime. Instead we find that increasing one or both of these variables may drive the action into hiding where the criminal activity continues but is harder to detect or regulate. Thus, rather than deterrence on prostitution, we see displacement.

3.3 Consequences and Costs of Hiding

By forcing prostitutes to hide, the government creates new opportunities for crime and violence. Recall that an important aspect of the prostitute's profit equation involves the likelihood of apprehension. As shown, if the prostitutes must avoid detection by the police, we must expect them to choose unsafe, darker areas to meet customers. The great drawback to these areas is that by being less likely to be able to screen their customers, prostitutes face a greater likelihood of assault than they would in a more secure area. Similarly, by seeking services in unsafe areas, the customer is exposed to a greater chance of being a victim of crime.

By forcing prostitution underground, the workplace is less likely to be safe. In turn, we should also expect prostitutes to become targets of rape and other violent assault. This is the case; as one former prostitute recalled:

> I had been working eight months when I opened the door for the wrong person...I guess I was off my guard...He pushed his way in and another man followed. One put a knife to my throat and they raped me...I don't understand why people always assume that, when a prostitute talks about being raped, she's describing a situation in which she has sex and then she doesn't get paid. Short of physical torture, the threat of murder and torture is the most traumatic element of this type of rape. [148]

Now consider other consequences of forcing prostitution to be illegal. Due to the need for secrecy, a certain sense of futility sets in. Among the consequences, we must expect a lack of communication. Indeed, this prostitute continues,

> After I was raped, I learned from some of the other women that these men had been doing the same thing to women at other parlors in town. No one passed the information around, I guess, from a feeling of hopelessness...[149]

But rape is a crime. So why don't prostitutes report these crimes to the police? The answer follows directly from our analysis of the economic costs. As this prostitute states,

> I couldn't call the police after I was raped. The owners of the parlor where I worked begged me not to, as it might focus attention on our parlor, which could result in my co-workers getting busted, the parlor being closed down and my co-workers being forced out on the street.[150]

It is even worse; the police, far from offering protection from assault, may condone violent acts against prostitutes, and have been known to abuse the prostitutes themselves.[151] The experience of the 1993 arrest and abuse of prostitute Michelle Vuong on a night in which she was out but *not* working, is unfortunately typical.

> [A] police car pulled alongside and one of the officers shouted at her, "No hooking." Michelle said nothing... Apparently this was the wrong response. The police car cruised behind her, the same officer leaned from his window, "Faggot," he called, and then arrested her. In the course of the arrest, Michelle was pushed against the wall and punched

---

[148] Leigh, (1995), 1.
[149] Ibid.
[150] Ibid.
[151] Davis and Shaffer, 1997, 14.

several times in the side and stomach leaving bruises on her ribs, her breasts were scratched hard enough to leave long welts that were visible two weeks after the incident...Michelle was cited for jaywalking and taken... for booking, after which she was released... [H]er boyfriend Frank called... to register a furious complaint only to find the arresting officer was untraceable. His signature was illegible, and...the badge number which must be entered on each arrest ticket was found to be one belonging to an officer long-retired from the Police Department and perhaps even dead.[152]

Forcing prostitution into the underground strips the prostitute of legal protection.[153]

The surprising, conclusion of this analysis is that criminalizing prostitution does not lead to a reduction in crime and violence, but instead, it can lead to an increase. This assertion is compatible with claims of experts on prostitution laws who argue that higher conviction rates will not decrease the problems, but may make them worse.[154] On the personal scale for prostitutes, criminalizing prostitution can generate a vicious cycle. For instance, many prostitutes turn to the profession for economic reasons and intend to pursue legal activity when they have sufficient funds. But if a prostitute is arrested, he or she will have a criminal record which will decrease the possibilities of obtaining subsequent legal work.[155] As the economic situation for the prostitute further deteriorates, the prostitute may have no recourse other than to continue to engage in prostitution. Thus, unfortunately, criminalizing prostitution can have the unintended effect of increasing prostitution.

3.4 Pimps for Illegal Prostitution

Already, we have explored the insecurity in the prostitute's workplace, the economic choice of an unsafe environment, and how prostitutes can be stripped of legal protection. The question remains, what do prostitutes do to obtain necessary protection? They turn to pimps.

In recognition of the fact that prostitutes can be victims of their own profession, laws have been created with the intent of protecting the prostitutes. Although well intended, it is possible, as critics claim, that these laws all too often harm the prostitute. For example, the Anti-Pimping laws created to protect the prostitutes from exploitation from pimps were made with good intentions. Part of the reasoning is that although pimps may offer a prostitute protection, they also can be a source of greater problems for the prostitute and for society.

The serious hazard is that prostitutes may be controlled by pimps or by organized crime. When this is the case, the prostitutes receive only a portion of the

---

[152] Hay, 1994, 6.

[153] In recognition of this problem, several organizations, such as the San Francisco Task Force on Prostitution and Maggie's – the Toronto Prostitutes' Community Service Project have been striving to increase police accountability.

[154] Davis and Shaffer, 1997, 7&57.

[155] San Francisco Task Force on Prostitution, 1996, 1.

gains made from their work, and they are often coerced into the occupation, or threatened against attempting to leave it. We are no longer talking about a choice of prostitution made with "free will" nor of rational economic decisions; we are discussing enforced servitude supported by threats that can range from threats of being reported to the police to death or bodily harm.

By recognizing that prostitution is an important source of their income, it is easy to understand why it is in the interest of organized crime, or pimps, to keep prostitution illegal. If illegal, then the prostitutes have less legal recourse against those for whom they work. Consequently, the prostitutes have less control, while their employers have more.

Even from a "supply and demand" analysis, we can understand why pimps prefer the illegal status; by prostitution being illegal, the employers can keep the proceeds to themselves instead of losing them and their prostitutes to the free market and competition. By making prostitution illegal, the state essentially restricts the supply creating the basis for black market supply of the service along with high (or even monopoly) profits. In other words, we encounter the economic setting that when a government creates shortages, it creates situations in which there is a "mutual advantage" to break the law; both sellers and buyers can gain from black market trade.[156]

As economic reasoning transcends national boundaries, we should expect the move to keep prostitution illegal to occur elsewhere. Indeed, the journalist, Arkady Vaksberg claims that, in the Soviet Union, the mafia was instrumental in keeping prostitution illegal.

> Freely elected democratic politicians appeared who wanted to take control away from the mafia and to release the prostitutes from dependence on the underground and from the fear of mistreatment. These people understood perfectly well that high moral principle would never bring the oldest profession to extinction. What happened, as expected, was that the all-powerful mafia, supported by 'public opinion', assumed the role of guardian of human morality and national tradition and blocked the legislation whilst continuing (for the time being!) to monopolize the income from this flourishing trade.[157]

When the mafia or pimps gain from black market trade, then society as a whole becomes a victim. As Vaksberg notes, the profession is not going to disappear. But if it were legalized, then the government -and not the organized criminals - would control it; and the government could gain from taxing it. Arguably, legalizing prostitution would not put organized crime out of business, but it would decrease one source of revenue and one area in their realm of control.

---

[156] Olson, 1995, p.11.
[157] Vaksberg, 1991, p. 163.

3.4.1 Anti Pimping Laws

In recognition of the deleterious effects of pimps, the government has imposed Anti-Pimping laws. These laws have often resulted, unfortunately, in negative effects. One difficulty lies in the wording; the broad terms under which a person could be defined a pimp tends to harm, rather than help, the prostitute. For example, a pimp is broadly defined as anyone who lives wholly or in part on the earnings of the prostitution of another person, or as anyone who lives with or is frequently in the company of a prostitute.[158] As a result, any person who is in contact with the prostitute risks the label of pimp. For example, a boyfriend, family member, roommate, or child over the age of 18 would qualify as a pimp, and may be punished under the law.[159] The natural consequence is that as most people are unwilling to take the risk of this label, they are unwilling to associate with a prostitute. In turn, the safe associates of the prostitute are legally barred. All too frequently, the only people willing to take the risks of contact with the prostitute are actual pimps, who seek to profit from the prostitute. So the laws intended to protect the prostitutes from pimps can deprive them of safe, legal help and increase the dependency of the prostitute on pimps.

Another harmful effect of these laws comes from the fact that prostitutes receive little or no protection from the police. Because of the pimping laws, they cannot band together for protection nor rely on protection from close friends or family. So what is left? Often the only remaining source of protection is from pimps. Thus, if a prostitute fears assault or breach of contract (generally refusal of payment for services) then he or she must accept the services of a pimp. Because the gains to be made from pimping can be lucrative, the incentives to provide these services are large, and many people are available. Pimping is another form of extortion.

3.4.2 Pimp Model

While the life of a prostitute may make the need of a pimp obvious to him or her, this need can remain a mystery to the rest of us. To better understand the incentives to become or to rely on a pimp, let's examine the options in terms of the simple Prisoner's Dilemma (PD) model described in the introductory chapter.

To use this game to understand the interactions between the players, consider their options. Here, the prostitute or her client can choose to either play Honest or to Cheat. (i.e., the client can pay or not, additionally the customer can cheat by assaulting the prostitute; and the prostitute can perform services for the money or not, or assault or rob the customer.) Each player, has an incentive to cheat, because by cheating, his individual payoff would be even higher, regardless of what the other player does. To put number values on these actions, let $\alpha>1$ represent the

---

[158] Section 212 of the Criminal Code, Canada, 1994.
[159] Davis and Shaffer, 1997, 9.

gains from cheating an honest opponent, and let -β be the loss to the honest victim.[160]

The game is as follows:

To reach an outcome, each player selects a strategy. If player 1 (row player) is Honest and performs the act, and player 2 (column) is also Honest and pays, then they collectively receive a high payoff, represented by the value 1. If player 1 is Honest and player 2 cheats, by refusing to pay, then 1 receives her worst payoff, -β, while player 2 receives his best, α. The result is the opposite if player 1 cheats and 2 plays Honest. If both players cheat (no services and no payment), then they obtain no gains from the interaction, 0.

	Honest	Cheat
Honest	1,1	-β,α
Cheat	α,-β	0,0

where α>1, β>0

Fig. 3.1

The model approximates the situation facing prostitutes and clients in terms of an agreement because it replicates the incentives each has to cheat the other. If a customer makes a payment for services, then, in a one-shot deal, the prostitute has an incentive to leave with the money without performing the act. If the customer promises to pay afterwards, then that person has an incentive to avoid this payment.

If the game is repeated, where the same prostitute and client interact several times, it can be shown game theoretically that, within certain constraints, any path of payoffs is possible. This means that the dire trap of the PD can be avoided and cooperation can be possible. The prostitute is paid and the customer is satisfied. It is standard, both in practice and in theory for people to focus on the strategy Tit-For Tat (TFT), which specifies, roughly, that cooperation can be maintained if one player's strategy is to respond to any defection (playing Cheat) of his opponent with a defection, and vice versa. If both players use this strategy, then neither has an incentive to cheat. However, if the game has a known endpoint, then, theoretically, the cooperation will not occur in the last round of the game. For instance, if a prostitute has been paid and knows that the client will never return, then why perform the services? Knowing this, the string of cooperation unravels until both players cheat at every round of the game.

Although long-term cooperation is feasible this cooperation depends on the desire of both players to realize gains in future interactions. If one player perceives that he or she can obtain a larger payoff by cheating in the first transaction, then only one round of the game will be played.

---

[160] The payoffs are assumed to be the same for the sake of simplicity. They may differ from each other, so long as each stays within the constraints $α_i>1$, $β_i>0$ i=1,2 without changing the basic results.

Now, due to the presence of competition among prostitutes, a prostitute is not likely to see a client again. So, what is to keep the client from cheating - not paying? One natural extension of this game theory analysis is to replace one particular prostitute with a group of prostitutes. For this system to function, the prostitutes would have to organize and convey information about their clients to one another. The intent is to capture the information necessary to play a strategy of TFT such that if a customer cheats one prostitute, then all the rest will be aware of the act. Although relatively uncommon, some prostitutes have organized to a sufficient extent that information about a cheater is spread throughout the prostitute community. One source[161] describes a newsletter for prostitutes compiled by an aging prostitute. The newsletter lists customers who have cheated a prostitute and gives a detailed description, even down to the person's license or credit card number. That person later finds it nearly impossible to do business with anyone who has read the paper.

The above anecdote suggests that information within the community can assist members in terms of long term cooperation in repeated interactions. If sufficient information regarding which players have cheated in the past is passed among members of a community, then cooperation between prostitutes and clients can be maintained over time in a group.[162]

This analysis demonstrates how the profession can adapt a self-policing approach that can free the prostitute from certain contract enforcement services provided by a pimp. Unfortunately, laws regarding pimping, which make it illegal for prostitutes to live or work together, can constrain the amount of information available to prostitutes from members of their profession. In addition, when forced into underground activity, the necessary secrecy may prevent them from establishing sufficient contact with one another. In turn, the information flow is limited and prostitutes have less knowledge regarding who is a potentially dishonest or dangerous client. Without access to informal resources, a prostitute may find a need for a more formal form of protection and contract enforcement. Ironically, the Anti-pimping laws again can force the prostitute into the arms of the pimps.

To better understand this argument from a political science perspective, recall how in legal activity, institutions are frequently used to provide a basis for contract enforcement. If one party to an agreement refuses to meet the terms specified, the other can take legal action to require that the contract be met. The court will often impose a cost on both parties and will charge a penalty on the negligent party. To be a deterrent, the penalty needs to be larger than the cost of meeting the terms for the contract. For instance, we see this effect in lawsuits where in addition to legal costs a penalty charge (which often is very high) is also imposed. In terms of the model, the case would be as follows.

---

[161] Maggie's, 1997.
[162] For proof see Saari-Sieberg, 1998, and Milgrom, North, and Weingast, 1990.

	Honest	Cheat
Honest	1-C,1-C	-β+P,α-J
Cheat	α-J,-β+P	0,0

where α>1, β>0

Fig. 3.2

To explain the terms, a charge of C<1 would be imposed on both parties; this could be interpreted as court costs. Thus, if both play Honest and go to court, the (Honest, Honest) entry means that they leave with income level of 1-C. A penalty of J>α would be imposed upon the cheating party. From this charge, the honest party would gain P<J. The payment from the penalty would be such that P-β>0, so the honest party would gain from his counterpart's mistake, and the cheating party would lose. The remainder of the penalty (J-P) would go to the court. Using this system, the payoffs have been changed in such a way that it is in both players' interest to be honest. No matter what the opponent does, each player will always do better (obtain a higher payoff) by being honest than by cheating. In this way, just the existence of an opportunity to use legal action can help to enforce contracts.

But, without legalization, prostitutes do not have recourse to legal protection. Without any protection whatsoever, they would be trapped in the Prisoner's Dilemma in which they would either try to cheat or be cheated. This is where the pimps can offer their services. The pimps function in the same way as the courts, but they offer services to only one party in the contract - the prostitute.[163] The model is similar to the one above.

	Honest	Cheat
Honest	1-C,1	-β+P,α-J
Cheat	α-C-F,-β	0,0

where α>1, β>0

Fig. 3.3

To explain the entries, if the prostitute has the protection of a pimp, then she pays a fee for protection, C<1. In turn, she receives P-β>1 if she is honest and has been cheated. Her cheating customer will be penalized J>α. The pimp will collect C at each period of the game, regardless of the actions of the players, and will collect J-P if the customer cheats. If the prostitute cheats, the pimp will fine her F (α-C-F < 1-C). This fine will be imposed on the prostitute to penalize her for the expense of losing a paying future customer. In this case, the pimp will keep the fine, F.[164] Now to find what actions to expect, just compare the expected winnings.

---

[163] This model is also used in Saari-Sieberg, 1998.

[164] The pimp is interested in maintaining a stream of payoffs from the prostitute's earnings, so it is in his interest to maintain customers. If the prostitute cheats the customer,

Once again, it is in the interest of both players to play Honest if the other does. Because the prostitute will be fined if she cheats, she has a dominant strategy to play Honest, and so both parties will have an honest transaction.

In this way, we have the surprising result that the pimp fills the role of a surrogate institution. If society fails to protect the prostitute, the prostitute needs to find other means of protection. Namely, because contract enforcement cannot be provided through legal means, the prostitute is better off using a pimp. But also notice that the larger the sums of C, J, and F the pimp can charge, the more lucrative his position.[165] Thus, by making prostitution illegal, a situation is created in which another illegal profession, that of extortion in the name of pimping, is given the incentives to emerge.

Why is pimping illegal? If the government provides a similar function through the court system, then why is a pimp a criminal? Political science defines a legitimate government as one that has a monopoly on coercive action. With this definition, a pimp steps outside of the law. He is not entitled to use coercive action - to collect fines or to otherwise punish cheating customers or employees. If a pimp functions outside of the range of legal action, he may (and often does) rely on threats or the use of extra-legal means, including violence, to maintain contracts and to collect penalties.

Furthermore, because of the black market profits to be made in selling prostitutes' services, the pimp is understandably unwilling to lose an employee. Thus, instead of a situation in which a person may choose to engage in prostitution for a limited time, earning sufficient money to be able to choose another profession, prostitutes may find themselves trapped by a pimp who will use any means necessary to prevent them from leaving. There are scores of stories of pimps who trap prostitutes into working indefinitely, in fear for their lives.

> Barbie got mad and told Nick [her pimp] that he couldn't keep us prisoners and we were just going to leave. That's when Nick pulled out a big gun... He twisted back on Barbie's hair and held the gun to her throat. She had tears running down her cheeks and sweat was dripping off her forehead...Nick told us that there were three other ungrateful girls buried in his back yard. He said that no one would miss us because no one even knew we left town. He said not to expect any help from the police...Nick said that girls like us should be grateful that he gave us a job. The scariest thing he told us was that we were completely expendable because there were lots and lots of [whores] in this world.[166]

By making prostitution criminal, and further, ironically, by making pimping illegal, the government increases the chances that the prostitute will be forced to

---

that person will not be likely to return. Therefore, it is in the interest of the pimp to charge a fine if the prostitute cheats, making it in the interest of the prostitute to play honestly.

[165] The pimp will most likely charge larger fees and penalties than would the court system.

[166] Anonymous. 1997.

continue to engage in prostitution and to rely on a pimp. The prostitute becomes the victim. Furthermore, with the emergence and growth of extortionists in the form of pimps, and with the violence associated with them, society becomes the victim as well. Rather than containing or curtailing crime, we are providing the incentives to encourage its growth.

3.5 Unilateral Legalization

A standard reaction is that, ideally, we should not have prostitution. But, it is a fact of life. And, as argued in this chapter, making prostitution a criminal act creates a worse situation than if it were legal. Faced with the potential drawbacks from criminalization, legalization appears to be a preferable option.

There are, however, arguments against the legalization of prostitution, and these are also based on economic theory. If one country unilaterally legalizes prostitution, then those who wish to partake of the services will be drawn (either in visits or permanently) to that country. In other words, they will vote with their feet. Unfortunately, in the case of prostitution, as is frequently the case with legalizing drugs, many patrons of the services are somewhat 'less desirable.'[167] For example, Estonia legalized prostitution, but has recently considered making it illegal in an attempt to limit the influx of prostitutes and customers into the country.[168]

Observing the game theoretically, it would be ideal if prostitution were legalized everywhere, because then one country would not be overrun with the occupation. If prostitution were legal everywhere, then prostitutes and customers would be able to stay wherever they were and would not have the incentive to flee elsewhere by voting with their feet. On the other hand, this fact provides each country with an incentive to make prostitution illegal in order to encourage prostitutes to move to where it is legal. So, since every country has an incentive to cheat on a theoretical international agreement to legalize prostitution, then it will remain illegal everywhere, and the mafia/pimps will gain from the proceeds and grow stronger from the ability to control more services. The problem becomes an international prisoners' dilemma.[169]

3.6 Conclusion

From the above examination, we can see that prostitution can be understood through economics, political science, and game theory. From economics, we learn that prostitution should, ideally, be legalized, because keeping it illegal creates the opportunity and incentives for a black market. If it were legalized, then the supply

---

[167] For instance, after Zurich began a policy of tolerating drugs, the city experienced an influx of crime as people who wished to buy and sell drugs entered the city en masse.

[168] World Sex Guide, 2001. This idea can also be compared with the experience of states, such as New York in the 1960s, who created generous welfare programs for their residents, and then experienced an influx of people who moved there strictly to partake of the benefits, without supplying the state with additional income.

[169] This model is developed in more detail in Chapter 4.

would eventually equal demand, through the free market, and monopoly profits would be unavailable. Legalization would give the prostitutes more control over their profession, and would thereby reduce the spread of disease.

What we learn from political science is the need for legal enforcement structures. Extending this idea, we learn that in the absence of such institutions, surrogate and possibly illegal structures can emerge. Namely, with legalization prostitutes would be able to use the legal system for protection and for contract enforcement, so pimps would lose some control over them. The legal system would presumably cost the prostitutes less (in taxes and court fees) and would allow the prostitutes more freedom in career choices.

Game theory, however, explains why the suggestions of economics are unlikely to be followed. By analyzing the issue through the tools of economics and game theory, we can avoid moral issues, and can focus on what the problem is and why it exists. The explanation of the situation rests on theory instead of on subjective ideas.

3.6.1 Policy

Prostitution, the oldest profession, is not a trade that is likely to disappear. The United States government spends millions of dollars annually in fighting prostitution.[170] Regardless, the number of prostitutes has not decreased. Critics deem the current policy a failure. Not only has the expense been unjustified, but also spending the money on the fight against prostitution has left fewer resources for fighting other types of crime. If this policy truly has failed, what policies would be more successful?

If, for moral or other reasons, legalization is not an issue, then policy should not be directed only at stopping supply. As long as there is demand for a good or service, there will be an incentive for others to provide it. Thus, in addition to taking steps to stop prostitutes from providing their services, attention should be paid to stopping demand. The city of Chicago has made an effort to do just that. The city arrests the customers as well as the prostitutes. Furthermore, policy has been directed at stopping demand by humiliating the customers. Names of people arrested for soliciting prostitutes have been published in the newspapers.[171] The intent is to decrease demand in order to achieve a decrease in supply.

From an economic perspective, the object of this policy is to increase the customer's cost by adding court costs and the cost of social stigma. What can we expect to happen with such a policy? Applying the previous cost analysis to the customer, we can expect the customer to try to find ways to avoid apprehension. Thus, we would expect such a policy to be effective only in the short run. This is

---

[170] Cities spend an average of $7.5 million on prostitution control every year. New York has spent as much as $23 million annually to fight prostitution. Prostitution Education Network: Statistics. 1997.

[171] Chiem, 10/28/96, Sec. 2, p. 1.

the case. The policy may help to reduce prostitution, but only temporarily until it slips further underground.

> "[The enforcement] discourages the men for a short time, then they just come back and do it again," [police officer] Camp said. "They're just more cautious the next time. They ask more questions. But eventually, they'll give in to their physical needs."[172]

The further hidden prostitution becomes, the more crime we can expect to be associated with it. Consequently, legalization of prostitution is arguably the best alternative available in terms of reducing crime.

3.6.1.1 Limited Control

By legalizing prostitution, the government gains a greater amount of control over it. Some areas have legalized prostitution with that aim. However, minor modification of the earlier analysis proves that the wrong kind of restrictions can be counterproductive. This is what has happened. Authorities have erred in asserting too much control over the prostitutes. In counties of Nevada that do not exceed a given number of inhabitants, prostitution is legal, but the restrictions placed upon them are stringent. Prostitutes are forced to live in their place of employment and are allowed out only at prescribed times during the day and then only to a small set of places. The prostitutes' contact (including visits and conversations) with people other than their customers is denied or severely limited.[173] The aim is not only to ensure that the prostitutes are safe and healthy, but also, according to some sources, to stigmatize them and to keep them away from "pure" society.[174] It is not hard to understand why these policies encourage prostitutes to work illegally in order to maintain some amount of control over their own lives.

Furthermore, we can expect that if prostitution is legalized but controlled so rigidly that supply does not accommodate demand, then there will be incentives for prostitutes to illegally meet the surplus demand. Thus, policies that only go part way, in an attempt to satisfy everyone, will satisfy no one. Instead, prostitution will be semi-legal, and the problems associated with it will persist.

This assertion is demonstrated in Australia's experiment with incomplete legalization. In Victoria, Australia, partial legalization, in the form of regulation, was attempted; but authorities were unable to detect any subsequent decrease in crime nor in illegal prostitution.[175] The mistake was that the municipalities, in attempts to limit the amount of prostitution in their areas, limited the number of licenses for brothels. Those holding the licenses found themselves in the position of oligopolists. With the number of available brothels insufficient to meet demand,

---

[172] Chiem, 10/28/96, 1&2.
[173] World Sex Guide, 1996.
[174] Ibid.
[175] Davis and Shaffer, 1997, 24.

the owners could charge exorbitant prices. Additionally, recalling the detrimental effects of competition on earnings and job safety, since legal jobs in prostitution were scarce, the brothel owners were able to exert an enormous amount of control over their employees. Wages were low and working conditions were poor.

> Women working in legal brothels have to submit to "house rules" which includes the operators taking 60 percent of all client fees and some have been asked for money up-front for employment in brothels. Owners have increased their profits by imposing a system of fines for various misdemeanours such as lateness, not shaving legs and not having matching nail polish on fingers and toes.[176]

The costs of working in the brothels became so large that many prostitutes found the risk of arrest preferable to working in these conditions, and chose to work illegally.

The above idea follows simple economic logic. Each employer was, to an extent, a kind of monopsonist - a single buyer of labor. Under monopsony, we can expect fewer workers hired at a lower wage than under perfect competition. In contrast, the prostitutes were numerous sellers of labor and had to not only compete with one another for a job, but also had to accept the low wages offered them. Had this simply been the case, the prostitutes would have had to accept the situation. However, the government tried to restrict the number of brothels. In so doing, they failed to provide sufficient supply to meet demand. As we should expect, the surplus demand created the incentives for prostitutes to work illegally - not only filling the excess demand, but additionally seeking better wages and working conditions. The presence of illegal prostitution created incentives for pimps to emerge.

3.6.2 Regulation

The above scenarios indicate that legalization will not be effective if it is done only partially. If the government attempts to undercut the market by asserting too much control or by restricting the number of available prostitutes, then problems will arise. If the government treats prostitution as it would a restaurant or another business - requiring a license[177] and that health standards are met - then supply will meet demand. If this is the case, then problems such as violence, disease, public disturbance, and spread and use of illegal drugs will not be associated with prostitution.

This solution may not be morally the most preferable. "Subconsciously we dislike the word 'legal'. It has such respectable undertones..."[178] As stated above, however, morality is not the issue here. The intent here is to analyze the effects of different policies and to determine which tend to reduce associated crime. The

---

[176] Davis and Shaffer, 1997, 25.
[177] This entails that licenses are not restricted in number or impossible to come by.
[178] Riddel, 1997, 7.

current policies, those of criminalization of prostitution are morally acceptable but can have the effect of not only continuing prostitution but also of increasing associated crime. The policies suggested here might offend those who view prostitution as criminal. They additionally have the effect of allowing prostitution to continue. However, as long as there are people who desire, and cannot otherwise obtain, sexual gratification and are ready to pay for it, there will be others who will be willing to provide it. Making prostitution illegal does little to stop it from persisting.

Legalization policies would allow the government more control over the profession, and would also lead to a decrease in crime. In the case of prostitution, trade-offs must be made. No policy will eliminate prostitution. The best policy will decrease the problems associated with it. Legalization is that policy.

Chapter 4

Drugs

4.1 Introduction

An old adage claims that sometimes the cure is worse than the ailment. This appears to be the case in our insistence on the illegal status of certain varieties of drugs. We would never advocate the use of a cancer-causing medication to treat the flu. Yet, in an attempt to limit drug use, and thereby curtail addictions and other debilitations arising from drug use, we stand resolutely behind the refusal to tolerate the use or sale of illicit drugs. We take this position despite growing evidence that the illegal status of drugs creates incentives for, and profits to, enrich the growth and spread of crime and criminal organizations. The problem we must confront is whether we have created a serious international disease that is becoming larger and more powerful every day merely to treat the afflictions of a few.

4.1.1 The Ailment

This assertion is not intended to downplay the enormity of the ailment. It cannot be denied that illegal drug use is a serious problem for society. Legislation has been created to prohibit drug use for many reasons. The use of illegal substances can have harmful effects. Used recreationally or to feed an addiction, drugs have a negative impact on the user. Furthermore, because some drugs allegedly induce violence in the user, those in contact with the user may also be harmed. Due to the fact that many illegal drugs are addictive and debilitating, a legitimate fear exists that "experimentation" with drugs, may lead to the inability to discontinue the use. Additionally, it is well accepted and documented that millions of dollars per year are spent on treatments for babies born with addictions that have arisen due to their mothers' drug use while pregnant. More funds will be spent in the future, to cope with the possible medical and behavioral problems of these children, who are innocent victims of this abuse. Many of the effects of drug use during pregnancy are still unknown, but evidently they may be crippling. These problems entail social and economic costs for families and for the community. Arguably, if drugs were unavailable, then these difficulties would not exist.

Drug related problems do not stop with physical effects to the user. The addictive nature of many drugs prompts some users to go to extreme lengths in order to be able to purchase them. The illegal status of drugs creates shortages of supply in the market, making drugs expensive. When their money runs out, users have been known to resort to prostitution, theft, robbery, or burglary in order to obtain the funds to support their habits.

"It degrades you to where you're selling your body," Cynthia McBride said...

Ms. McBride said she had begun sniffing cocaine as a 10-year-old...By the time she moved to crack, she said, "I was married, cheating on a husband and sleeping with men to get high."...

"When the drug dealers start dissing you," she said, "when you can't get a $2 hit because they don't want you, that's when it's time to [quit]."[179]

4.1.2 The Cure

However, the "cure" appears to be worse than the disease. The most notable problem with drugs comes from the violence involved with their sales. Drug sales and their distribution are crimes that spawn ancillary criminal behaviors. Crime enters the equation in many ways. Because drugs are illegal, those who provide them must be willing to step outside of the law. Due to this requirement, many of today's drug providers include organized crime groups. Lured by the prospects of high profits, these groups provide organization and distribution and are understandably unwilling to lose their proceeds to competitors. The associated violence and deaths resulting from battles over "turf" have been astounding.

As of 1994, the United States government has spent more than $50 billion, by one estimate,[180] in fighting the war against drugs. Yet this war has resulted in only limited reduction in domestic drug use and addiction. Approximately $75 billion is spent annually in drug related health care costs, including drug treatment and rehabilitation.[181] In monetary terms alone, the toll of drugs is staggering. However, as described below, the "solution" to the problem appears if anything, to create a worse situation than we had to begin with.

A review of these difficulties indicates a need for the current situation to be assessed through research to provide insight into managing these societal dilemmas. An ideal policy would eradicate all of these problems. Yet it appears that this ideal is unobtainable. No policy will be costless. Every action will have certain drawbacks. Arguably, drugs will be used and users will become addicted regardless of policy until and unless there is a radical change in attitude. An important step in consideration of the issue is to accept the possibility that there may be no absolute "solution" to the problem. Despite our ideals, we must select the policy whereby society can effectively manage the problems associated with drugs, procurement, and usage. No policy will eliminate all of them.

Entire books have been written on this subject alone. In recognition of this fact, the chapter does not profess to examine all of the social and economic factors involved in drug abuse and the war on drugs nor to find the ultimate solution to the problem. Rather, it uses simple concepts from economics to examine the potentially intended and unintended effects of policies from both sides of the drug legalization debate. In consideration of the above goals, I argue that legalization of

---

[179] Wren, 3/4/97, A10.
[180] *The Economist*, 12/24/94 – 1/6/95, 21. and Duke, 12/21/93.
[181] Califano, 1/29/95, 40.

drugs would minimize the problems associated with drugs. This policy is disturbing from an emotional stance; however, after having considered the theoretical arguments for and against legalization, it appears that legalization would present fewer social and economic problems and that it would be manageable for society. Finally, some policies are suggested that might reduce drawbacks associated with legalization.

4.2 Illegal Versus Legal Drugs

4.2.1 Illegal

Any discussion of the drug legalization debate must describe the goals and concerns of the different policies. The policy of making drugs illegal, or prohibition, is the simplest to explain. Because drugs are responsible for so many problems, the best solution would appear to be to make it impossible to consume them – or curtail their supply. With this goal in mind, standard governmental policy is aimed at supply reduction tactics such as destroying coca crops and marijuana plants as well as stopping drug smugglers and imprisoning drug dealers.

The illegal status of drugs is also directed at saving people from others who would use drugs. This can be very important. Drugs can have very different effects. A person under the influence of a drug that causes violent or destructive behavior can be dangerous to others. Similarly, if drugs are used while working or driving, judgment and/or ability could be impaired, leading to potential injury or death of the user and others. Users may be aware of the risks and choose to take the drugs anyway, and the victims of their actions can do little to stop them. Legislation advocating criminalization of drugs is partly an attempt to protect the innocent.

Legislation based on these grounds, however, may also be contradictory. Recent studies have shown that the consumption of alcohol produces many of the same effects in some people.[182] In fact, some studies have shown that alcohol can produce more violent reactions in certain individuals. Consumption of alcohol is responsible for approximately 80,000 deaths each year, due to driving under the effect of alcohol and due to other accidents caused by impairment due to alcohol consumption.[183] Nonetheless, alcohol is legal. Critics argue that the existence of restrictions on certain types of drugs and not on others is an arbitrary and inefficient policy.

The failure of these policies is that they have been implemented without consideration of the basic economic aspects of the drug trade. The forces of economics are not repealed simply because the commodities are criminalized. Instead, drug dealing and consumption involve the same economic exchanges as any other product market. The existence in society of consumers of illegal products provides economic incentives for trade. So, destroying crops in Hawaii when the same crop can be grown in Jamaica, Afghanistan or elsewhere, and smuggled in

---

[182] Schaffer, 1999.
[183] Ibid.

through uncountable avenues, is counter productive and should be reassessed. The roots of a nation's local problem are located in a global economy.

4.2.1.1 Hidden but Available

If the government attempts to control the drugs market, it must expend resources to interdict two groups: black market agents and consumers. This is the tactic taken by those who criminalize drugs. The government attempts to prevent each group from access to each other to prevent a flow of goods from one group to the next. This war on crime is costly and must be maintained over time.

A basic economic approach to the problem of drugs would assert that if we crack down on producers and dealers, then it will become too inconvenient or costly for them to continue in that line of business. In other words, through tactics such as arrests, and destruction or seizure of the drugs, drug policy should make the costs outweigh the expected gains of drug-related industry. This policy is based on strong economic grounds. Indeed, it recalls equation (1) from Chapter 1.

Approaching the problem from a standard supply-demand perspective, however, yields additional intuition. We know, in general, that there exists a certain demand and supply for drugs. This demand and supply will dictate the equilibrium price P_1 and quantity Q_1 for the product. If current popular punitive tactics such as arrest are used against drug dealers, we would expect to see some dealers removed from the market and incarcerated. Under this scenario, we would see a shift in of supply, leading to a lower equilibrium quantity, Q_2, supplied.

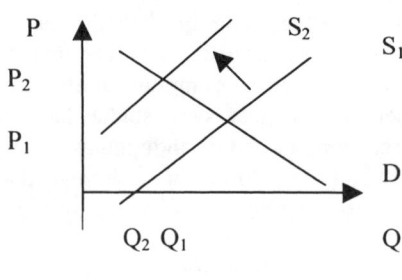

Fig. 4.1

Initially, the decrease in the quantity supplied appears successful. Unfortunately, this appraisal overlooks the fact that the equilibrium price also rises to P_2. Although the imprisoned dealers are incapacitated, remaining dealers are (at least temporarily) free to ply their trade. The price increase creates incentives for residual dealers to take the risks to acquire an even larger profit. Thus, rather than providing an overall deterrent, policies such as arrest may *increase* incentives to participate in the drugs market.

The assumption that these tactics will reduce drug dealing and consumption drastically underestimates the relative gains to be made at all stages of the drug trade. It further underestimates imaginative ways to avoid detection. If the expected profits associated with drug production, transport, or sales (accounting for possible losses and penalties) are large enough to outweigh the gains to be made from another type of employment, then we can expect a significant number of individuals to undertake the risks, despite the best efforts of anti-drug officials.

Indeed, this is the case. The result of anti-drug policies is that drug manufacturers and dealers at all stages of the trade have become more sophisticated and more careful. They have not, however, discontinued their trade. Coca farmers shoot at planes that are sent to kill their crops; and more recently align themselves with armed guerillas who provide security at a cost. To avoid being hit, planes, bearing herbicides, are forced to fly higher, where the herbicides are dropped everywhere but on the coca plants.[184] Smugglers hide their wares more effectively, and have even resorted to hiring or coercing individuals, or "mules," to smuggle their products by swallowing condoms filled with drugs.[185]

Faced with the difficulties of importing marijuana into the United States, the expected economic response has been the emergence of a domestic industry. Domestic marijuana growers have moved indoors to avoid detection and are capable of growing a greater number of more potent crops than they could previously produce. As an example, marijuana growers have begun to breed strains that are shorter than the previously grown outdoor variety, yet able to produce more yield in a single plant than in several of the older type. This selective breeding is done to avoid the stiffer legal penalty that is imposed if one is caught breeding a larger variant of marijuana.[186] If penalties are meted out according to plant height, the growers' market responds by breeding a shorter, higher-yielding product. The result is a strain that yields a far more potent drug, with a THC (delta-9-tetrahydrocannabinol) content of between 8 and 10 percent, as compared to the average 1970s level of between .5 and 2 percent.

Dealers, facing increased arrests, may leave the streets; moving indoors, hidden from view.

> These days, the police see more organization and sophistication among dealers, whose operations have been forced from the streets into apartment buildings by years of enforcement pressure. Narcotics officers say knots of street dealers have been replaced by a handful of "steerers" on the sidewalk, directing customers to apartments outfitted as sales offices.[187]

In short, drugs become harder to find or more expensive, but they remain available, despite the best efforts of US officials. If anything, instead of raising the costs for those involved in the drug trade, anti-drug officials have found that reactions to the policies have increased their own costs of labor. This, too, is to be expected. After

---

[184] *The Economist*, 8/17/96, 36.
[185] Navarro, 11/2/95, A1&A12.
[186] Pollan, 2/19/95, 32.
[187] Purdy, 1/2/95, 10.

all, if significant profits can be made, legal efforts must counter the imaginative and creative efforts of the illicit drug industry.

4.2.2 Legal

The government does have another option. If making drugs illegal appears problematic, why not legalize? Economic theory argues against the use of price or quantity constraints, arguing that the market should allow supply to meet demand. Following these suggestions, the government can legalize drugs, open its market, and allow prices to be determined by supply and demand. There are costs and benefits to this type of action as well.

The costs are obvious. As stated above, many drugs are addictive, requiring a significant amount of rehabilitation therapy to recover. With continued use, for example, the effects of a given amount of heroin decrease, forcing the user to consume more of the drug to obtain the same high. If the user abruptly stops consumption of heroin, he or she can experience painful withdrawal symptoms.[188] These physical effects, and the intense psychological dependencies on other drugs such as cocaine can make it very difficult for an individual to discontinue use. The statistics regarding drug rehabilitation are not encouraging.

Furthermore, although the risks are under debate, the use of illegal substances can be dangerous and detrimental to the user. For instance, cocaine abuse can have a major long-term effect of a paranoid psychosis, one that is frequently indistinguishable from a schizophrenic reaction. The victim of this psychosis can become agitated and violent.[189] Thus, even if the user does not become addicted, drug use may lead to short or long-term ill effects. These sobering issues can make the prospect of legalization unpalatable.

Moreover, it most surely is true that if drugs were legalized, the government will see a quantity of drugs supplied that is higher than had been intended under the zero-tolerance policy and more people would be willing to try them. In the short-run, more people would become addicted.[190] This result implies that the ailment that the government sought to solve will continue or even grow. Most proponents of legalization accept this fact; legalization is not without serious costs. However, drug use and addiction are not the only issues involved. The crime and violence associated with our "cure" for drugs impose an immense cost upon the entire globe. As long as drugs are relegated to criminals, these problems can be expected to continue.

By legalizing drugs, we could reduce the negative results of the "cure." Legalization would allow us to appropriate the market from the gangs and organized crime groups, directing it instead to licensed businesses, as discussed later. By allowing entry into the drug market, current high prices would theoretically decrease to those approximating perfect competition. In turn, this

---

[188] Simon and Witte, 1982, 268.

[189] Ibid, 164.

[190] Califano gives that dire prediction that cocaine addiction will increase by 10 times the current amount if drugs are legalized. Califano, 1/29/95, 40.

reduces incentives for individuals to supply drugs and minimizes gang "enforcement" approaches discussed below.

The debate is difficult to resolve. However, the current system is riddled with opportunities for circumvention. If we insist upon keeping drugs illegal to decrease the number of addicts, we must be willing to accept that a large part of the price we pay as a society will be domestic crime and geopolitical instability that accompanies the risks, dangers, and competition of black market dealings.

4.3 Supply Versus Demand

Economics dictates that equilibrium price and quantity of a good is determined by the supply and demand for that good. Most policy on illegal drugs has focused on attempts to eliminate the supply. Until 1988, at least 70% of federal funding for the war against drugs was earmarked for "supply-side" control. Even after the percentage allotted to demand control was officially increased to 50%, in practice, little was done to decrease demand.[191]

4.3.1 Demand

As long as demand for illegal drugs exists , it always will be in someone's interest to take risks and supply them. The United States' market is extremely profitable for drug dealers. Americans use cocaine alone at the rate of 240 tons a year.[192] If demand could be reduced, then drug production and supply would be less profitable. If drug policy were extended to reduce the number of users, we might see some marginal decrease in demand.

Evidence shows that information about cigarettes can cause a decrease in smoking.[193] This highlights an important fact: *education* about a substance can lead people to make informed decisions regarding its use. There is indication that education has affected drug use; following increased information about the negative effects of LSD, consumption of the drug decreased significantly. Thus, education can be used as a deterrent tool; if people are aware of negative aspects of certain substances, they may avoid them.[194] Education alone will not solve all drug-related problems. Arguably, however, that education combined with rehabilitation and a moderate amount of regulation is a policy that is superior to the one in place

Of course, no policy will ever eradicate demand. However, "demand-side" laws that place more penalties on the users mean that these people, and not simply the dealers, would bear more of the risk. This risk might be sufficient to deter some from consumption of the drug. But in any population, there are extreme cases - those who will use drugs regardless of the laws and those who will never use them.

---

[191] Bagley, 1992, 3-4.

[192] Wren, 3/4/97, A1.

[193] Stevenson, 1994, 105.

[194] Richard Stevenson fears that the opposite may occur. He claims that increased information may lead people to feel that drugs are safer than they had believed, and that instead of decreasing use, more people may be willing to risk drug use. Stevenson, 1994.

It is the people between the extremes that form the moderate center; these are the people who can be affected by policy and, thus, form the group we must consider when evaluating proposals.

What types of laws will affect this group? Economic analysis suggests that an increase in the costs of procuring the goods should eventually outweigh the benefits of obtaining them. Moderate people can be deterred from drug use for a number of reasons. If drugs are illegal, some might be unwilling to assume the risks associated with illegal action. Others might be deterred because of the negative effects an arrest might have on their social or professional status. Still others might avoid drugs because they are unwilling to seek out or associate with those who might supply them. The latter is no small issue; consider the dangers involved in approaching a stranger on a dark street corner in search of drugs. If the buyer can be penalized, these risks increase. Now, in addition to fears of being robbed or harmed, the prospective buyer must determine whether the stranger he assumes is a dealer might be an undercover policeman.

A federal law enforcer argued that because this group of people can be affected by the legal or illegal status of drugs, a policy that kept drugs illegal would effectively dissuade them from purchasing drugs. An extension of her argument posits that if buyers risked penalty, they would be more likely to avoid drug use. As a result, we might expect that this type of policy would produce a decrease in the number of people addicted to drugs.[195]

Variations of this type of policy have been used with encouraging results. In Washington D.C., and in other areas around the nation, "drug courts" have been created, which have devised a scheme to decrease drug use. Drug takers, brought to court on minor charges, are offered the chance to be put on probation, or even have their charges dropped, if they successfully complete a program designed to wean them off of drugs. The defendants are obliged to take drug tests twice a week. If the test is positive, then the defendant is punished. The punishments are small, but they increase in severity for each infraction. Researchers Harrell and Cavanagh of the Urban Institute think tank found in a preliminary study that whereas only 13% of defendants who pass through the ordinary court system are free of drugs in the month before sentencing, of those who used the "drug courts," 32% were free of drugs.[196]

If this type of sentencing does prove to be effective, then it could reduce a large percentage of the demand for drugs. Before we accept it too enthusiastically, however, all of the potential consequences must be examined. Unfortunately, the success rate of this type of policy is threatened by the addictive nature of narcotics. Secondly, this approach of imposing risks on the consumer retains effectiveness as long as the buyer must purchase the drugs in an area where he or she can be apprehended. We have learned, however, that we should never underestimate the inventiveness of a supplier searching for profits. We should expect the dealers to

---

[195] Interview with a Federal Law Enforcer, September, 1995. I am grateful for her comments and suggestions.

[196] *The Economist*, 3/29/97, 26-7.

create new drug distribution approaches to lure back the buyer. Thus, the best scenario for keeping drugs illegal appears flawed.

4.3.2 Supply

As stated, the majority of drug enforcement policies are directed against the supply side of illicit drugs. Unfortunately, instead of successfully eliminating supply, these policies can make drug production and distribution more lucrative than before. Although the highest earnings are reserved for only a few, many find that supplying drugs can be a more rewarding profession than any others available. Farmers in Columbia, for example, make far higher wages growing coca leaves than they would from other crops.

> "We do this because you can't raise cattle or corn in this region," Mr. Restrepo said... As a cane cutter, he said, he was lucky to earn $35 a week. For processing coca leaves he was promised $10 to $15 a day, plus a dormitory cot and food.[197]

Although the pay is not great in comparison to the earnings made by drug lords, it is better than most can obtain legally. A large percentage of cocaine is produced in Columbia and Mexico. Legal pay in these countries is so low, that many are willing to take the risks associated with drug supply. Drug lords take advantage of the situation to produce and transport the drugs at low costs.

> Mexico's economic problems and double digit unemployment help in recruiting smugglers for a relative pittance. One smuggler was offered $500 to smuggle a load to Los Angeles and promised another $500 if he made it back, an antidrug agent said.[198]

> Spotters [who observe customs agents and alert smugglers as to which lanes to use or avoid] earn $25 to $50 a day for working the bridge, far more than the $25 to $40 a week that they might earn in a Juarez factory.[199]

Proceeds are available in every stage of drug sales, with an increase in the price of drugs roughly corresponding to the amount of risk borne by the seller. Street dealers, although by no means taking the most lucrative share of drugs transactions, can reap immense gains.

> When he was arrested last September by federal authorities, Valenzuela admitted that in 1991 and 1992 he had been selling $15,000 to $20,000 a day in crack and cocaine...

---

[197] Wren, 3/4/97, A10.
[198] Ibid.
[199] Ibid.

"He said it was unbelievable how much money he was making," Thomas Murphey, a special agent for the U.S. Bureau of Alcohol, Tobacco and Firearms, testified... "He didn't think there was that much money in America."[200]

Evidence does not uniformly support the notion that wages from drugs can be as high as Valenzuela reported. In a rare opportunity to track a drug-dealing gang's financial activity, Levitt and Venkatesh found an extremely skewed distribution of earnings. On average, however, they did not find drug dealing to be extremely lucrative. Although gang leaders earned up to $10,900 a month in profit and officers earned about $1,000 per month, the lowest ranking members were paid only up to $11 per hour. The authors attribute the low pay partly to benefits (such as weapons and funerals) received from the gang and partly to hopes of earning the higher wages of the leaders in the future. They also note that the lowest wages were substantially higher than the members would have earned legally.[201]

In general, the difference between legal and illegal wages can be perceived to be so large that even the possibility of penalties is insufficient to cause the expected gains of this type of work to fall below those of legal prospects. Because this is an economic fact of life, we can expect a large number of people to be willing to assume the risks associated with the drug trade.

4.3.3 Illegal Drugs - Negative Effects

The illegal status of drugs, has additional negative effects. The crime and violence, mentioned above, that are associated with drugs are, theoretically, to be expected. We already know from the United States' experimentation with the prohibition of alcohol that designating certain goods illegal may deter some, but not all, individuals from using them or from profiting from their commerce. In fact, Miron and Zwiebel found that although alcohol consumption decreased in the first years of the Prohibition, during the next several years it increased sharply to about 70 percent of the pre-Prohibition level.[202] The profits and the risk involved in the trade provide a further incentive for these people to resort to violence to protect their market share and their interests. Analysis by Warburton of the price of alcohol during the Prohibition suggests that prices were about three times higher than they had been before the Prohibition.[203]

What we observe in practice is amply supported by the theoretical work of Mancur Olson, an economist, who claims that corruption will tend to arise in societies that do not follow a market system. By restricting prices or quantity, the

---

[200] O'Connor, 3/11/97, Sec. 2, 3.
[201] Levitt and Venkatesh, 1998. The authors also mention that despite the low wages, participation in gang sales may be rational in terms of other benefits such as status, protection, companionship, and increased success in attracting the opposite sex (fn. 22). See Chapter 5 for more analysis of gang behavior, duties, and organization.
[202] Miron and Zwiebel, 1991.
[203] Ibid, p. 245.

government creates shortages, thus creating situations in which there is a "mutual advantage" to breaking the law: both sellers and buyers gain from black market trade.[204]

To explain this point, notice that when goods, such as drugs, are restricted, societies destroy the incentives of a subset of their inhabitants to obey and work with the law. In market societies, in which goods are not restricted, some people commit crimes and, in doing so, work against the government. However, for many kinds of crimes, most individuals have an incentive to aid the authorities. For instance, in the case of theft, if he/she is not caught and brought to justice, a criminal can gain from a single criminal act. The victim of that act, however, has an incentive to cooperate with and use the system to work against the criminal, either to avoid the crime in the first place, or to gain retribution from the criminal. Thus, at least one party has excellent reasons to support the rules of the government.[205]

By restricting certain goods, however, the government creates a situation in which *both parties* to the crime have an incentive to undermine the law. This logic is applicable to the case of drugs. Dealers break the law by selling illegal drugs. Buyers do likewise by purchasing them. Since both parties can gain by their transaction, neither has an incentive to obey the law. This is a complicating factor because, in general, only the buyer and seller are knowledgeable about the details of the criminal transaction, and neither wants to disclose them. As far as the seller and the buyer are concerned, drug dealing is a victimless crime. In this manner, a crucial component of law enforcement is hampered. If the government wishes to enforce the law, it must work against part of the public with little expectation of the help on which it can normally rely in fighting crime. Thus, the government can hurt its own enforcement policy by restricting access to certain goods.

4.3.3.1 Quality

The action of restricting supply imposes a cost on the government and on society. This is especially true in the case of drugs. We can expect that, due to the provisions of the external market, governmental control over drugs will decrease. Not only are drugs still available, but the government is unable to control for their quality. Quality control can be a serious issue. Bureaus such as the Food and Drug Administration and the Bureau of Alcohol, Tobacco and Firearms test for the quality and safety of products to protect the consumer. The consumer, however, has no such protection in consumption of black market goods. Instead, it is generally understood that drug suppliers manipulate their product with other substances in order to increase the amount or potency that they can sell.

This practice should be expected. It was common and documented during the Prohibition of alcohol. Miron and Zwiebel note that:

[F]ederal regulation required manufacturers of industrial alcohol to adulterate their product with poisonous wood alcohol, knowing that

---

[204] Olson, 1995.
[205] Olson, 1995, 11.

> much of this product was diverted to illegal consumption...In one case, an adulterant used by bootleggers...turned out to cause permanent paralysis, victimizing thousands.[206]

The possibility of poisoned alcohol was recognized during the Prohibition and was attributed to the lack of quality constraints. According to one source, the national death rate from poisoned alcohol increased over time. In 1925 it was 4,154, as compared to 1,064 in 1920.[207]

This trend, then, should come as no surprise in illegal drug production. As a consequence, by the time the drugs reach the average consumer, the purity is significantly reduced.[208] The consumer is unaware of what products are used to mix or to treat the drugs. This uncertainty can have devastating effects.

> This problem came to a head in the late 1970s in the Southwest when regular users discovered that much of the Mexican marihuana they were smoking had been sprayed in the fields with the herbicide Paraquat by Mexican authorities. The possibility that Paraquat could cause an irreversible fibrosis of the lungs touched off a serious panic among the millions of regular users in the Southwest.[209]

Thus, an ironic effect of quantity constraints emerges. In an attempt to gain complete control over the consumption and sale of drugs, the government, instead loses control. Instead of protecting the public, the policy exposes drug users to greater risks, in terms of quality, than they would otherwise face.

4.3.3.2 Youth

Alcohol is a substance that, as noted, can produce negative effects in its users. Alcohol is a legal product, but its distribution is regulated. There are undeniable cases of children gaining access to alcoholic beverages, (According to a Monitoring the Future survey, in 1999, 52.1% of 8th Grade students, 70.6% of 10th Graders and 80.0% of 12th Grade students reported use of alcohol.[210]) However, the government can control access to liquor licenses to persuade merchants to refrain from selling alcohol to minors. This power does not extend to control over drugs. Drugs are illegal, so rather than regulating the production and distribution of drugs, the government is outside of this process. Consequently, the government does not have the same leverage – in the form of licenses –to control for the age of users. Without regulation, there are a large number of children selling, purchasing, and using drugs long before they are sufficiently mature to make decisions about the risks of their actions, nor about the potential harmful effects of the chemicals

---

[206] Miron and Zwiebel, 1995, 179.
[207] Thornton, 1991, 3.
[208] See Simon and Witte, 1982, chapters 6, 7, and 8.
[209] Simon and Witte,1982, 182.
[210] Johnston, O'Malley, and Bachman, Table 1a, 2000.

they are using. This means that youth are exposed to these substances, and all of their risks, and, users who fear punishment, have an incentive to *avoid* seeking help if they develop a drug abuse problem. Thus, problems associated with abuse go uncorrected.

These concerns are well founded. Children, spurred by a culture of consumption and lured by the prospects of high earnings, are frequently willing and eager to aid in the sale of drugs. They are also willing to ingest. Drug use by teenagers has been increasing. In a 2000 survey of a nationally representative sample of 45,000 students, 54.7 percent of the graduating high school class said they had tried an illegal drug. Additionally, 22 percent of eighth graders, 40.9 percent of sophomores, and 49.7 percent of seniors claimed to have used marijuana at least once.[211]

> "Nowadays the younger generation starts smoking [marijuana] and dealing as young as 10," said Luther Syas, 26, an Austin resident at the New Beginnings Drug Recovery Home. Syas said he spent his later teen years peddling drugs and using marijuana and heroin. "They are coming up quick. Even if they don't get into the heavy drugs, they are exposed to it."[212]

4.4 Violence

The drawbacks to the criminalization of drugs mentioned previously are serious and merit concern. The most notable drawback to this policy, however, is the incentives for crime and violence that it engenders. Theoretical analysis indicates that the illegal nature of drugs spawns the violence associated with their sales. Because black market prices are high, dealers have the opportunity to earn large profits.

The profits are no secret, however, and many people are willing to take the risks in order to secure the benefits of drug dealing. Richard Freeman describes the labor market of drug dealers as one in which there is a potentially high elasticity of supply of people to crime.[213] This fact cripples arguments by those who advocate eliminating the supply of drugs. This policy is inherently flawed. The reason behind this failure is that much of the violence associated with drug dealing stems from the unlimited supply of dealers combined with a limited territory in which to sell drugs. Each criminal removed from the streets is replaced by another.[214] Policies that seek to disrupt the supply of drugs through arrests only assist other dealers who take the place of those arrested.

---

[211] Ibid.

[212] Poe, 10/21/96, 12.

[213] Freeman, 1996, 36. Freeman describes an elastic supply to crime in general, of which drug dealing is an example.

[214] Freeman, 1996, 36.

> Jovan had to compete to get a job with [the dealers]. He would wake up early and stand outside his building hoping one of the older boys, most of them members of the Vice Lords street gang, would choose him to be a lookout. He could make $75 a day just watching for the police...
>
> He began as a sidewalk dealer but had to move whenever the bigger fish decided to take his spot. He found fighting the gangs over street corners a losing battle. Unable to beat them, he joined the Vice Lords, in drug-dealing terms entering the big leagues.
>
> Soon he was making $800 a day. It was not a lot of money for people in his business, he said.[215]

It is precisely this elasticity of supply and competition among dealers that leads to violence. We hear many reports of the violence related to drug dealers, and frequently make the assumption that this violence is symptomatic of the wares sold and of the types of people selling them. Instead, arguably, the root of violence lies in the illegal status of the drugs and the constraints – or lack of – that this status places on drug dealers.

4.4.1 Anti-Competitive Strategies

> Corporate executives look to developing countries like China and see huge new markets for their products. So apparently, do mobsters.[216]

Territory is crucial, and the less competition, the better. Simple economics dictates that, with a few exceptions, so long as the profits of doing business in a new area are at least equal to the costs, new firms will have an incentive to join the market. This makes sense; if, for example, there is only one restaurant in a town, then it can charge high prices. Despite the costs, some people will dine there because they have no alternatives. If the restaurant makes lots of money, another restaurant has an incentive to go into business in the same area. If the newcomer charges slightly lower prices, it can capture a large percentage of the customers resulting in a reduced profit for the original firm.

Drawing from the restaurant analogy, there are striking parallels between legal and illegal business strategies. In the business world, new companies frequently plan to move into the territory of an already established company to capture some of that company's profits. When this happens, the original firms may engage in a limited number of tactics to drive the newcomer away. The most common tool used by firms is what is known as a "price war." The original firm will slash prices in an effort to drive a potential competitor out of the market. The logic behind this activity involves reducing the profit level for the competitor. If profit is calculated by the following equation

---

[215] Wilkerson, 12/13/94, [A], B12.
[216] *The Economist*, 10/11/97, 29.

$$\pi = pq\text{-}cq \tag{12}$$

(where p, q, and c, are respectively the price of a good, the quantity sold of a good, and the cost of producing the good), then to increase profit, a firm would seek to minimize costs, cq, and increase revenue, pq. However, if the price drops considerably, then eventually, the competitor will reach a situation in which

$pq < cq$.

In other words, the gains of production will be insufficient to cover the costs, and the competitor will drop out of (or refuse to enter) the market.

The use of price wars entails a short-term loss of profits for the original firm as well. However, the action is logical in terms of future gains of the firm. If the original firm is financially strong enough to bear this short-term loss, then price wars can serve as a deterrent to potential competitors. Eventually, however, if the newcomer is not deterred, the original company must accept its competition.

Dealers, like firms, recognize that competition can lead to an unwelcome decrease in profits. Drug dealers also have access to the use of price wars to deter rival dealers. However, a drop in prices would reduce profit in a market that already has a high cost (in terms of risk) of labor.[217] Dealers, as described below, are both unprotected and less constrained by the legal market. Consequently, they have an expanded range of tools that they can use to deter newcomers. This unfortunate situation arises as a consequence of the illegal status of drugs. With these tactics, dealers are able to sidestep the laws of economics by availability of the option to use the threat or use of force as a deterrent against potential competitors. In this way, and in others, violence enters the equation.

4.4.1.1 Legal Behavior

The above assertion may be explained with reference to the profit equation.

$\pi = pq\text{-}cq$.

Legal firms deter competition at a loss to themselves. Legally, they must suffer this loss of profit because they are constrained to affect their competitors *indirectly*. In the corporate world, we don't anticipate tactics such as burning down the new company or threatening the lives of the owners; and if the original firm tries them, this becomes a criminal offense. The newcomer can then take the issue to court and

---

[217] Levitt and Venkatesh surprisingly observed a decrease in drug prices during gang wars. They suggest three possibilities for this drop: First, the low price could be a strategic move – price war – designed to punish the rival group. Second, the low price could exist to compensate buyers for disruption during the war. Third, they noted that city-wide prices of drugs during the period of study fell by more than the drop in prices during gang wars, so the decline could simply represent a city-wide trend. (1998, 22-23.)

collect damages. Economically, this potential would reduce the expected utility for the original firm and could increase utility for the competitor.

To clarify this statement, consider the options faced by a legal firm in a decision whether to use legal (PW) or illegal (DW) tactics to deter a competitor. If the firm wishes to fight the entrant legally, it can drop its price from P_M to P_L for a certain number of periods, m. If it is successful in deterring the entrant (with probability ε) it will then return to its original price. If it is unsuccessful, the price will fall to P_C, and the firm and the competitor will share the market, each selling Q_C.

To represent this decision mathematically, a legal firm would compute the expected utility for each strategy. The expected utility of legal action, EU(PW), would take into account the probability of success in a price war, ε, and the probability of failure, 1-ε. In each case, the firm would calculate the present discounted value of dropping the price to P_L and later raising it (to P_M if successful in driving off the entrant or P_C otherwise). The variable δ represents the firm's discount factor (how much the firm values the future).

$$EU(PW) = \varepsilon\{ P_LQ - CQ + \delta(P_LQ - CQ) + \delta^2(P_LQ-CQ) + \ldots \\ + \delta^m(P_LQ-CQ) + (\delta^{m+1}/1-\delta)(P_MQ-CQ)\} + (1-\varepsilon)\{ P_LQ - CQ + \\ \delta(P_LQ - CQ) + \delta^2(P_LQ-CQ) + \ldots + \delta^m(P_LQ-CQ) \\ + (\delta^{m+1}/1-\delta)(P_CQ_C-CQ_C)\} \quad (13)$$

If the firm wishes to fight the entrant illegally, it bears a cost of aggression, A, and faces a certain probability (1-λ) of being caught and penalized Q and losing its business. If it is successful, it can maintain its high price and profits. The expected utility equation, then, would include the probability of successfully avoiding arrest, λ, multiplied by the present discounted value of continuing (infinite) sales at monopoly prices, P_M, minus the cost of aggression, A. This amount would be added to the probability of arrest, 1-λ, multiplied by the costs of penalty, Q, and aggression, A.

$$EU(DW) = \lambda\{(\delta/1-\delta)[P_MQ-CQ] - A\} - (1-\lambda)\{A+Q\} \quad (14)$$

The important point to note is that the entrant has the ability to influence the value of λ by contacting the authorities and reporting aggressive behavior. This incentive is even increased, because the entrant would presumably gain the original firm's market share if that firm were penalized and legally forced to leave the market. If this is the case, the entrant will attempt to make λ as small as possible (this making the probability of arrest, 1-λ, as large as possible, presumably by reporting suspicions to the police). This action would make the expected utility of illegal tactics, EU(DW), negative, on average. Thus, the legal firm would be better off engaging in price wars. Because both players have the ability and incentive to appeal to a legal judicial and enforcement system, the use of force or violence is deterred in the legal market.[218]

4.4.1.2 Criminal Behavior

The deterrent effect of sanctions on a legal firm provides a crucial distinction between strategies selected by firms and dealers. Due to their illegal status, drug dealers' businesses are unprotected by the legal system. However, it is important to note that *they are also unconstrained by its niceties*. Unlike a legal enterprise that may eventually accept competition, dealers may use other means to deter newcomers. A common means of deterring competition is through violence; newcomers are threatened if they attempt to introduce their product into a territory that is already claimed by another group.[219]

If dealers wish to reduce the profit of their competitors, they may attempt to do so by affecting the *cost* (rather than revenue) side of the equation. In other words, a dealer can attempt to make doing business more costly to a rival, in order to drive the rival out of the market. The end result – for the competitor – is similar. Increasing the costs again results in a situation in which

$$cq > pq.$$

The costs of doing business are greater than the returns. The rival may be forced to shut down.

While the result – in terms of reduced competition – remains the same in each case, the cost of deterrence may be lower for the illegal dealer. In affecting the cost side of the equation for the rival, the profits to the original dealer should remain unaffected.[220] Thus, the fact that the products are illegal serves to expand the tools available to the dealer. He can fight or deter competitors with minimal corresponding loss in profit.

Unfortunately, the dealer's expanded set of tools can be used with violence. In attempting to increase the costs of a competitor, the dealer must affect the rival directly. The various means of increasing costs include: theft of the competitor's

---

[218] Note the similarities between this model and the simple expected utility model regarding the choice between crime and no crime (equation 1) in Chapter 1. Direct action against a legal rival may constitute criminal behavior and can generally be deterred by standard tools of probability of arrest and severity of punishment.

[219] In their study of gang activity, Levitt and Venkatesh found that any attempt of one gang to disturb the drug distribution activity of another was followed by a gang war – a prolonged period of violence. (1998, 20.)

[220] Profits may, in fact, suffer some setbacks if customers are frightened away from the area in response to a violent exchange between rivals. Notice, however, the motivation to hit a rival dealer but to leave the customers alone. This theoretical presentation also serves to explain a previously mysterious phenomenon in which organized crime groups would attack one another but would not attack outsiders.

goods and physical force – either to drive the rival out of a given area, or to otherwise harm the rival so that he or she is unable to sell.[221]

We know from analyses of price wars that despite the tactics used by the original firm, a rival firm may enter the market in an attempt to beat the original at its own game. Along these lines, it is easy to imagine that a rival dealer might resist the tactics of the original dealer and try to maintain his share of the market. Thus, the "price wars" that can erupt in legal markets bear some resemblance to the drug wars that break out periodically. Both types of "war" share the goal of driving out a competitor. However the blood shed in wars over drug turf - by dealers and occasionally by others, not party to the dispute - bears little relation to the drop in prices that results from a "price war."

The violence and destruction must be expected given the anarchic nature of the trade. Dealers, for obvious reasons, do not take one another to court to protest actions nor to challenge monopoly profits in a given territory. Although they do have the potential to report these actions to the authorities, doing so would expose them to the risk of arrest and punishment. Individual dealers are aware of their counterparts' unwillingness to appeal to the authorities, and thus find the practical bounds on their behavior expanded.

Since both the dealer and his rival are resistant to appeal to the legal system to protect them, they must develop their own means of force or protection. This source of power is generally derived from strength in numbers. Similar to the behavior of the legal entrepreneur - if a dealer wishes to engage in rival deterring behavior, he must start from a position of sufficient power or strength. A lone dealer - even a heavily armed one - will be defenseless against a similarly armed group. So the dealer has an incentive to increase his group size. For his protection, or in an attempt to seize "turf" the dealer's rival has the same incentive. The result is large aggregations of individuals - generally referred to as gangs or the mafia - that emerge in response to a desire to protect - or conquer - a share in the market for illegal drugs.

4.4.1.3 Organization

In the battle over territory, we would expect that membership in a group should have its advantages. As described in greater detail in Chapter 5, individual action is risky. Groups provide the important security of protection in numbers. This is particularly critical for individuals whose economic activity places them outside of the protection of the law.

We can further envision that sophisticated groups would have the ability to steal the market from other groups that are not as well organized. To clarify this assertion, recall that since drugs can be addicting, an uninterrupted flow of supply is a key asset in sales. If one group is better organized and has greater access to

---

[221] It should be noted that engaging in violent or destructive activity may also be costly for the initiator. The assumption is that a dealer will choose an activity that entails the lowest cost – violence or price wars – while maximizing the likelihood of deterring competition.

drug supply than another, then that group would be expected to outperform the other, and thereby win the customer base.

In fact this is frequently the case. The Chicago gang, the Gangster Disciples have been known to expand into other areas where, due to the lack of structured and reliable competition, prices for their wares were higher.

> "They could sell an ounce of crack in Chicago for $1,000," said one narcotics investigator. "Down here, [in Missouri] they could get $8,000 for that same ounce."[222]

The gang allegedly took control of the new market by offering superior services. Unlike the local groups, the Gangster Disciples were highly organized and, through their links to the gang in Chicago and through an endless supply of recruits for sales, were able to ensure continual delivery of the goods.

> "Normally, local dealers would have some crack for a while, and then when they sold out, there would be a gap before they had more. The Disciples were dependable. They always had it."[223]

As in the business world, membership in a gang, or network, can yield the advantage of superior marketing and delivery. Unlike the legal world, however, membership in a group can be crucial. As stated, violence becomes a pragmatic and effective tool to deter competitors. An individual facing offensive action by a gang has little chance of survival in life much less in the business. Thus, if gangs adopt strong measures to deter competitors, then the decision to become a member, rather than a competitor, can help protect the very life of the drug dealer.[224]

Forcing all dealers to become members of a given network may not be efficient policy. Although increased membership can create an expanded source of income and power for a gang, it stands to reason that the members impose certain costs on the gang as well.[225] This means that the gang must balance these concerns with the need to control competition. In this case, a natural solution would be the development of a type of "free-agent" policy, in which gangs would allow unaffiliated individuals to sell drugs in their territory for a fee.[226] In other words, using terminology from the business world, franchises are being sold. Such a system would permit the gang, or network, to avoid the costs of an additional member while continuing to deter competition, and to reap the gains from sales in the area.

---

[222] Possley, 12/17/95, 12.
[223] Ibid.
[224] For more detail, see Chapter 5.
[225] Some costs include weapons, protection, and wages. Levitt and Venkatesh note that gangs bore the costs of funerals and related expenses, such as compensating the victim's family, which could be costly for the gang.
[226] *The Economist*, 12/17/97, 22.

Evidence exists that this type of system is put to use. Larry Hoover, the leader of the Chicago gang, the Gangster Disciples was recorded discussing

> ...[C]ollecting street taxes from non-gang members, called 'neutrons' by Gangster Disciple members...He allegedly directed followers to collect the equivalent of one day's narcotic sales each week from dealers for the 'privilege' to sell drugs in the Gangster Disciple territory. If any drug dealers refused to pay, Hoover warned that the gang would shut them down...[227]

Hoover estimated that the gang could garner between $200,000 and $300,000 a day from street taxes alone...[228]

Thus, through an expanded range of tools, where some parallel the legitimate business world and others manifest the lack of legal recourse, dealers have a greater ability to organize and to deter competition. Individual rivals can choose to: stop dealing in the area, join the group, or, if possible, provide heavily taxed free-agent labor for the gang. If the rival is another group, then, as we see in legal businesses, matters such as relative levels of organization and supply can affect the prospects for the dueling groups. However, in contrast to the legal world, the results also hinge upon which group is larger and/or better armed. Due to their illegal status, the competition reducing options of dealers are not constrained by legal protocol. Through these means, groups that organize to sell drugs have an expanded possibility to create and maintain a type of monopoly. Just this application and expansion of violence indicates that the fact that drugs are illegal is creating more problems than it solves.

4.4.2 Anarchy

The previous section suggested that power must be anticipated to apply to a large range of issues. Violence, in the world of illicit drugs meets many of the functions that are filled, in a legitimate society, by a system of enforcement or arbitration. The illegal status of the drug dealer, however, creates an environment in which this use of power should be expected as "natural." Indeed, the circumstances of the world of drug dealers correspond closely with the concepts of power and anarchy found in political science. Theorists claim that the international system is anarchic because there is no credible international police to enforce agreements, nor any international judge and jury that have any real power to apply and enforce judgments on a country which chooses to break an agreement with another. Because this is the case, states must cope with the possibility that other states will renege on deals with one another. In the effort to hold others to their agreements, power is a key resource. If one state breaks an agreement, it may become subject to military action by another.

---

[227] O'Connor, 1/4/96, 17.
[228] Ibid, 1.

4.4.2.1 Contracts

This system, although abstract, can mirror the world of drug dealing. In addition to the impact on anticompetition strategies, the illegal status of dealers affects interactions with consumers. Dealers hold an illegal status, therefore they cannot make use of legal systems (the police or the courts) to enforce contracts with customers. Subsequently, we can expect that, as in the international system, when informal means are ineffective, many dealers will resort to the use of power as a means to enforce contracts. Indeed, this is what happens; power is a tool both for punishing someone who cheats in a business transaction and for deterring others from attempting to do so.

> Nelson Sepulveda's testimony was a rare instance of a gang leader describing how he ran a murderous criminal enterprise...At one point, he described exacting revenge against a 'regular customer' who had apparently crossed him while buying a large amount of crack cocaine. "I saw a couple of the bills were counterfeit," Mr. Sepulveda said of the money the man had paid for the drugs. "I had a gun; Stanley had a gun," Mr. Sepulveda continued... "We approached the guy's car. We was talking to him about the counterfeit money. Stanley told him that he jerked us. He said he gave us straight-up money. I shot him. Stanley shot him."[229]

But, how is this power obtained? Obviously, one person, even if well armed, cannot serve as a formidable opponent to a large number of others. The insecurity of individual action in a world of force and power-play has prompted many dealers to develop networks or gangs.[230] This network exists to produce and sell the drugs and to enforce payments. Dealers must determine their own, extra-legal means of ensuring that their contracts are upheld. It goes without saying that they will not make use of the judicial system to help them. The drug trade is a subculture of a society that possesses a judicial system, however, drug dealers will only be hampered by this system and cannot use it to uphold agreements.

Reliance on gang members for protection and to enforce agreements results in violence and disorder. Consider the situation; because juveniles receive lower penalties for criminal behavior, a larger number of very young children are recruited and used by the older members both to sell drugs, and also to punish cheaters. The notion of justice exacted at the whim and hands of a nine-year-old is disturbing, at the very least! Combine this scenario with the potential for retaliation by a rival gang, and the chance of violence escalates. So, due to the fact that dealers are unprotected and unconstrained by the legal system, the potential for widespread death and destruction is overwhelming.

---

[229] Hevesi, 3/1/95, B1.
[230] See Chapter 5 for a detailed discussion on the development and role of gangs in contract enforcement.

4.4.2.2 Informal Mechanisms

The threat of power is ever present, but dealers may also use other means of contract enforcement. The use of nonviolent measures is rational both in terms of safety and to create good business conditions. It is easy to imagine that some customers might be scared off otherwise. To avoid some of the bloodshed, dealers develop their own rules of sale to ensure that they won't be cheated.

> "They passed the money under the door," [the gang leader] said, adding a cautionary business procedure, "Always get the money first, then pass the change or the work [drug]."[231]

Although their illegal status keeps the price of drugs artificially high, dealers are reportedly constrained to sell within the loose range of the street value of the drug. Although dealers may wish to charge artificially high prices, the customer won't be cheated twice; if a customer learns he has been overcharged, he may discontinue business with the dealer. Despite efforts to destroy competition, customers have other options. If one dealer proves to be unreliable, another dealer in another territory can be found. Thus, repeated interaction is important, as neo-liberals in political science stress in their related analysis of trade and cooperation in the international system. In fact, repeated play is so important that producers mark their wares with special seals, so that the dealers will recognize them, and, if the drug is of high quality, demand them again.[232]

> Mr. Sepulveda's ring utilized 'red-top and orange-top' crack vials to differentiate their product. At one point in the fall of 1991, a rival gang began selling 'yellow-top' on [their gang's] turf... "I put a hit on them," Mr. Sepulveda said, referring to the Dec. 16, 1991, killing of one rival gang member and three bystanders.[233]

Yet, as the cite reveals, despite the slight lapse in the use of force that informal mechanisms can create, violence continues to loom in drug trade. Even the informal mechanisms are subject to break down. As the population grows, and anonymity allows a customer to cheat and then disappear, dealers will come to rely on power to support their trade.

4.4.2.3 Employee Relations

Power is also used to deter employees from making mistakes. As described in the next chapter, a careful system of rewards and punishments is implemented so that employees have every incentive to fulfill their duties actively and carefully.

---

[231] Hevesi, 3/1/95, B4.
[232] Interview with a Federal Law Enforcement Officer, September, 1995.
[233] Hevesi, 3/1/95, B4.

Lose a load [of drugs]...and a smuggler can be forced to work for nothing to make it up, or the smuggler can be disfigured or killed.
"The level of violence is like nowhere I've ever seen," said a federal agent...[234]

Why is this important? One answer involves consideration of the costs and high gains of drug trade. An error or loss on the employee's part can be costly for the employer. It is easy to envision that to avoid these expenses, an employer has an incentive to use tactics to strongly discourage any failings on the part of employees.

Another reason behind the use of force in the treatment of employees can be derived from the issue of supply of labor. Due to the seemingly endless supply of employees throughout the drug trade, individual workers may be viewed as disposable. If this is the case, we might expect that the liberal use of punishments could serve as a type of signal to potential employees regarding the level of capability and responsibility expected of them. It is simple to imagine that this open threat can serve to weed out those who do not feel adequate for the task.

Finally, the use of force in punishment should deter those who might otherwise steal the drugs for themselves, either to use or to sell, and claim to have been apprehended or robbed. This possibility poses a risk for the employers. Employees could make larger gains by selling the drugs themselves without giving a share of the proceeds to a superior. If the employer were under the impression that the drugs had been stolen from the employee, then he would not expect to receive any proceeds from the sale. To avoid this chance of being robbed by one's own employees, we can expect many employers to take steps to ensure that the punishment for losing the drugs, through robbery or through arrest, is so high that it would outweigh any potential gains from theft and sale. With this cost/benefit perspective, employees would avoid real or false losses.

4.4.2.4 The Cure?

If the above analysis is correct, then violence appears to be a natural consequence of the illegal status of drugs. If this is the case, it is difficult to assert that keeping drugs illegal is a reasonable policy. Instead, we continue to see drug users and addicts, and a policy that creates the incentives for the growth of criminal groups and the spread of violence. And the situation is becoming worse. As we learned from the analogy to businesses, drug networks have a motivation to expand into other areas, in which they can charge a higher price for their wares. Thus, gangs and other criminal organizations have an incentive to spread and to penetrate a growing number of areas. This prospect is extremely disturbing! Indeed, instead of protecting people from drugs, we are motivating dealers to seek new clients and to tempt them into trying drugs. Instead of treating the ailment, we seem to be

---

[234] Wren, 3/4/97, A10.

fostering its spread. If this is the case, reversing the "cure" through legalization would be the best policy.

4.5 Legalization

4.5.1 Undercutting the Black Market

Benefits to opening the market are numerous. If the market is allowed to dictate prices, then the price will occur, as dictated by economic theory, where supply meets demand. There will be no shortage of goods. Consumers would have no incentive to turn to the black market, because they could obtain the goods legally. Thus, by relaxing price controls, the government can essentially *undercut* the black market. Instead of inducing illegal activity, the black market agents must compete with the market.

> Underselling drug dealers and supplying clean needles, [A. Robert Kaufman, a candidate for the City Council of Baltimore, Maryland] argues, would end turf wars, reduce violent crime, ease the strain on the criminal justice system and curb the spread of diseases like AIDS and hepatitis.[235]

> No one could ever justify a legalization argument on grounds that drugs are harmless. But as a tactic to upset the economic realities of the drug marketplace, it could work by sticking government right in the middle of the demand-supply equation.[236]

However, in order for legalization to be accepted, we must demonstrate that it can address some legitimate concerns. Among these are fears that legalization will lead to experimentation and also to an increased number of addicts. The following section addresses these concerns and suggests types of policy that could reduce the potential drawbacks to a legalization policy.

4.5.2 Experimentation

As stated, critics of legalization argue that if drugs were legalized, a larger percentage of people would experiment with increasingly "harder" drugs. This concern is not borne out in evidence. Holland, which has a tolerant policy on soft drugs, does not experience a large problem with hard drugs. Indeed, comparing results from a 1997 National Household Survey (SAMHSA) in the US to one run by CEDRO in the Netherlands, a greater percentage of Americans reported having ever used cannabis, cocaine, inhalants and heroin than had their Dutch

---

[235] Janofsky, 4/20/95, A16.
[236] Madigan, 9/22/96, 10.

counterparts.[237] Instead of a progression from soft to hard drugs, some evidence suggests that the use of harder drugs may be encouraged by dealers with their eye on potential profits. For instance, the DEA has reported that distributors working with the Cali drug organization have required customers to purchase heroin along with cocaine.[238]

4.5.3 Addiction Control

The prospect of undercutting the black market has other advantages. Currently an enormous problem in consideration of the drug issue is that drug addiction is very difficult to overcome.

> Fewer than 25 percent of the individuals who need drug or alcohol treatment enter a program. On average, a quarter complete treatment; half of them are drug- or alcohol-free a year later. In other words, with wide variations depending on individual circumstances, those entering programs have a one-in-eight chance of being free of drugs or alcohol a year later.[239]

Proponents of keeping drugs illegal cite these statistics to argue that the risks of legalization are greater than the potential benefits. They claim that because addictions are so difficult to overcome, any increase in drug use would entail a significant social loss.

4.5.3.1 Inelastic Demand

The addictive nature of drugs ensures that many tend to be willing to purchase them regardless of the price. This willingness can be seen in numerous anecdotes of people who have lost everything because of their need to feed their addiction.

> Although Crack is widely derided as a loser's drug, its customers include people like Thomas DeGrace, 35, who had a restaurant and a music company and whose five-year addiction wiped out all he had achieved.
> "Crack is the only drug in the world where the more you take, the more you want." Mr. DeGrace said. "When you take your first hit, you're chasing that hit for the rest of the day."

---

[237] Centrum voor drugsonderzoek, 1997. (The statistics for "Ever used" are cannabis: 32.9% US, versus 15.6% NL; cocaine: 10.5% US, versus 2.1% NL; inhalants: 5.7%, versus 0.5%; and heroin: 0.9%, versus 0.3%)
[238] *The Economist*, 12/24/94, 24.
[239] Califano, 1/29/95, 40.

98

Eventually, Mr. DeGrace lived on the street, bartering for crack by holding the drugs so the dealer could avoid arrest if the police swooped in.[240]

This willingness is often referred to as inelastic demand. Representing this scenario with a graph, a perfectly inelastic demand would entail that a person will be willing to buy a certain amount, q*, of a drug at any price, no matter how high.

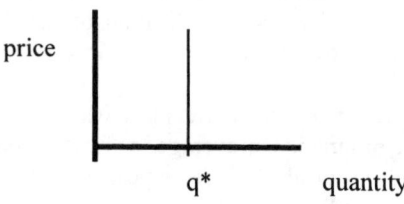

Fig. 4.2

Simon and Witte have argued that the demand for illicit drugs is not perfectly inelastic.[241] However, even a moderately inelastic demand curve can be profitable for dealers. Stories exist of dealers who take advantage of addiction to obtain and keep customers. They offer "free samples" to new customers. Once the person becomes addicted, he or she will continue to purchase the dealer's wares.

Rehabilitation for alcohol addiction is difficult. The problem is exacerbated for illicit drug addicts. Oddly enough, the illegal status of drugs may *increase* the problem for drug users who wish to overcome addictions. Many advocates of decreasing drug use through illegalization miss an important point. Drug dealers and suppliers *have an economic incentive in creating and maintaining demand*. Dealers recognize and rely on the addictive quality of their wares to keep their customers buying.

> "Have you ever been in love?" Harris [a drug addict] asks. "You can let go of somebody you love easier than you can walk away from a cocaine problem."[242]

Many dealers don't just rely on the addiction of their customers, they actively encourage it and work to destroy the effects of rehabilitation programs.

> B.L. Harris, who is struggling to quit, knows just how easy it is to find the drug. In his little corner of Halifax County [North Carolina], it's hard to hide from crack. ...Harris has to avoid the convenience store just

---

[240] Wren, 3/4/97, A10.
[241] Simon and Witte, 1982, 134-138.
[242] Stocking, 8/13/95, 11A.

beyond his driveway because drug dealers accost him there. If he turns in the other direction, he's heading toward a neighborhood he calls 'Drug Town,'...

If he stops on some of the side streets there, Harris says, dealers will swarm his car, boasting of the quality of their merchandise.[243]

The actions appear menacing, but are entirely rational from the perspective of the supplier. Drug dealers need their customers in order to make a profit. If demand disappears, they will be out of business. Indeed, that is the goal behind eliminating demand. But, if the government tries to fight dealers by destroying demand, through rehabilitation or through other measures, dealers will fight back to maintain it. Unfortunately, statistics regarding success in overcoming addiction are in the dealers' favor.

This issue can put pause to arguments made against legalization which claim that legalization of drugs will create more addictions. Certainly, if drugs are legalized with the same restrictions as alcohol, we will see an increase in people trying drugs. Also certain drugs are more addictive than others, so a large number of people may become addicted. Conversely, by removing the encouragements of dealers, we may find it easier to rehabilitate addicts if drugs are legal. Legal stores do not have the same incentives as drug dealers to pursue and tempt former customers. We do not hear stories of liquor store-owners actively pursuing and tempting recovering alcoholics with samples. Without the pressure, offers of "free samples," and harassment that haunts drug addicts today, we may discover an improvement in rehabilitation if drugs were legalized.

This optimism may be unwarranted, however. Recovering alcoholics face constant temptations from the easy availability of alcohol in stores and social events. It is easy to imagine that legalization of drugs might eliminate the pressures from dealers only to have these pressures reemerge unwittingly in a social context from friends or acquaintances.[244]

4.5.4 Control

Many of the above arguments suggest that legalization is not as threatening as it appears. There are also benefits associated with the policy. If the market is open, then the government has, ironically, more control over consumption than if the market is closed. In the case of drugs, the government can impose age restrictions, as it does with the consumption of alcohol and tobacco, so that children will encounter more difficulties in attempts to purchase drugs. The restrictions are not foolproof; some children will be able to obtain the prohibited substances. However, as argued previously, the government has a greater influence if the goods are sold legally than it does otherwise.

There are further ways to control drug use. Licenses, similar to those for liquor sales, could be required in order to sell or distribute non-prescription,

---

[243] Stocking, Ben, p. 10A.
[244] Thanks to Dr. W. Lutz and Dr. B. Weinmann-Lutz for this point, July 2000.

recreational drugs. Drugs could be labeled, as are cigarettes and alcoholic beverages. For greater control, users could sign a waiver, (similar to those required by bungee jumping companies) which acknowledges that the user understands the risks. This waiver not only entails that the user take responsibility for his or her own actions, but also serves as a register of those who have purchased the drugs.

Drug sales should be taxed. To ensure that the government does not "gain from the use of improper substances," the taxes could be designated towards drug rehabilitation funds. In this way, the tax serves as a type of insurance for drug users and social insurance for society.

Other controls are more controversial. Studies have shown that drug use can impair the user's ability to drive or to operate machinery. The effects range from distorted perceptions of time and distance and hallucinations, due to LSD use; to attention lapses, higher sensitivity to light, and anxiety from cocaine consumption; to decreased ability to perceive and respond to hazardous situations, due to use of cannabis.[245] In Sweden a register is kept of those people who are prescribed heavy drugs. Based on the effect of the drugs, those whose ability to drive or operate heavy machinery may be impaired by the drugs must refrain from doing so while taking the drugs.[246] Similar measures could be used for those who wish to use certain drugs recreationally.

This restraint may appear too restrictive on individual freedom; however, it could solve many problems. Currently, the use alone of drugs is illegal. The suggested measure would allow drug use, but would curtail driving privileges for those who risk being impaired while under the influence. After all, it is illegal to consume alcohol and drive.[247] If drugs were to be legalized, laws should be created to protect the public from drivers under the influence of drugs. This policy suggests an extension of existing laws to heavy drugs.

The law could improve conditions in two ways. It would reduce the number of people who would use drugs and drive or operate machinery. This would protect the public. Furthermore, since the restrictions are placed upon the buyer, it could reduce - although not eliminate - the number of people willing to purchase drugs for others.

It should be noted that a careful balance must be made when placing controls over substances. Some controls are useful, but if too many exist, then incentives for the black market reemerge. If it becomes too difficult or expensive to purchase drugs legally, then users will seek other sources. Along these lines, if the number of stores are insufficient to meet demand, consumers will find the product elsewhere.[248] The quantity supplied must meet the quantity demanded.

---

[245] ARF Marketing Services, [A] 1992.

[246] Professor A. Andersson, personal communication, August, 1997.

[247] In fact, several states are considering making it illegal to talk on a cellular phone while driving.

[248] This problem has been evidenced in the case of legalized prostitution in Australia. The number of legal brothels was severely limited, leaving a surplus of customers. These customers provided incentives, in terms of higher pay, for prostitutes to meet their needs

4.5.5 Resources

A significant benefit of legalization is that the government no longer must invest money or resources into fighting the black market. By relaxing price control, the government can let the market eliminate the black market. This scheme has been successful in the past. Violent crime dropped 65 percent in the year following the repeal of the Prohibition.[249]

Using a cost/benefit analysis, the method of eliminating price controls far outweighs that of fighting black market activity. Taking the potential savings on the normal costs of factors such as enforcement (domestic and international) and incarcerations, a conservative estimate of the savings due to legalization yields $37 Billion in annual savings.[250] In support of this assertion, a representative from the John Howard Institute expressed frustration that the growing number of drug-related court cases overwhelmed the judicial system and left little resources available to combat more serious, violent crimes.[251]

Legalization has been tried in an attempt to combat smuggling of other goods. Brazil, Argentina, and Uruguay have created a trading bloc, Mercosur. The bloc is gradually making goods in those countries cheaper. The effect is that the sophisticated smuggling rings of Paraguay, who sold or smuggled cheaper goods, are slowly being put out of business. Now the new prices are as low as those found in Paraguay, and citizens of the above countries no longer find it necessary to go to Paraguay, or to "import" its products.[252]

Legalizing drugs would very likely take its toll in an increased use of drugs. This fact is recognized by proponents of legalization.

> Legalizing drugs would not be cost free. We could expect somewhat more use of presently illicit drugs and, all other things remaining the same, more drug abuse. But... [v]ast sums would be freed for prevention and treatment of drug abuse...[253]

Although there would be an increase in drug use, more funds would be available for remediation. The taxes gained and the money saved from fighting drugs could be designated for rehabilitation programs.

As stated in the introduction, there is no optimal solution to this problem; the tradeoffs are considerable. Fighting drugs involves investing resources into fighting both the supply and demand sides of a market. It also inadvertently encourages criminal activity. In the fight against drugs, the government must provide funding for rehabilitation, the benefits of which drug dealers will try to negate.

---

outside of the brothels. Thus, problems associated with illegal prostitution continued. Davis and Shaffer, 1997, 24-9.

[249] Schaffer, 1999.
[250] Ibid.
[251] Private conversation, December 1997.
[252] Matt Moffett, 5/30/95, 1&A9.
[253] Duke, 12/21/93, 3.

Legalizing drugs would involve a possible social loss of a higher number of addicts and the monetary cost of providing rehabilitation for them. Drug addicts may resort to crime to support habits if drugs are legal, but punishments should be severe, and programs, such as the ones in Zurich, which provide free heroin while requiring the recipients to undergo drug counseling, can be created to attempt to cope with these people.[254] If drugs will be used and addicts will be created under both scenarios, then legalizing drugs seems to be the better alternative.

4.6 Legal -The Zurich Problem

Despite legitimate concerns in consideration of the prospect of legalizing drugs, the above analysis indicates that it is the optimal policy. If this argument is correct, are we likely to witness legalization in the near future? Unfortunately, the probability is low. The emotional aspect of the drug debate alone ensures that the subject will be debated for years to come. However, there are other factors that have the potential to create significant and daunting problems with the prospect of legalizing drug use. These problems are typified in the case of Zurich, Switzerland.

Until 1992, the city of Zurich tolerated drug use. The policy of toleration was designed in hopes of undermining the black market to thereby decrease the crime in the area.[255] These hopes were not fulfilled. Instead, Zurich has seen an increase in violent crime and a large increase in drug use as well as turf wars that resulted in the deaths of several dealers. Addicts and dealers menaced the neighborhood.

> "It was like an Oriental bazaar," said the principal of a nearby school..., speaking on the condition of anonymity. "You heard shots sometimes. They were all over the sidewalk. Shops went out of business. Restaurants went out of business. People moved away. The dirt and pollution were incredible. The whole district died off."[256]

If the policy was intended to improve matters, why did the situation become worse?

In the case of Zurich and of Holland, a crucial problem was that drugs were *tolerated* but not *legalized*. Given that drugs were not officially legal, the government could not control their distribution in the way that it can control alcohol. Had the government given licenses and restrictions for the sale of drugs, dealers would have to cooperate with the state, as must liquor store owners. In this case, the main problem would be rehabilitation. By merely tolerating drug use, dealers remained free agents who could cooperate with the state or not. Furthermore, by not providing legal networks for access to drugs, the state essentially ensured that dealers would have to seek access to criminal groups to acquire their merchandise. Rather than attracting business people, this type of

---

[254] For example, in Zurich and in other areas, drugs and clean needles are given to addicts.
[255] Cowell, 3/12/95.
[256] Ibid.

policy generates incentives for petty criminals and members of organized crime to enter the market for drug supply. Given the constraints, it is unsurprising that the policy of toleration resulted in a rise in crime.

4.6.1 Voting With One's Feet

Unfortunately, even if the cities had fully legalized drugs, they would have experienced many of the same problems. The circumstance can be illustrated with two models. The first, used in political science, is known as "voting with one's feet." The model states that people will frequently choose to live in a place that has laws that appeal to them. If drug use is tolerated in Zurich, but not elsewhere, then people from outside of Zurich who wish to sell or use drugs will go there, either permanently or temporarily. This was the case.

> Based on the figures, only about one-fifth of the addicts came from Zurich while the rest came mainly from among the 30,000 addicts elsewhere in Switzerland.[257]

The Netherlands, a country that is well known for tolerating drug use, has experienced similar problems. Although officially, only soft drugs may be consumed, and only in set quantities, drug dealers eagerly make other drugs available.

> ...[T]he soft policy on soft drugs serves as a magnet for criminal dealers, who supply the drugs, both soft and hard, and have made the Netherlands a European haven for dealers and takers.[258]

Unfortunately for Zurich and for Holland, people who use drugs are not often the most productive.

> ...[A]ll the financial lures and prods and all the job training in the world will do precious little to make employable the [people] who are addicts and abusers.[259]

Furthermore, as drugs are expensive, addicts without sufficient funds may choose to resort to criminal activity, such as theft or prostitution, to support their addiction. Additionally, many professional dealers are attracted to the areas. These people are frequently also involved in other types of organized crime.[260] Thus, by creating laws which attempt to decrease crime, Zurich found itself faced with even more.

---

[257] Cowell, 3/12/95.
[258] *The Economist*, 10/12/96, 58.
[259] Califano, 1/29/95, 40.
[260] *The Economist*, 10/12/96, 58.

The governments of Zurich and of Holland sought to eliminate the illegal status of their residents who did drugs and to undercut the profits of the drug dealers. However, the policies did not apply only to the current residents of the city. The policies attracted people who lived outside. Within this group of people, a subset has a tendency towards crime, to make sufficient money to support their habit. So, by doing "the right thing", the governments made their situation worse.

4.6.2 International Prisoners' Dilemma

The important drawback to Zurich's problem, was that other cities did not also change their policies on drugs. Had all of the other cities in the area, or even a large percentage of them, legalized drugs, the Zurich's problem probably would not have been so large.

"Zurich is just not in a position to look after all of Switzerland's addicts," [Giorgio Prestele, a city spokesman on drug policy] said.[261]

If other cities have similar legislation, then either people won't need to vote with their feet and move to a different city, or at least they will have a number to choose from, so the impact on a particular place will be diminished.

The problem is that these other places have little incentive to do so. If Zurich legalizes drugs and the neighboring city does not, then those who wish to consume or sell drugs will move to Zurich. Thus, the neighboring city is better off. Not only is it avoiding Zurich's problem, but it is also losing residents of its own that engage in crime and use drugs. Using this reasoning, most cities have a powerful incentive to avoid legalizing drugs.

Here we have a dilemma; if everyone legalized drugs, everyone could be better off. But if only one state (or few states) legalize drugs, they will be worse off while the others will profit at their expense. This problem is captured by the Prisoners' Dilemma described in the introduction. In this case, if there are only two players (for simplicity) then each can choose to either legalize drugs or make them illegal. If both players legalize, then they both have the second best payoff. If player **a** legalizes and **b** does not, then **a** gets its worst payoff, and **b** gets its best. If neither legalize, they both get the next worst payoff. Because both have an incentive to keep drugs illegal, they will both do so. Thus, they will lose out on the potential better payoffs, but they will not get cheated and receive their worst payoffs.

Although the models are very simplistic, they can provide a good explanation for why legalizing drugs can have very negative effects, and for why it is unlikely that we will see many places do so unilaterally.

---

[261] Cowell, 3/12/95.

4.7 Conclusion

The analysis presented here demonstrates that a policy that criminalizes drugs creates a cure that is significantly worse than the ailment. To counter the associated problems of the "cure," three recommendations are offered.

1. Legalization: If the cure is worse than the ailment, then we should forgo its use and treat the ailment in a different manner, using means such as rehabilitation.
2. Education: Educating the public allows us to deter some potential drugs users in a manner which is consistent with the notion of individual responsibility.
3. Regulation: Regulation, in a similar manner to the restrictions placed upon distribution and consumption of alcohol can allow us to control for issues such as quality and age of the consumer. Reasonable controls should aid our goals to protect users and those around them. However, restrictions should be carefully designed to allow supply to equal demand, so that we do not produce incentives for a black market to reemerge.

Drawing from the analysis, these suggestions appear to be the best solution to the problems we have created by criminalizing drugs.

Chapter 5

Gangs

The issue of gangs is troubling for today's society. Stories of gang violence fill newspapers. Rival gang members shoot one another over drugs, over turf, or in retaliation for the injury, or death, or even insult of another member.

> ...[T]he evidence suggests that when bullets fly and bodies fall, something other than the profit motive is usually at work...Often that something can be absurdly trifling. Kody Scott, for years, a famously cruel leader of Los Angeles' Eight-Tray Gangster Crips,...recalls that "one of the biggest wars inside the Crips goes back to when a young girl had a leather coat taken by a guy in my neighborhood. It erupted into a full-scale war..."[262]

With all the violence and bloodshed why would anyone join a gang in the first place? Why would a person choose to join a life of crime, in which the probability of early death is so great that nineteen-year-olds are considered old-timers?

From the perspective of many of us, who face few, if any, of the choices and constraints that confront inhabitants of environments controlled by gangs, even the idea of gang membership is rejected. What we will discover, however, is that by evaluating the alternatives that many potential gang members face, joining a gang may be the best option. The intent of this chapter is to explore the question from a rational choice perspective - to examine the motivations behind decisions as well as the options available to those making the decisions. Hopefully, in this manner, we can better understand what is needed to combat this serious problem.

Somewhat surprisingly, an appropriate analogy for gang behavior comes from political science. In particular, the analogy lies in the large portion of the literature that focuses on alliances in the international system. Similar to the roles international alliances, gangs define coalitions of individuals where a part of a gang's function is to take offensive or defensive action against other groups. The analogy can be extended further; membership in either an international or local criminal alliance entails a cost. Self-defense or aggressive behavior can yield rewards but also entails effort. Hence, individuals have an incentive to free-ride on the actions of the group. Just as governmental alliances create systems that can be held together in a state of anarchy, gangs must seek to develop mechanisms for attracting new members and for discouraging dropouts.

Exactly what these mechanisms that enhance the existence of coalitions involve is the subject of much debate. When describing international coalitions, many authors propose that punishment strategies discourage states from "defection" from an alliance. Compare these theories with the grizzly tales of

---

[262] *The Economist*, 12/17/94, 22.

gangs' reactions to a member who wishes to leave the gang; punishment strategies appear, indeed, to be a critical mechanism to enforce continuation of membership.

Applying the above intuition to the problems facing inner-city youth, the example takes on a chilling reality. A *New York Times* article describes decisions concerning gang membership which face Chicago's youth as a choice resembling that between life and death. One problem is, as one youth stated, that most gang members will assume that a person is in a gang. Thus, if a gang sees someone who is not in their gang, they will fight him. The safest bet for most people, therefore, is to join some gang,[263] as membership will at least provide the protection of others. Unfortunately, once a person is in a gang, it becomes close to impossible to leave.

Protection is not the only motivation for gang membership. The prospect of profits from drug sales draw many into the fold. Admittedly, drugs can be sold independently of a gang, but competition from the gang can substantially circumscribe gains. Additionally, constraints on the actions and recourses of the dealer, due to the illegal status of illicit drugs, can create a situation in which a dealer is forced to rely on the protection and enforcement of a gang in order to successfully complete his or her drug sales. Elsewhere,[264] I examined the development and use of extortion in the context of international relations. It is interesting how this model is applicable to the situation facing gangs; through the gangs' offers of protection and enforcement to dealers, contingent on their joining and remaining in the gang, we discover behavior that bears a striking resemblance to that of an extortionist.

Finally, I use a model from macroeconomics to examine the options available for many urban youth. Through this model, I attempt to demonstrate that, in some cases, crime may be a rational choice.

The natural reaction remains: *Why would anyone join a gang? Gang membership is dangerous and counterproductive.* The above examples, arm us with mathematical analogies for answers to this question - a question that was previously asked and analyzed mostly by sociologists. With this new approach, we may not only obtain a new understanding, but also derive new answers for new questions. For instance, what conditions lead to the development of this system of alliances (gangs)? Can we counteract the punishment strategies and the incentive strategies of gang membership? What would we have to do to do so? The models allow us to combine anecdotal evidence and straightforward analysis to obtain insight about concerns which previously were out of our grasp.

5.1 Motivations for Membership

The presence of gangs has become commonplace - if not accepted - in most urban settings. However, the crime and violence generally associated with gangs leads one to question why anyone would choose to join one. The reasons for membership are varied. For instance, these groups fulfill many functions for those

---

[263] Terry, 8/18/94, 26.
[264] Saari-Sieberg, 1998.

who join which range from economic gain, to power, to protection, to a sense of family that is absent in the lives of many.

> Another 15-year old Black Disciple who called himself Will said that he was afraid of going to jail and of dying violently but that he had no desire to leave the gang. "Being in an organization is like being in a big family," he said "They are always there for you when nobody else is."[265]

5.1.1 Structure

Gangs provide needed institutions in a part of the world where every other institution; the family, the church, and the schools; has deteriorated and collapsed. In light of the conditions, it is unsurprising "that children who are poor, ill-educated and, typically, raised by a single parent (of whom a depressing number are unemployed, alcoholic, drug-addicted or some mixture of the three) should flock to gangs."[266] Some join because an older brother or sister is already a member.[267] Some join out of an emotional need - to feel a sense of belonging. Others join to gain a sense of structure in their lives that is otherwise lacking.

> Chill said the gang cared about its members like a family would and kept them in line: "They told us we can't even sell drugs around here if we don't go to school. I know one brother who was broke all summer because he messed up in school and couldn't sell."[268]

Distinctly hierarchical systems, organized crime groups provide structure for their members. Through a careful system of rewards and penalties, they even offer incentives for their members to become educated. In different environments, these incentives typically come from other sources, such as parents, schools, or churches. But if these traditional sources do not provide this motivation, gangs can do so.

> Chill said the boy improved his school record and was back on the corner selling. "It's no different than your mama making you go to school," Will said.
> "And anyway," Chill added, "a lot of mamas don't care if you go. The organization does. It don't want no dummies. The organization ain't all negative."[269]

In this way, the gangs serve as a sort of surrogate parent for those who need them. Yet, in spite of how it is perceived by the members, this encouragement is not

---

[265] Terry, 8/18/94, 26.
[266] *The Economist*, 12/17/94, 23.
[267] Ibid.
[268] Terry, 8/18/94, 26.
[269] Ibid.

simply based on paternalistic sentiment. Instead, the gangs, like any organization, seek education and talent among their members as part of a long-term plan to develop sharper and more effective means of action.

5.1.2 Protection in Numbers

Positive aspects of gangs aside, a large number of members do not join gangs merely for their fraternal, or paternal, aspect. Some are coerced, and some join for protection from the gang itself and from other gangs. Recall the alliance analogy from political science. Just as states in the international system must weigh the pros and cons of alliance membership, individuals in heavily gang-populated environments must make similar choices. In the international arena, if states reject alliance membership, they face potential aggression coupled with a lack of protection. Individuals contemplating gang membership encounter these and other constraints. Unlike individual states, while individuals are numerous, they are relatively powerless and anonymous. Consequently, we can expect that, unless all gang members are distinctively recognizable, any unallied person risks being mistaken as a member of some gang. If that person inadvertently crosses the territory of any gang, then at a minimum, he risks punishment for trespassing.

Indeed, this "if you are not one of us, you are probably against us" attitude has the potential to affect anyone who strays into a gang environment. In December, 1996, a graduate student from Mexico, who was enrolled in a Chicago university, was on his way to do the family grocery shopping when he was mistaken for a member of a rival gang. He never knew what hit him; when he awoke, he was in the hospital with a brain concussion.

This incident was an isolated happenstance for a member of the university community, whose students are generally sheltered from gang activity. Unfortunately, for those who reside near gang territories, these are the daily problems that face those who reject membership.

> "Around here, if you're not in a gang, they still think you're in a gang," [an 18-year-old Black Disciple member] said. "You can't walk to school. You can't go where you want, when you want, so you might as well be in a gang. Then at least when trouble starts, you ain't by yourself. You got some aid and assistance. You got a chance to live."
> He added with a sigh, "If I didn't have to, I wouldn't be in no gang."[270]

In this case, it makes sense to join a gang. Consider the options: the costs of membership may be high, but the costs of acting independently are even higher. The gangs serve as mandatory alliances where members join for protection against other alliances.

Evaluating gangs in terms of alliances allows us to analyze the issue in the abstract - apart from disturbing emotional aspects that can cloud or distort the

---

[270] Terry, 8/18/94, 26.

question. To do so, it is important to see how alliances function. Then these functions are compared to gangs to determine if the analogy fits. If it does, then we have a means of understanding and analyzing gang behavior.

To start, recall that alliances form to provide greater opportunities for aggressive or defensive action. In order to be effective in this objective, an alliance must recruit members. This requirement makes sense; an alliance of one or two (medium sized) countries is likely to be relatively ineffective when faced with an opposing alliance of 5 or more similar sized countries. Consequently, an alliance must ensure full participation of its members; it must take steps to avoid any member quitting the alliance.

To achieve these goals, alliances generally apply a system of rewards and punishments to their members to ensure that each member has an incentive to join, participate, and remain. Since the benefits come from the strength of an alliance, each member is motivated to ensure that other members do so. After all, deterioration in any of these aspects (membership or activity) could decrease the strength of the alliance and, correspondingly decrease the level of protection of its members.

What we learn from these comments is that if alliances serve as an appropriate analogy for gangs, then we must anticipate that gangs would develop similar goals. We should also expect the gangs to adopt similar strategies to achieve these goals.

The individual choice regarding gang membership is very personal. From the list of motivations to join gangs, every member has his or her own incentive. So, an attempt to analyze the formation and maintenance of gangs based on these myriad decisions would be close to impossible. Instead, I create a model based on simple cost/benefit reasoning, to identify the gang structure by examining a gang member's decision-making processes.

As already described, for various reasons, some people simply desire to become gang members. If everyone held these sentiments, then gangs would have no problems recruiting and maintaining members. It is the enticement or coercion of unwilling individuals that is interesting; this is the action modeled here.

To describe the strategies and outcomes, I narrow the game down to two main players, the gang and the unwilling person. Initially, for the person, the costs of membership are higher than those of remaining independent. These costs should not be understated. It cannot be overlooked that, from the idealized *West Side Story* to today's harsher depictions, gangs are generally associated with violence.[271]

Initiation itself can be costly. Initiation into a gang, where a candidate must prove to be worthy of acceptance, can be dangerous for the new member. This is because the forms of proof of worth may range from the commission of various crimes to physical abuse at the hands of current members. As related to me by members of one community, the initiation task of one young boy from Chicago

---

[271] Levitt and Venkatesh found, in the gang studied, that active gang members had an estimated one in four chance of dying. (1998, 25.)

involved shooting point blank into an approaching car. The boy's membership resulted in the death of a high school student from a nearby suburb.[272]

Membership also exacts a hefty price. Members are assigned duties and are severely punished if they make errors or do not complete the task.

> A Black Disciple...describes the role the youngest members play: "He's this small little punk but wants a name, right? So you make him do the work. 'Hey homey, get me a car. A red car. A red sports car. By tonight. I'm taking my woman out. Or hey, little homey, go find me $50. Or hey, little homey, you wanna be big? Go pop that nigger that's messing with our business."[273]

> ...the gang's enforcer does not want excuses. No matter whether it was the police who took the dope or a holdup man with a .357, nobody messes with the gang's money, rules or reputation...legend has it that one Black Disciples leader beat his own brother to the ground for violating the rules.[274]

Additional risks include the possibility of arrest and penalty if the member is caught fulfilling an assignment, or of becoming the target of a rival gang.

In consideration of the dangers of gang life, it is easy to envision that an individual would evaluate that the costs are higher and the benefits are lower for gang membership than for those with a life on the outside. Left alone, this person would remain outside of a gang. But should too many people select this option, then gang membership would suffer.

Similar to the concerns facing an international alliance, as the numbers in a gang decrease, its ability to fill its role in either aggressive or defensive action deteriorates. This decline in power presents a precarious situation for the current members - if the gang is not sufficiently potent to act against rival gangs, then the safety of the members is threatened. This argument is intuitive; if gangs offer protection in numbers and if the gang's size is small, then it may be unable to offer sufficient defense against the actions of rival gangs. For their own protection, gang members must actively recruit and retain participants. From a cost/benefit perspective, the task for the gang is to change the payoffs so that membership, rather than independence, becomes the more attractive option. In other words, the gang must alter the costs and benefits of both joining and remaining independent.

To change the payoffs, the gang can either increase the benefit of membership, or the cost of nonmembership. There is evidence that gangs do both. As previously described, the dangers associated with life outside of a gang's

---

[272] Personal conversation, Chicago, 1996.
[273] Gibbs, 8/19/94, 30.
[274] Terry, 8/18/94.

protection can encourage many to seek membership. Membership benefits include kinship, structure, protection, and permission to sell drugs in gang territory.[275]

The mere presence of members is not sufficient to ensure the effectiveness and viability of the gang. Considering the duties involved in the various gang activities, it is understandable why some members might seek to minimize their personal input. In other words, gang members have an incentive to free-ride on the contributions of others without providing any labor or services themselves. These incentives, if unchecked, would leave the bulk of the responsibility on a small number of members.

Not only would this free-riding situation prove to be costly for those who did choose to contribute, but it would also be detrimental to the gang's survival. Just as the gang must maintain membership to protect itself, the gang also must ensure the loyalty and activity of its members. By neglecting to do so, the actual power of the gang declines, if only because there are not enough active members to cover all of the activities necessary to fulfill the role of the gang. To avoid this organizational decline, we should expect gang leaders to exploit rewards and penalties in such a manner to make it in every member's best interest to do his fair share.

Indeed, the gangs act as expected. Rewards are allocated for exemplary contributions to the gang, and punishments are meted out for shirking duties. Gangs generate hierarchical structures organized like a corporation. Positions in the gang range from rank and file members to the gang's leader. In between, there are ranks such as Enforcers, who enforce the rules and punish violators; Regents, who assist in narcotics distribution; and Governors, who control drug sales over a large region.[276] Levels and titles vary from gang to gang, but the structure is similar.

Members who perform exceptional levels of activity for the gang are rewarded with a higher position in the organization.[277] As an example of exemplary gang behavior, Gary Knox, a gang researcher, analyzed the shooting committed by a ten-year-old gang member.

> If it was just an initiation ceremony, he'd do it from a car. But to go right up to the victims, that means he was trying to collect some points and get some rank or maybe a nice little cash bonus.[278]

Rewards alone, however, would be insufficient to guarantee the cooperation of all members. To discourage shirking, those who seek to avoid activity are duly punished.[279] A simple cost/benefit analysis shows that a member can gain through active participation and can lose without it; thus, participation becomes the better strategy. Through use of these reward and punishment tactics, the gangs avoid the

---

[275] Levitt and Venkatesh also mention status, and increased success with members of the opposite sex.. (1998, fn. 22)
[276] O'Brien, O' Connor, and Papajohn, 8/1/95, 1, and Levitt and Venkatesh, 1998.
[277] Ibid, 12.
[278] In Gibbs, 8/19/94, 31.
[279] Nieves, 12/25/94, 13.

traditional collective action problem, in which few have an incentive to participate. Instead, gangs provide members an incentive to strive to outperform one another.

Once the goal of attracting new members and ensuring their active participation has been achieved, the remaining job of the gang is to prevent them from leaving the group. Again, we could expect that a similar system of rewards and penalties would apply to this task. Most frequently, gangs use punishment as a deterrent to attempts to exit.

> For example, someone who wants to quit might be shot in the leg before being allowed to leave. Or be thrown out a 6th-floor window. Or receive a "pumpkin-head," a beating so bad the head swells to the size and shape of a jack-o'-lantern.[280]

Some moderation, however, must be placed upon recruitment goals. Every new member, if productive, provides a benefit to the gang but also imposes a cost.[281] Given this constraint, we would, from an economic perspective, expect gangs to seek an optimal balance, in terms of size, that maximizes returns from gang membership subject to the individual costs. Indeed, we have evidence that gangs do operate in this manner. Instead of forcing all drug dealers, for example, to join a given gang, gangs will frequently allow individuals to sell drugs in the territory in return for a certain percentage of the proceeds. Gangs have also been known to hire mercenary fighters (non-gang members who are paid for short periods to fight for the gang in drug wars.)[282] These tactics allow the gang to gain revenue and support without incurring the cost of additional members.

The above analysis offers new insight about gang recruitment, which can change our perspective on gang members. Instead of the traditional view of gun-slinging, blood-thirsty killers, we should recognize that some people are forced to join gangs for survival. Gangs provide individuals the same type of security that alliances provide nations. Like alliances, gangs, for their own survival, must ensure that their members contribute and that they remain in the group. By a careful application of rewards and punishments, the gangs can make any other alternative to membership and involvement in gangs less attractive until they have achieved an optimal size. Lest this analysis be mistaken as portraying all members as hapless victims, however, it should not be ignored that many members actively desire and pursue inclusion in a gang. In addition to the function of protection in numbers, the gangs provide other services. Some of these services, and the accompanying incentives they provide for membership, are discussed below.

---

[280] Terry, 8/18/94, 26.

[281] Some of the costs described by Levitt and Venkatesh (1998, 15) include the provision of weapons and covering the costs of funerals and compensation for the victim's family for deceased gang members.

[282] O'Connor, 1/4/96, 17, and Levitt and Venkatesh, 1998, 13.

5.1.3 Economics

Despite the risks, some people join gangs for power or respect. Still others are lured by the prospects of lucrative gains from drug sales.

> Ask [a gang member] about crack, and he will tell you about the seductive idea of being somebody when you have nothing. "If you weren't selling drugs, you weren't nobody," Jovan said. "If you sell drugs, you had anything you wanted. Any girl, any friend, money, status. If you didn't, you got no girlfriend, no friends, no money. You're a nothing."[283]

Enormous profits can be made from drug sales. As explained in the last chapter, by controlling all drug sales within given boundaries, the gang can avoid competition from rival drug dealers. By the use of force to create an artificial monopoly, gangs are able to reap higher profits.

Given the economic actions of the gangs, the decision to join a gang for economic purposes can be rational. Consider the costs and benefits associated with the options of a drug dealer. If the dealer wishes to work alone, his expected gains include the income that he can reap from selling drugs. His expected costs include the likelihood that members of a gang that controls the territory in which he chooses to work will punish or fine him, and also includes the possibility of arrest. The closer our independent drug dealer is to gang territory, the more likely it is that he will be apprehended by gang members. If the expected costs of independent dealing outweigh the gains, then the dealer can choose among three main strategies. He may discontinue his work, pay a percentage of his proceeds to the gang, or join the gang. Simple economic logic dictates that the dealer will select the option with the largest net gain. In many cases, especially when we add in the recruitment analysis described above, the optimal choice is membership.

As an example, consider an individual who can earn more from dealing drugs than from any legal wage available to him. This individual must choose between the alternatives of paying "street taxes" to the local gang or of joining its ranks. (This choice assumes that the former option is available; otherwise, the dealer must choose between legal employment or membership.) The profits of independent dealing include the costs due to the "taxes" coupled with the drawbacks of nonmembership. Evaluation of gang-endorsed drug dealing must account for the costs due to gang life. If the net gains of independent action are lower than those that can be made as a gang member, then we would expect a person to join.

5.2 Extortion Model

The constraints imposed by gangs on profits and safety are not the only difficulties faced by independent drug dealers. The previous chapter examined how

---

[283] Wilkerson, [B] 12/13,94, B12.

the absence of legal constraints expands the range of mechanisms dealers can use to avoid competition. The illegal status of drugs also expands the scope of possible actions of the customer. Unlike consumers of legal goods, the customer of illegal drugs can refuse payment or rob the dealer, knowing that the drug dealer has no legal recourse. This lack of constraints on both parties makes drug dealing a precarious occupation.

Reality dictates that, for the single dealer, the risks involved in selling drugs can outweigh the gains. Thus, we could either expect the dealer to discontinue sales, or to change the environment by finding some means of protection. At times, the former action will be chosen. But, drug sales are very profitable. So in a quest to obtain and protect these riches, we must expect some mechanisms to be developed, to substitute for the absent legal protection.

This situation can be modeled with a simple prisoner's dilemma (PD) game. In the game, we have two players, the dealer and the customer. The players can choose to either play Honest or to Cheat. In other words, the dealer can provide the drug, or she can withhold it, and the customer can pay for the drug or not. Each player, has an incentive to cheat. This is particularly so if by cheating, his or her individual payoff would be even higher.

The game is as follows:

	Honest	Cheat
Honest	1,1	$-\beta,\alpha$
Cheat	$\alpha,-\beta$	0,0

where $\alpha>1$, $\beta>0$

Fig. 5.1

To explain the entries, if both players play Honest, (the dealer provides the drugs and the customer pays) then they both receive their highest payoff, denoted 1. If the dealer (row player) plays Honest (gives the drugs) and the customer cheats (takes the drugs without paying) then the dealer receives her worst payoff, denoted $-\beta$, and the customer receives his highest, represented as α. The value of α is selected to be greater than one to represent the gains achieved by cheating. β is positive (so $-\beta$ is negative) to capture the costs of being cheated. The situation is the reverse if the dealer takes the money and refuses to give the drugs. If both players cheat (no drugs and no money) then both players receive their second lowest payoff, 0.

The model approximates the situation facing dealers and buyers in terms of a contract (an agreement to pay or provide goods at a later date). Obviously, both players would be better off acting Honestly, but each has an incentive to cheat the other. If a customer makes a payment for future drugs, then, in a one shot deal, the dealer has an incentive to leave with the money. If the customer promises future payment for drugs today (as is more often the case) then that person has an incentive to avoid this future payment. If both players follow their best (dominant) strategies, then no drug transaction will occur.

Yet, drugs are sold despite the conflicting incentives and constraints. Since this is the case, some subtle, hidden mechanism must be in use which overcomes the obstacles. In fact, several mechanisms are available.

As described in the previous chapter, repeated interactions with the same customers can induce cooperation. This makes sense; if a dealer and a customer wish to do business with one another on a continual basis, then it would be in neither player's interest to cheat the other. If one party cheats, then the other can refuse to do business in the future. Indeed, it can be shown game theoretically, that, if the game is repeated, within certain constraints, any path of payoffs is possible. This means that the PD result of Cheat/Cheat can be avoided and cooperation can be possible. There are a large set of strategies, such as TFT, a strategy in which a cheat by one player is punished by a cheat by the other in the next round, that can help maintain cooperation. The emphasis on a need for mutual cooperation in order to continue a pattern of future joint gains is similar to the situation described in the previous chapter, in which dealers and customers develop a reputation over time with one another for providing good quality drugs and for paying for the merchandise.

Unfortunately for the dealers, as the number of dealers and customers grow, it becomes easier for customers to cheat. This action is facilitated by the fact that the cheater can avoid interaction with the dealer that he has robbed and purchase from other dealers. Unless dealers are sufficiently organized so that information regarding a customer's honesty is widely exchanged, chances are that the person can cheat with impunity. Thus, the system of mutual cooperation between the dealer and customer breaks down and the dealers (and customers) once again face the unappealing result of the Prisoner's Dilemma. When informal mechanisms no longer function, formal ones must be developed.

What mechanisms can help maintain a system of fair trade? In legal commerce, sellers and buyers rely on the legal system that has costs, C, penalties, J and compensation, P, to support contracts. In particular, the court system offers a means of contract enforcement. As described in Chapter 3, this enforcement can be modeled as follows.

	Honest	Cheat
Honest	1-C,1-C	$-\beta+P, \alpha-J$
Cheat	$\alpha-J, -\beta+P$	0,0

where $\alpha > 1$, $\beta > 0$

Fig. 5.2

By changing the payoffs through penalty and compensation, the existence of the court converts the previous PD into a game where it is in both players' interest to play Honest, because both do better by doing so, regardless of the other player's actions. So, as described in Chapter 3, an important role of the court is to provide incentives for the players to avoid cheating one another.

However, as stated above, drug dealers cannot take legal action against theft because they have no access to the court system;[284] a fact which is problematic for them. Without the opportunity to use the courts to uphold contracts and agreements, drug dealers must develop other means of enforcing contracts. This is where the protection offered by a gang can be helpful. Just as the gang serves as a replacement for such institutions as the family or church, gangs can provide services that substitute for inaccessible legal institutions.

> That year, the drug spots in the neighborhood were plagued by a string of holdups by a certain crack addict. The word was that the man was wanted by the gangs and should be shot on sight. The day the man was caught, Jovan said, he stood frozen as older gang members cornered the robber and extracted street justice with 17 bullets from a semiautomatic.[285]

When creating a substitute for the legal system, a gang provides protection and contract enforcement, but charges a price. Although this activity may sound benign, it bears a striking resemblance to extortion.[286] As noted above, like the proffered services of an extortionist, the gang's "offer" of protection through membership often is one that cannot be refused. Payment for the protection assumes the form of services to the gang: through obtaining weapons, protecting other gang members, or disposing of members who have made some fatal error. Additionally, similar to an extortionist, a gang is generally unwilling to lose its members.

In return for the payment, the gang provides the promised protection. In filling the role of a substitute institution, the method of contract enforcement is very similar to the court system. This similarity is captures by the following game.

	Honest	Cheat
Honest	1-C,1	$-\beta+P, \alpha-J$
Cheat	$\alpha, -\beta$	0,0

where $\alpha > 1$, $\beta > 0$

Fig. 5.3

In this case, the dealer is protected by a gang, while the buyer is unprotected. Again, the dealer (row player) pays a fee, C, to the gang. If he is Honest (provides

---

[284] The customers also face the unappealing fact that they cannot take a dealer to court if he has cheated them. Unlike the dealers, however, customers have the recourse of getting even by informing the police that the cheater is dealing drugs.

[285] Wilkerson, [A] 12/13/94, B12.

[286] This model is also used in Saari-Sieberg, 1998, to examine the role of extortion in business interactions.

the drugs) and is Cheated, then the gang will punish the customer, J, and compensate the dealer, P. Although the variables, C, P, and J representing the fee, compensation, and penalty, respectively, are the same as in the court model, gangs may choose to charge higher fees and penalties than would the court system.

In this model, the buyer will be penalized if he cheats and the dealer is honest, but if the dealer cheats while the customer is honest, then no punishment is made. Neither party has a dominant strategy in this case - neither party would be better off choosing to be either honest or to cheat, regardless of what the other player does.

To solve this dilemma, we would expect the substitute institution to structure incentives in such a way that it would be in both players' interests to be Honest. The reason a gang has an interest in providing this service is that a large percentage of gangs' profits are derived from drug sales. The desired effect can be achieved if the gangs will also punish a dealer if he or she has cheated a customer. Now the game becomes:

	Honest	Cheat
Honest	$1-C, 1$	$-\beta+P, \alpha-J$
Cheat	$\alpha-Z, -\beta$	$0, 0$

where $\alpha > 1$, $\beta > 0$

Fig. 5.4

This game is identical to the one above except for the inclusion of a penalty, $-Z$, for the cheating dealer. If the penalty is large enough, if $\alpha-Z > 1-C$, then it becomes in both players' interest to play Honest with one another, and cooperation within the underground economy is restored.

Once again, this analysis demonstrates how a careful use of rewards and punishments on the part of the gang can affect behavior. This strategy changes not only the actions of the member, but of the nonmember as well. The constraints of illegal activity provide the gang with an opportunity to increase membership by tactics that some might call extortion - offering protection and contract enforcement to those who are in need, and who, in absence of the gang, would have to function without. Through these tactics, the gangs swell their ranks, and, because the resulting system provides incentives for cooperation, also increase their profits due to drug dealing. Thus, it becomes easier to understand why it is rational for the gangs to be involved in illegal goods and services. The existing constraints for those involved in illegal activity provide fertile opportunity for gangs to enter the scene and to profit.

Drug dealers face other problems due to their illegal status. Because they cannot appeal to the law, they have no legal recourse against thefts by other drug dealers.

> Not only were the police after them, but so were rival dealers and the addicts. Gunpoint robberies by customers and other dealers happen all

the time because everyone knows that the dealers can't call the police. The only way to make up the loss is to do the same to someone else.[287]

In this case, the protection offered by a gang is more crucial. Here both parties may have this protection.

	Honest	Cheat
Honest	$1-C, 1-C$	$-\beta+P, \alpha-J$
Cheat	$\alpha-J, -\beta+P$	$0, 0$

where $\alpha>1$, $\beta>0$

Fig. 5.5

Using similar logic to that applied in the use of the court system, if both parties enjoy the protection of a gang, then both can deter the other from theft or other dishonest action.

But, if gang membership can deter theft and dishonest action among members, then why does this behavior still occur from time to time? The above model assumes identical penalties for the players. If one player correctly or mistakenly believes that his gang is stronger (more able to collect penalties) than his opponent's, that player now has an incentive to cheat. If he is correct, then he can do so with impunity. If he is mistaken, then the violence frequently associated with turf wars and gang struggles will be eminent.

If the above model and argument are correct, then when gangs establish reputations and become aware of each others' strengths, we should expect a decrease in mistakes and, correspondingly, a decrease in violence. This is the case. Drug researchers claim that violence rises as a new drug is introduced into an area, as drug dealers fight for turf. Over time, they state, territories and strengths are established, and violence declines.[288]

At first glance it might appear that once a gang rival strengths have been established, then an equilibrium would emerge in which gangs refrained from competitive or violent behavior. Theoretically, however, this equilibrium cannot be maintained in a situation in which new players can enter the system. As each gang absorbs more members, uncertainties can arise as to the relative strengths of the rival gangs. This lack of information changes the situation from a deterministic game into a game that involves reputation, "types," and Baysian updating. Without addressing specifics here, one can imagine the effects that uncertainty and reputation would have on strategies of the players.[289] Reality reflects these results. If one gang believes that it is strong enough to defeat the other, then it may choose to fight in order to gain the rival's profits. Thus, the use of violence does not decrease over time. Instead, due to uncertainties created by the dynamics of the situation, it becomes clear that this violence might even grow.

---

[287] Wilkerson, [B], 12/13/94, B12.
[288] Myers, 12/13/95, 6.
[289] As an example, see Kreps and Wilson, 1982.

5.3 Job Search and the Market for Crime

The above discussion gives the impression that some people actively choose to become drug dealers. Although the prospects of drug profits are enticing, it is not the case that all dealers originally intended to enter this profession. Consider the constraints placed on an individual in which there are few legal venues for earning money.

> "What got me selling drugs," said a 16-year-old B.D. [Black Disciple] who calls himself Chill, "was the day I filled out 14 job applications and not one of them stores called me back. I said, 'I got to make some money.' My mama was struggling. I let my mama keep her little money. This year, I didn't ask her for no school clothes, books, nothing. This year, I was a man."[290]

In contrast to typical criminal analysis, we can imagine that as the costs of *avoiding* criminal action, such as drug dealing, outweigh the benefits, then the individual will eventually choose to commit crime. In other words, if the legal wages of the individual are insufficient to cover his costs, whereas, in contrast, even taking risks into account, his expected earnings from crime are greater, then the decision to commit a crime becomes a rational decision.

This decision process may be modeled in the following way. Imagine an individual who is selecting a job, and making her choice based upon her costs of living and wages offered. To make the image more vivid, consider a single parent of four, who has not completed high school. Our job seeker must either choose to remain with her current job, which pays a risk-free wage of w (which could be zero, if she is unemployed), or search for another.

The search itself introduces risk, because the alternative wages may be lower than her current wage. If she selects a criminal wage, the prospective profits are high, but she also faces risks such as the potential cost of arrest or physical harm.[291] If we posit that the person is unable to meet her costs of living with the available wage, then, theoretically, we must expect the person to search for a job in the legal and the criminal market until she finds one for which the expected benefits are greater than or equal to her costs of living. If (due to some reason such as lack of skills, training, or education) the legal wages available are insufficient to cover

---

[290] Terry, 8/18/94, 26.
[291] Additional costs to criminal employment can include the pain of stigma, ostracization by the family, among other, personal costs.

costs, then we can expect her to choose a criminal profession.[292] Recalling the above analysis, the easiest venue for criminal activity may come through gang membership. Thus, by examination of the realistic legal opportunities, costs, and constraints, we appreciate the choices individuals must make. We also gain insight into another potential target for recruitment by the gangs.

5.4 Conclusion

The many lurid descriptions in the press suggest that gangs and their members are savage entities that are raging out of control. The analysis offered here, however, indicates that reality is quite the contrary. Far from raging out of control, gangs appear to be tightly controlled, coldly calculating economic and political enterprises. But rather than offering comfort, this fact should make us more nervous.

Given an environment in which gangs exist, they are able, through threats, rewards and penalties, to recruit and maintain membership. Through similar means, gangs are able to ensure that their members actively participate and fulfill their duties. These duties can range from drug sales to executions.

How can we predict where gangs are likely to emerge? The extortion model suggests that gangs have an incentive to develop anyplace where illegal activity takes place. Quite simply, the absence of recourse to a legal system of enforcement places constraints upon illegal entrepreneurs. The extreme profitability of providing a substitute system of enforcement creates an incentive for gangs to emerge. This scenario can explain why organized crime groups, such as gangs and the mafia, tend to be involved in the provision of illegal goods and services. Indeed, this sentiment was expressed by the Gangster Disciple leader Larry Hoover who stated, "Everybody who was doing something wrong in our community had to pay us."[293]

A disturbing aspect of this conclusion is that, as described earlier, gangs are beginning to expand and spread out to reach a greater range of regions. The expansion motivation follows simple economic logic. Once the concentration of drug sales in any region becomes saturated, the prices, and correspondingly the profits, will drop. Consequently, dealers have an incentive to expand to areas with less competition. The chilling result is that drug dealers will infiltrate a wider range of cities and towns and the gangs will follow.

How do we avoid this specter? The previous chapter argues that legalization of drugs will decrease the crime and problems associated with drug dealing. The

---

[292] A rough mathematical representation of this choice is: max $\{w, \frac{1}{1-\delta} \int G(l)dl, \frac{1}{1-\delta} \int F(c)dc\}$, where w is the current wage, δ is the discount factor, G(l) is a distribution of the available legal wages, and F(c) is a distribution of criminal wages.

[293] Papajohn, 8/1/95, 12.

results of this chapter support that argument. Recall that, in absence of available legal services, a critical source of a gang's power and support is derived from the need of illegal entrepreneurs for protection and enforcement. If drugs were to become legal, then dealers would have recourse to the legal system. In turn they would have no need to accept the services of gangs.

So, legalizing drugs removes part of gangs' abilities to recruit members and to earn profits. This decrease in profits could have extended effects. With fewer resources, gangs would have fewer rewards to offer. In this manner, we would further eliminate some of the economic incentives for membership and for active participation. A decrease in profits would also decrease the funds available for purchase of weapons. Thus, the awesome power of the gangs could be somewhat curtailed. Drug legalization would not destroy gangs, but it could effectively decrease their sphere of activity and, consequently, their power.

Other means are also available to decrease the influence of gangs. The above analysis indicates that the easy targets of gangs are those who, due to reasons such as lack of skills or education, cannot support themselves through legal activity. Social programs that provide opportunities for training and employment could be effective to dissuade these people from entering the market for crime. Additionally, recalling the alliance analogy, police enforcement and protection in gang-populated areas could provide an alternative to reliance on the protection of a gang.

When portrayed as an organization, gangs can lose their aspect of lack of control and unpredictability. However, this clearer picture is no more comforting than the wilder image. The benefit to analysis of this type is that if the framework and tools used by gangs can be identified, then steps can be made to decrease their control.

Chapter 6

Gun Control

6.1 Introduction

As gun control is a controversial, emotional topic, it has become increasingly difficult to resolve. Should guns be limited or made illegal, or should the population be allowed to bear arms, as some argue is permitted by the US Constitution?[294] The pros and cons for this debate are numerous. A sample of arguments from each side will be provided here. Then, they are analyzed in a game theoretic format to show how this analytic approach helps facilitate an understanding of the subject.

The issue of handguns and gun control is one of the more controversial and emotional topics facing the American public. Because of the dangers and violence associated with criminal use of firearms, particularly in urban settings, opposing sides frequently find it difficult to compromise. Without question, some people feel threatened by the presence of handguns, while others feel vulnerable without their protection.

Gun control advocates stress that firearms facilitate murder and that more guns lead to more deaths.

> Will allowing handguns make it likely that otherwise law abiding citizens will harm each other? Or will the threat of citizens carrying weapons primarily deter criminals? To some, the logic is fairly straightforward. Philip Cook argues that, "[i]f you introduce a gun into a violent encounter, it increases the chance that someone will die."[295] A large number of murders may arise from unintentional fits of rage that are quickly regretted, and simply keeping guns out of people's reach would prevent deaths.[296]

Gun control supporters believe that if firearms are controlled and eliminated, then we will experience a decrease in violence. The sense of their argument is obvious. If guns were completely unavailable, people would not be able to shoot others (although they could, and often would, be able to kill others in different ways).

---

[294] The actual wording in the second amendment of the Constitution refers to the rights to form a militia and to bear arms within these groups. "A well regulated Militia being necessary to the security of a free State, the right of the people to keep and bear Arms, shall not be infringed." "The Supreme Court has stated that today's militia is the National Guard." U.S. Department of Justice, Federal Bureau of Investigation Home Page, "Three Myths Used Against Gun Control," January 5, 1997

[295] In Lott, and Mustard, 1/23/96, A8.

[296] Lott, and Mustard, 1997, 1.

Opponents, on the other hand, argue that gun control policies hurt only the potential victims of crime. If legal means of obtaining a weapon are eliminated, they claim, criminals will seek illegal sources. Thus, the criminals will be armed, but those who desire handguns as a form of protection against criminals will be denied access to this protection.

Which side is correct? This chapter examines the issues through a game theoretic perspective in order to determine which argument is best supported theoretically.

The disturbing fact is that every year a large number of Americans are killed by handguns. In 1994, of the 23,305 homicides in the Unites States, 15,456 involved firearms and 13,483 of these involved handguns.[297] In 1993, 39,595 people died due to firearms.[298] This figure includes not only criminal activity, gang, and drug related shootings, but also children playing with found pistols; angry, drunk family members; and other accidental or unintentional deaths from the use of firearms. According to a *Chicago Tribune* article, the number of firearm related deaths of children in the US was 1.66 per 100,000 children between the period of 1990 and 1995. That figure is 12 times the average of other countries studied.[299] Although the number of unintentional injuries in children have decreased since 1950[300], the possibility of accidental gun related deaths or injuries in children understandably increases concerns over ownership of firearms.

The fundamental question regarding gun control is over whether the possession of a firearm serves as either a form of protection or as a menace. Will people be safer if they own the means to protect themselves against an armed criminal population? Or, will the ownership of guns facilitate the acquisition of guns by criminals and also lead to more accidental deaths? As both sides tend to view the issue as a question of personal safety, the rise of emotion in tackling the issue is understandable.

6.2 Gun Control

The purpose behind gun control is to reduce crime by reducing the availability of firearms. Because handguns are responsible for both purposeful and accidental deaths and injuries, the belief is that accompanying a decrease in the number of guns will be a reduction in both types of problems. Support for gun control measures range from those who wish to totally eliminate the use and distribution of firearms to those who wish to strictly control this distribution.[301]

Recent gun control policies include the Brady Law, which imposes a five day waiting period on handgun purchases, so that the applicant's criminal records may be checked. While even some supporters viewed its passage as more of a token

---

[297] U.S. Department of Justice, [B], 1/5/97.
[298] U.S. Department of Justice, [D], 1/5/97.
[299] Reuters, 2/7/97, 12.
[300] Ibid.
[301] Don Kates refers to those who are completely opposed to the possession of firearms as "anti-gun." See Kates, 1991.

advance of a first step, this law can claim some success. Background checks of applicants have blocked attempted gun purchases of more than 40,000 criminals.[302]

Other gun control measures include an attempt to ban the use and distribution of specific types of firearms. These categories include assault weapons, plastic guns (which are used to avoid detection with usual scanning procedures such as those used in airports), "Saturday Night Special" handguns and "cop-killer" bullets[303]. Because roughly half of U.S. households have a gun of some type, these laws, which target the kinds of weapons owned by a smaller subset of voters, are less likely to be confronted with resistance. The argument used against these types of weapons is generally that these weapons are more often used for criminal purposes than for lawful reasons, and that these criminal uses outweigh any positive effects these weapons could have.[304]

Firearms are unquestionably dangerous instruments. Given these dangers, it is not immediately apparent why any law-abiding person would wish to own or carry one. Opponents of gun control argue that law-abiding citizens need guns as a protection against potential gun wielding criminals. But many anti-gun advocates disagree with the belief that the possession of firearms will deter crime.

> "We will not be a safer nation, a safer state, if people are carrying guns around shopping malls and restaurants" [U.S. Senator] Durbin said.[305]

> Many argue that the debate [over the deterrent effect of handgun ownership] is frighteningly beside the point. "The issue is not whether people are carrying concealed or unconcealed," said Richard M. Aborn, president of Handgun Control Inc. "It's that they're carrying them at all. More guns mean more death."[306]

The argument, then, rests on the concern that access to a handgun will result in more intentional and accidental deaths, causing more harm than good.

This theme has ample justification with newspaper articles which detail tragic stories of accidental death. The stories include people who mistakenly shoot their own children, or family members, thinking they were burglars. One story tells of a man, who was reluctant to own a gun in the first place, who accidentally shot his stepdaughter who was playing hooky from school. The man was alerted by the authorities that his burglar alarm had gone off. Searching the house, he eventually reached his daughter's closet.

> "He was very frightened, very nervous, as generally most people would be," [detective] Smith said. "When he opened the door, he saw a person,

---

[302] U.S Dept. of Justice, [G].
[303] Kleck, 1991, 3.
[304] Ibid.
[305] Secter, and McRoberts, 10/1/96.
[306] Verhovek, 8/3/95, 1.

he saw movement, instinctively brought the gun up and pulled the trigger."

"He still had an open line with his wife on the cellular phone. He said something to the effect of: 'Oh my God, I've shot Sheree'"[307]

Even a slight likelihood of killing a member of one's own family understandably deters many from ever wishing to own a handgun. The possibility of accidentally being killed by someone else serves as a strong motivating force to seek to deter others from owning firearms as well.

Several individuals believe that being armed will not solve the problems.

Mrs. Phillips-Taylor's 17-year-old son Scott, was shot six times, first in the back, then execution style in the head, with an AK-47, fired by an 18-year-old classmate, an Eagle Scout who was "obsessed with guns," she said....

"It's made me physically sick," Mrs. Phillips-Taylor said, clutching her abdomen and starting to sob. "What was I supposed to do, arm my poor child? That's ridiculous.

"They're saying they want to arm themselves to protect themselves," she added. "So do you arm the 17-year-olds to protect themselves? Do you arm the 15-year-olds to protect themselves? When the hell is it going to stop?"[308]

Her point is strong. Few would argue that children are sufficiently responsible and mature to arm themselves and to make decisions with firearms. The logic that frequently drives the adults' claim for the right to bear arms is that criminals will be armed. As the argument continues, if honest people are denied the right to weapons, then they will be unprotected. But if we apply this reasoning unquestioningly, we encounter a serious problem. Children face the same hostile interaction problems with their peers: We do not wish to arm our children. Therefore, some form of gun control must be taken seriously in order to protect these children from their armed cohorts.

Several gun control supporters believe that, in states that allow concealed handguns, the laws which are intended to protect the public from criminal acquisition of firearms do not go far enough. Evidence of this problem is seen periodically. For example, in February, 1997, due to flaws in the enforcement system, a foreigner was able to illegally purchase a handgun in Florida. The man subsequently used the gun to shoot into a crowd of tourists on the Empire State Building in New York and then to kill himself.[309] What was the flaw in his purchase? Only that he had been in the country less than the federally required 90 days limit before a handgun may be purchased. The ease with which he obtained

---

[307] Associated Press, 12/13/95.
[308] Seelye, 4/1/95, 26.
[309] Krauss, 2/25/97, A14.

the weapon caused many, including New York City Mayor Rudolph Guiliani, to criticize "the laxness of Florida's gun control laws."[310]

Advocates of gun control argue that, because they are instruments of violence, access to guns should be severely restricted. One coherent argument for this position involves envisioning the population as a sort of bell curve in terms of the desire to possess a firearm. The curve represents the number of guns in certain segments of society. At the extreme right of the graph are those who will always want a gun. These people include legitimate gun owners such as Vermont hunters and target shooters, as well as criminals. These people probably possess several guns, and will not decrease their possessions, even if possession is illegal. This number is small and relatively limited.

Fig. 6.1

At the extreme left of the graph, we find others who will never purchase firearms; again, this also is regardless of the laws. These two groups of people serve as the extremes. The majority of the population, which lies in the middle, are those who would be most affected by gun laws. Arguably, some of these people will be deterred from owning a gun if they are illegal. If we were to legalize guns, however, then these people would have easier access to them. The availability and legality might provide an incentive for such people to purchase guns (or less deterrence from purchasing them). Continuing the cycle, with greater access to firearms, a greater number of people could use the gun in a criminal act, or could accidentally shoot or kill another person. These very real possibilities prompt gun control advocates to argue that the deterrent effect of gun control on the marginal people, at least, is enough reason to support the policy.

6.3 The Right to Bear Arms

6.3.1 The Criminals Have Guns

Firearm supporters, on the other hand, claim that the right to bear arms should be protected. These supporters use a remarkably similar analysis to that detailed above. Their version of the argument claims that if guns are made illegal, then practically the only people who will own guns will be criminals. "By definition, laws are most likely to be obeyed by the law-abiding, and gun laws are

---

[310] Krauss, 2/25/97, A14.

no different."³¹¹ Their potential victims, therefore, will be unarmed and less able to defend themselves.

While this argument is controversial, it does have some research support. In countering the fact that the Brady bill has deterred 40,000 individuals (criminals or those considered unacceptable for possession of firearms) from purchase, statisticians argue that gun laws have done little to restrain criminals from obtaining firearms. According to Polsby and Brennen:

> In surveys of prisoners, a majority report that they had owned a handgun prior to their imprisonment. But only 7 percent of criminals' handguns are obtained from legitimate retail sources. Three-fourths of felons surveyed report they would have no trouble obtaining a gun when they were released, despite legal prohibitions against firearms ownership by convicted felons.³¹²

This kind of evidence suggests that, beyond the inept or uninformed criminals who stumbled into the Brady law, the people who will be deterred by handgun laws are mainly law-abiding citizens who seek to obtain handguns as a form of recreation or self defense. Firearms supporters believe, then, that instead of denying access to criminals, gun control is punishing or restricting the law abiding potential weapons owners. The problem is aggravated, they feel, because these law-abiding people are less likely to use their weapons in criminal acts. The law abiding are also more likely to use their weapons carefully and responsibly.

> It does seem to have been demonstrated, though, that people who apply for a permit to carry a handgun do not necessarily become gun-slinging vigilantes when the permit is issued. They appear to exercise as much responsibility with guns as with any other potentially dangerous piece of equipment.³¹³

6.3.2 Guns for Self Defense

There is evidence that handguns have been useful as a form of self-defense. Although the statistic is not as well known as that for accidental deaths, criminologists Gary Kleck and Marc Gertz claim that each year guns are used by adults approximately 2.5 million times for protection. For every life that is lost due to a gun, they claim that at least 65 are saved because of possession of a handgun.³¹⁴

---

[311] Kleck, 1991, 6.
[312] Polsby, and Brennen, 1995, 3.
[313] *The Economist*, 4/15/95, 27.
[314] Cited in Polsby, and Brennen, 1995, 3.

> While Sharon-Jon Ramboz was a teen ager, she was home one day when a man broke into the home, beat her and left her for dead...Years later, in 1989,...another man broke into her home...This time she was ready.
> "I calmly walked to our closet where the firearm was stored," she testified... "I took my Colt AR-15 semiautomatic rifle" and "inserted the magazine while I was in the closet.
> "I walked to the top of the stairs. Then I pulled back the bolt and, letting it go, chambered a round."
> That act, which loaded a bullet for firing, produced a sound loud and distinctive enough that the intruder uttered an expletive and fled.[315]

Kleck and Gertz claim that each year potential victims kill 2,000 - 3,000 criminals and wound between 9,000 and 17,000.[316] Kleck further states that there are approximately 600,000 - 1 million defensive uses of guns each year. This figure, he states, is comparable to the number of crimes committed with guns.[317]

Is there a need for this degree of defense? Several people believe that there is. According to Polsby and Brennen, approximately 83 percent of the American population will be the victims of a violent crime at some point in their lives. They state that in any year, serious crime affects 25 percent of all households. According to them, this crime goes largely without protection. Part of the reason is that there is, on average, only one police officer on patrol for every 3,300 people.[318]

> [Texas State Senator Jerry Patterson]...sums up the case for his [right to bear arms] bill as follows. "All the criminals have guns, and the United States] Supreme Court has ruled that the government is under no obligation to provide police protection services to any individual citizen. No longer are we able to find solace in the fact that the government can take care of us as individuals..."[319]

The negative effect of limited police protection is made more severe by recent court cases which insist that it is *not* the duty of the police to protect individual citizens.

> ...[T]he fact is that the police do not function as bodyguards for individuals. Rather the police function is to deter crime in general by patrol activities and by apprehension after the crime has occurred. If circumstances permit, the police should and will protect a citizen in

---

[315] Seelye, 4/1/95, 1.
[316] In Polsby and Brennen, 1995, 3.
[317] Kleck, 1991, 5. This finding is supported by Kates, 1991, who argued that the number of times per year that handguns are used in self defense slightly exceeds the estimated number of crimes attempted by or committed by handgun armed felons each year. p. 12.
[318] Polsby and Brennen, 1995, 3&4.
[319] *The Economist*, 4/15/95, 27.

distress. But they are not legally duty bound to do that, nor to provide any direct protection -- no matter how urgent a distress call they may receive.[320]

The limits placed upon the legal duty of the police for protection of the people raises questions about the extent of protection they can actually provide. For instance, arguments have been offered in favor of abolishing guns which assert that self-defense with a weapon is unnecessary because the police will provide protection. Notice that the crucial assumption is "the police will provide protection." However, it is clear that the police are neither obliged nor always able to ensure the safety of individuals. By adding the fact that even the largest police force in the United States (the New York City police) has insufficient numbers to address all of the calls of women seeking help from threats made by ex-boyfriends/husbands and to also respond to other crimes committed in the city,[321] it becomes apparent that some form of individual self-protection, whether with firearms or otherwise, can be useful and necessary.

At this point, it is important to note that firearms are not the *only* form of self-defense available.[322] The issue addressed here, however, is not to examine these alternatives. Instead, it is whether or not the possession of a gun will be a net asset, in terms of self-defense, or if it will pose a threat. The threat to the household includes the risk of accidents or an escalation in violence on the part of the criminal, as a reaction to the victim's possession of a gun. Put more succinctly, do guns add to the safety of their owners, or do they threaten that safety?

Kleck claims that owning a gun adds to the safety of people. As he argues, people who use guns for self-defense are less likely to be injured or to have a crime completed against them. He compares these individuals both to those who use other forms of resistance *and* to people who do nothing to resist.[323] He uses this evidence to state that, contrary to popular opinion, nonresistance is *not* safer than self-defense with a gun.

Kates although more cautious than Kleck, also argues that advocates of non-resistance and of submission err in their claims that non-resistance is a safer option.

---

[320] Kates, 1991, 5. The limits of legal obligations of the police can be seen in: California Government Code 821, 845, 846, and 85, Illinois Rev. Stat. 4-102 construed in Stone v State. (Kates, fn 20.) Also in "Calogrides v City of Mobile, 475 So. 2d 560 (S. Ct. Ala. 1985) -- quoting with approval from Weutrich v Delia, 155 N.J Super 324, 326, 382 A.2d 929, 930 (1978) 'a public entity such as a municipality is not liable in tort for its failure to protect against the criminal propensity of third persons.'" among others. (Kates, fn. 16)

[321] Kates, 1991, 6.

[322] There has been, however, an unfortunate lack of research and development on alternative forms of protection and self defense. Kates attributes this lack primarily to the political resistance on the part of those "numerous and influential segment of anti-gun advocates who disapprove of every form of private self protection." He claims that the resulting political situation deters those from undertaking the costs of developing alternative forms of protection because of the fear that they will be banned. 1991, fn 6.

[323] Kleck, 1991, 5.

While he stresses that the use of a firearm in resistance may not be the best alternative in many circumstances, he also disagrees with those who posit that a victim will be safer if they "give in" to their attacker.

> Based on national crime victim survey data, a number of scholars who happen to be anti-gun recommend that victims eschew forcible resistance of any kind; if an attacker cannot be 'talked out' of his crime, the victim should submit in order to avoid injury... [This position's] scholarly critics have not been pro-gun nor have they urged gun-armed resistance specifically. Their criticisms involve issues of policy (that to advise victims to submit may encourage crime) and of methodological error (...it is not clear [from the data] how often victims are injured after they resisted; they may have been harmed prior to any resistance...) The latest, and probably the definitive, analysis concludes that the "data, when interpreted carefully, do not support any strong [general] assertions concerning the victim's safest course of action when confronted by a robber."[324]

Data[325] helps to explain this position. In a national victim survey, 22% of unresisting victims suffered injury despite the fact that they offered no resistance. In contrast, only 7.5% of victims who resisted with a gun suffered injury from their attacker.[326] This evidence contradicts assertions that resistance with a gun will lead to increased violence from the attacker. Kates cautions, however, that another possible cost of gun-armed resistance would be if the robber initially harmed the victim, who then pulled out a gun, in which case the robber would respond by inflicting even more severe injury than if there had been no resistance.[327]

A lesson that may be drawn from the evidence is that the positions taken by both extremes have some validity, but also some errors. The use of a weapon in resisting a crime is neither always detrimental nor always foolproof. While a firearm *may* be a deterrent, there is nothing that ensures that it *always* will be a deterrent. Instead, it could be that the presence of a firearm in a conflict is detrimental. "In short, a gun simply offers victims an option -- a dangerous option to be used only with discretion and/or because throwing oneself on the mercy of a violent attacker may be more dangerous yet."[328]

A frequent fear regarding public possession of firearms is that criminals will be likely to seize the weapons from their owners, and that the weapon, instead of protecting the owner will become a tool used against the victim. Addressing that fear, data indicates that criminals have been able to seize guns from their potential victims less than 1 percent of the time.[329] Polsby and Brennen state that these

---

[324] Kates, 1991, 13-14. and Cook, 1986, 405&407.
[325] Kleck, 1986.
[326] Kates, 1991, fn. 87.
[327] Ibid.
[328] Kates, 1991, 16.
[329] Polsby and Brennen, 1995, 3.

figures understate the effect of handgun ownership on crime because the numbers do not take into account the deterrent effect of handgun ownership on criminal behavior.[330] This issue will be taken up in more detail further in the chapter.

6.3.3 Firearm Accidents

A firearm is a dangerous weapon, and a logical fear is that accompanying an increased presence of these weapons in the homes of citizens will be an increased number of accidents in which innocent people are killed or injured due to mishandling of the weapon. Kleck and Gertz offer data that indicates that, contrary to the fears of gun control advocates, accidents caused by the use or ownership of handguns are relatively infrequent, occurring on average of only about 30 times a year.[331]

Polsby and Brennen cite additional evidence regarding accidents with firearms that, although larger than the number of accidents reported by Kleck and Gertz, still appears to be encouraging. They claim that between the years 1970 and 1991, the number of Americans that died from firearm accidents *decreased* from 2,406 to 1,441. This decrease took place despite a large increase in gun ownership. To give some indication of the infrequency of accidental gun deaths, the authors compare the annual rate of gun accidents in the U.S. in 1991 (0.6 per 100,000) with that of accidental drownings (1.6 per 100,000 in 1991.)[332]

It has been suggested that the number of firearms accidents has been artificially inflated. In part, this is because many gun suicides are routinely misclassified as accidents, possibly in an attempt to spare the feelings of the family.[333] If this is the case, then the actual number of accidents is even smaller than given by the official figures. If these figures or statements are correct, we are left with the sense that the natural emotion and hype attached to news reports of a firearm accident seriously inflate our estimation of the true danger.

6.3.4 Information

Banning guns can have other, unintentional negative effects. Alderman William Beavers of Chicago, Illinois notes that the 14-year ban on handgun registration in Chicago has done little to stop the flow of guns into the city. To make matters worse, the ban has made it harder for officials to track the number of guns owned by Chicagoans. As a consequence, officials believe that there are thousands of guns of which the police are unaware.[334]

---

[330] Ibid.

[331] Ibid.

[332] Ibid, 4.

[333] Kates, 1991, fn. 51. "for instance, an experienced medical examiner comments that he has never seen or heard of a death occurring 'by accident' in cleaning a gun that did not turn out, on examination, to be either a suicide or a murder." See also Rushford, Hirsch, Ford, and Adelson, 1975.

[334] Heard, 2/7/97, 1.

"We know now that criminals aren't going to register their guns," Beavers said. "But right now we have no idea how many guns are out there because even law abiding citizens aren't registering them anymore."[335]

Essentially, the government is trading information for hopes of some degree of control. Unfortunately, due to the availability of guns of the black market, the government forgoes this control as well.

6.3.5 Black Market

Firearm supporters argue that by restricting gun ownership, the government creates a black market. Much like the failed experiment of the Prohibition, supporters worry whether serious restrictions on gun ownership might not increase the problem. Because some people will be willing to pay large amounts in order to obtain the illegal items, it becomes profitable for others to supply them.[336] Thus, they argue, in our attempt to control and decrease crime, gun control laws can actually create the opportunities for more crime.

Support for this argument comes from basic economics. The economist, Mancur Olson claims that a black market economy is an inherent feature of a system that sets prices differently than the market system.[337] As described in Chapter 4, by setting prices lower than market clearing prices, the government creates shortages, and thus creates situations in which there is a "mutual advantage" to breaking the law: both sellers and buyers can gain from black market trade[338].

An example of this problem can be seen in apartment seeking in Manhattan, New York. Several apartments in the city are included in subsidized housing plans, and have extremely low rents relative to the other apartments. Because many rental agencies are reluctant to rent apartments at the low prices specified, fewer apartments are provided, often leading to a housing shortage. In this case, people are often willing to pay more than the specified price "under the table," or illegally, in order to obtain an apartment. In this manner, even actions that may have been designed to help Manhattan residents can result in shortage and an increase in illegal activity. In other words, illegal action is introduced into a situation in which it should not naturally occur. Most individuals seeking an apartment do not expect nor wish to engage in criminal activity, however, the constraints of the system - creating the lack of housing - may lead them to do just that. Thus, the system may encourage otherwise law-abiding individuals to break the law.

This analysis extends to our concern about gun control. Using gun control, the government effectively sets a quantity that is lower than the market-clearing amount. This action can be expected to result in shortages, causing many to be

---

[335] Ibid.
[336] See Olson, 1995.
[337] Olson, 1995.
[338] Olson, 1995.

willing to pay more in order to obtain the desired goods. Many critics have pointed out that gun laws are able to restrict only *legal* access to guns.[339] Accordingly, black marketeers, recognizing this fact, can gain by providing guns illegally, and citizens can gain by purchasing them. Some illegal sources include sale by legal owners, theft from legal owners, smuggling from foreign manufactures, and manufacture by illegal gunsmiths in the U.S.[340] The situation becomes one in which going outside of the rules creates "mutually advantageous trade". Neither the criminal nor the buyer has an incentive to assist the government. Thus, it is more difficult for the government to stop gun distribution.

This behavior can be explained by using standard supply and demand graphs found in the financial pages of a newspaper. The crossing of the lines in the graph indicates the equilibrium quantity, Q_o, and the corresponding price, P_o. These are the prices and quantities that will result if the market is allowed to function without restriction.

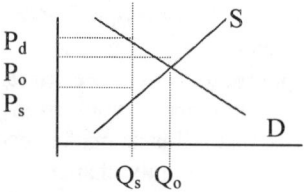

Fig. 6.2

In the graph we see that at the market-clearing price, where supply equals demand, the price is P_o and the quantity is Q_o.

But now suppose the supply is restricted to Q_s. Here, the same graph shows that the price that people are willing to pay will be higher. Similarly to what we noted from the apartment example in Manhattan, as supply becomes restricted, people will pay more for the desired good. In the graph, we see that customers are willing to pay P_d for guns, whereas suppliers are willing to sell them at a lower price, P_s. The demand for the product, and willingness to pay will create an incentive for some to supply more guns on the black market, at a high price.

6.3.5.1 Buyers

Just as an increased price for a particular type of car restricts the demand for the product, economics suggests that an increased price of (and difficulty in obtaining) guns will drive people out of the firearms market. Who remains interested in purchasing a weapon? If we assume that a gun is a necessary "tool of the trade" for a criminal, the answer is apparent.

Indeed, critics such as Polsby and Brennen claim that the extent of a shortage has fewer effects upon criminal purchase of handguns than one might expect. They

---

[339] Polsby and Brennen, 1995, 17.
[340] Polsby and Brennen, 1995, 17.

state that a difference between law-abiding and criminal demands for guns is that most law-abiding citizens have a relatively elastic demand for handguns; stated in other words, they are sensitive to price changes. If there is a large rise in the price of guns, then many law-abiding people will choose not to buy a gun. They state that criminals, on the other hand, have relatively inelastic demands for handguns. This assertion means that they will be more willing to pay higher prices for handguns.[341]

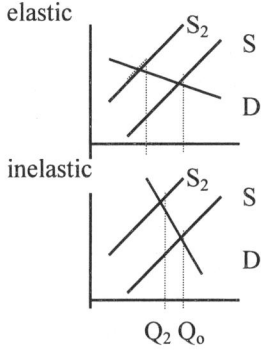

Fig. 6.3

To better explain this point, assume that the demand for a product - guns in this case - is elastic. If the supply of guns decreases (shifts to the left) the price for handguns will rise slightly and the quantity demanded will fall significantly. If demand is inelastic then the price will rise much higher for a given decrease in demand, and the quantity demanded will fall only slightly.[342]

If criminals have an inelastic demand for firearms, then they will obtain more of these weapons than law-abiding people. This can result in a precarious situation in which the 'balance of power,' seen here as access to firearms, rests in favor of the criminals.[343] This concern has support in the literature. Polsby and Brennen compare the issue to international relations.

> Thus, it appears that gun control laws will have the effect not of *disarming* criminals, but rather *increasing the ratio of firearms-holding criminals to non-criminals*. Unilateral disarmament does not have a good reputation in international affairs, because such a tactic on occasion has invited aggression by the better-armed party. What reason

---

[341] Polsby and Brennen, 1995, 16.

[342] Ibid, 17.

[343] This assertion is not made lightly. Evidence suggests that firearms can be very effective both in aiding a criminal to successfully carry out his crime and also in aiding a victim to deter the criminal. In both cases, the weapon does not actually have to be used to be effective. If one party is armed and the other is not, the mere display of the gun may at times be sufficient to awe the other. See Kates, 1991, 12 and fn. 71.

do we have to suppose that domestic unilateral disarmament would be more successful?[344]

If we agree with the above argument, then gun laws are not entirely successful in reducing criminal possession of firearms. They are mainly successful in reducing the number of law-abiding citizens who have access to these weapons. This fact can produce a disturbing ratio of armed criminals to similarly armed law-abiding citizenry. Additionally, because gun control creates the incentives for the formation of a black market, the laws could be contributing to more crime in a way similar to effects of the infamous alcohol Prohibition in the U.S. By creating a situation in which it is mutually advantageous for groups to break the law, the government may be reducing an important aspect in crime prevention and enforcement, the self-interest of individuals in avoiding crime and in aiding enforcement.

6.4 Deterrence

An argument frequently voiced to support legalization of the possession of concealed handguns is that these guns can deter criminals. Adherents to this idea range from those who believe that guns will always deter criminals to those who believe that guns may deter criminals only under certain circumstances.

6.4.1 Rural Versus Urban Characteristics

Support for the theory of deterrence is frequently based upon evidence that in many areas that have a high percentage of gun ownership, there is a lower level of crime. Although the presence of guns may, in fact, be a deterrent force, one must be careful about inferring this deterrence property from the data. A sense of this argument is captured by the following statement.

> [B]y the same token, there could probably be established an equally strong negative correlation between more cows...less crime. Before breaking into a paean of praise to Bessie the Great Protector, it might be wise to ask whether this correlation represents anything beyond a spurious artifact of rurality: cows tend to be found in rural areas and crime doesn't. Of course the low per capita crime rates in rural America may be attributable to its high rates of gun ownership. But for the rational and dispassionate observer more proof of that is required than the bald correlation between 'more guns... less crime.'[345]

The question of why crime is lower in rural countries poses an intriguing question. Attributing the property simply to an increased percentage of guns may

---

[344] Polsby and Brennen, 1995, 16-17.
[345] Kates, 1991, 9.

be misleading. It is possible that a very different phenomenon occurs in rural areas, as compared to urban areas. If this is the case, then by aggregating or comparing the two types of areas statistically, in any attempts to measure the effect of gun ownership on crime, we would make significant methodological mistakes.

What kinds of factors could influence the different crime levels between rural and urban areas? We may start by focusing on the differences between the two types of communities. Rural areas tend to have lower populations. Within these populations, the level of anonymity tends to be significantly lower in rural communities than in urban ones. As the models in earlier chapters suggest, the lack of anonymity should increase the likelihood of cooperation. These factors alone could have serious repercussions on the level of crime in the different areas.

By examining a person's willingness to commit a crime, violent or otherwise, we see different constraints in the different areas. In a rural community, if a person commits a crime (and is caught, either by the legal system or by being recognized by a community member), it is more likely to be the case that that information will be spread to a large percentage of the community. If this is the case, that person, and often his or her relatives, will be ostracized or otherwise punished at the hands of the community.

In an urban setting, a criminal, convicted or otherwise, has the benefits of anonymity. This person has a higher possibility of avoiding recognition, and thus of avoiding punishment. Furthermore, even if the person does receive punishment for the crime, he or she is less likely to suffer the additional punishment from the community.[346]

Taking this issue into account, we cannot avoid the possibility that social control can serve as an effective deterrent against crime, and that differences in the level of social control can have an important impact upon differences in the crime rate.

The following model helps to illustrate the point. Imagine that people gain from interactions with one another, but that they might further gain by stealing from one another. (Or by committing other types of crime.)

	Crime	Honest
Crime	2,2	4,1
Honest	1,4	3,3

Fig. 6.4

---

[346] Community punishment, whether ostracization or in other forms, should not be underestimated. The effect of this treatment has been used to argue against the imposition of "Megan's Law", a law which necessitates that a community be informed if a convicted sex offender will move into the area upon release from prison. The arguments against the law have centered around the issue that this requirement forces the offender to be "punished twice" for the same time. Thus, community action constitutes a formidable form of punishment.

Now we can use a kind of repeated prisoner's dilemma model. To explain the entries in this model, each square in the grid denotes the payoffs, ranked ordinally with 4 the highest and 1 the lowest, that people receive from a combination of their own strategies and those of others. The rankings are ordinal for convenience in comparing one outcome versus another without stating specifically how much more an individual values the various outcomes with respect to each other. For instance, if two players commit a crime against one another, they receive their second lowest payoff, 2. If the row player commits a crime against his neighbor (column player), while his neighbor does not, then the row player receives his highest payoff, 4, because he committed a crime with impunity, while the column player receives his lowest payoff, 1. The situation is reversed if the row player commits no crime, while the column player does commit a crime. If both players are honest, they receive their highest joint payoff, 3.

This game is accurately labeled a dilemma because if it is played only once, then both players have an incentive to commit crimes against one another. To understand this incentive, note that, regardless of the opponent's strategy, a player always does better by committing the crime than by being honest. Thus, although the players would mutually be better off by being honest, they will both commit crimes against one another.

The model is appropriate for our discussion, because it is easy to envision a circumstance in which a person may have an incentive to cheat (commit a crime against) another, but would be less likely to do so if he knows that he will repeatedly encounter that person in the future. This improved behavior arises because the cheated person will be unlikely to trust him, or may even punish him in the future.[347] In a community, a person may not have to interact with the same person forever, so it may appear possible that the person will risk cheating (or stealing from...) one or a few members of the society. However, if the society is sufficiently small and cohesive, to the extent that information about its members is shared, then the person will not risk criminal activity for fear of punishment.[348] If, on the other hand, the community is not small or is not cohesive, so that information is not available, then the person is more able to risk criminal action because the chance of encountering someone who will legitimately punish him for his action is low.

---

[347] It can be shown that if a player cheats another in a repeated PD game, then the other can respond with a strategy of Tit For Tat, TFT, or cheating in response to her opponent's having cheated, or by cheating 2 times, 2TFT, in response, to punish, or by using the Grim Trigger strategy and always cheating against the original cheater. These strategies can be shown to deter a player from cheating. See Myerson, 1991 for examples of strategies.

[348] Milgrom, North, and Weingast (1990) show that if information is perfect, i.e. if all members of a community share all of the information about the other members, then the using the strategy of ATFT (adjusted TFT) can produce cooperation. In Saari-Sieberg 1998, I show that even imperfect information, up to a certain limit, can help maintain cooperation in a community.

If community activity is, in fact, a deterrent to crime, then it calls into question the extent to which the presence of firearms in rural areas actually serve as a deterrent. Firearm possession in these areas is frequently used for hunting and also for protection of livestock against other animals. Although rural gun ownership is roughly three times larger than in urban areas, "there is evidence that in rural areas guns are less likely to be used in the commission of a crime."[349] It is possibly the case that the presence of the weapons bears little or no relation on the level of crime in these areas.

This is not to say that firearms possession does not serve as a deterrent. To infer that result for all areas, based upon potential results for rural areas would be a mistake. In areas that do not enjoy social control, the presence of armed citizens may, or may not, be a formidable deterrent. The argument here is that because different factors can have very distinct influences in various areas, we should avoid aggregating data from these areas. (similarly, we should avoid imposing the same policy in all areas.) If we do so, the results are likely to be incorrect, and could lead us to either overestimate or underestimate the true effect of weapons on crime. The results could also cause us to ignore or overlook effective alternatives in crime prevention.

6.4.2 Deterrence - the Fear of Armed Victims

Firearms are dangerous instruments and can be intimidating, both in the hands of criminals and victims. Much of the deterrence argument states that if criminals believe there is a possibility that their potential target may be armed, they may choose to avoid that person. The argument further states that if the criminal believes that many people may be armed, then she may choose to abandon crime altogether, or at least decide to choose non-confrontational criminal activity. In support of this notion, there is evidence that the presence of firearms among potential victims is worrying to criminals.

> ...[S]urveys of convicted felons in America reveal that they are much more worried about armed victims than they are about running into the police. This fear of potentially armed victims causes American burglars to spend more time than their foreign counterparts 'casing' a house to ensure that nobody is home. Felons frequently comment in these interviews that they avoid late-night burglaries because "that's the way to get shot."[350]

If this survey accurately reflects the mind-set of a typical burglar, we are left with the image of a small time entrepreneur in a high risk profession who is trying to maximize profits while minimizing costs - detection, capture, injury, or death. This depiction suggests that if citizens have any likelihood of being armed, criminals, in fear of their own safety, may be less willing to risk an attack. If this is

---

[349] Weisheit, and Wells, 1996, 380.
[350] Lott and Mustard, 1997, 3.

the case, then we could arrive at the conclusion that by increasing the number of firearms to law-abiding citizens we might decrease the numbers of violent crimes.

Many criminologists assert that this effect should not be underestimated. Kleck states that robbery, burglary, and rape rates might be higher than their present levels if some citizens did not form a deterrence factor by being armed. He notes that guns can be frightening and intimidating to whoever they are aimed at, victim or criminal. Thus, he claims, guns can either help a criminal commit a crime or can help a victim avoid having that crime completed.[351]

> ...[O]ne has to take seriously the possibility that 'across-the-board' gun control measures could decease the crime-control effects of noncriminal gun ownership more than they would decrease the crime-causing effects of criminal gun ownership.[352]

6.4.3 Open and Concealed Weapons

The debate, among firearms supporters, often centers around the issue of concealed versus open weapons. People argue that if the possession of guns is a deterrent to crime, then an openly displayed gun, as in the old West, would be a visible and powerful deterrent, which could stop crime attempts before they were even initiated.

> At the moment of a perceived criminal assault, a gun could of course be drawn in a last-minute bid to defuse the situation. Bob Ross, an Arizona man who testified in favor of the Texas law [allowing handguns], described an encounter with young men armed with aluminum baseball bats outside his neighborhood video store. As the toughs approached, Mr. Ross said, he drew his gun from a shoulder holster inside his coat. "Fortunately for me and them," he told Texas lawmakers, "they jumped back 10 feet and I convinced them it was a good night for them to go home." Still, if Mr. Ross had had a gun on his hip, the episode might never have escalated to the brink of confrontation.[353]

The choice between open and concealed weapons can be seen as a tradeoff in types of deterrence. Although most policemen are strongly against guns on the street, others say that open weapons would be preferable to concealed weapons. Their preference lies in the fact that, in the case of open weapons, they would be able to tell on sight whether or not a person was armed.[354] This is not a minor issue - the life of the officer could be at stake. In other words, although they feel that the choice is one between two evils, police would choose open weapons in order to have an issue of certainty in their interactions with people.

---

[351] Kleck, 1991. 6-7.
[352] Ibid, 7.
[353] Verhovek, 8/3/95, 1.
[354] Ibid.

Police are not the only ones who desire this kind of certainty; criminals would also benefit from it. If handguns were carried openly, criminals could avoid attempting crimes against armed people. In contrast, they would be able to better target those people who did not have a weapon.

> The use of concealed handguns by some law abiding citizens may create a positive externality for others. By the very nature of these guns being concealed, criminals are unable to tell whether the victim is armed before they strike, thus raising criminals' expected costs for committing many types of crimes.[355]

By allowing concealed weapons, the criminal is rendered uncertain as to whether or not his potential prey is armed. Just as the police would prefer open weapons, in order to be prepared, in advance, for whether or not a person is armed, criminals would, arguably, like to have the same information.

If we use concealed weapons to introduce uncertainty into the situation, the positive externalities noted by Lott and Mustard may be created. In other words, if the situation is indeed one in which criminals fear armed victims, then even unarmed people will be less likely to be attacked if criminals believe that there is a possibility that they are armed.

There exists evidence that this tactic may be effective. Following a series of brutal rapes in Orlando, Florida in 1966, a large number of women bought firearms for self-defense. In order to deter accidental shootings by these newly-armed women, the local newspaper co-sponsored a weapons training course, taught by the police department. A significant number of women were trained and the program was highly publicized. In the following year, Orlando was the only city in the United States with a population greater than 100,000 to show a decrease in crime.[356]

An additional story relates the success that retail merchants in a suburb in Detroit had in reducing crime. The merchants had suffered armed robbery on average every two or three days. Following a well publicized firearms training program, the crime rate dropped substantially.[357]

One important aspect of these examples is frequently overlooked. The deterrent property of guns seems most effective in areas suffering a large number of crimes, where the probability of having to use them is high. This possibility corresponds with ideas in the previous model regarding the deterrent properties of weapons in different areas. If we can differentiate in this way, we might gain a better perspective as to when the costs (including expense and inherent dangers) of owning a weapon are compensated by the need for deterrence.[358]

---

[355] Lott and Mustard, 1997, 4.
[356] Kates, 1991, 17-18.
[357] Ibid, 18.
[358] For instance, I may not feel the need for, and may even feel inconvenienced by a weapon in Sweden, but I may feel much more secure if I have one while walking through the Bronx in New York.

Others have used variants of this argument to claim that many researchers underestimate the deterrent properties of weapons because they themselves are not generally in areas in which they have to rely on them.

> In general, the submission position literature has avoided any discussion of rape and invariably it treats robbery and assault as the once-in-a-lifetime dangers which they are (at most) for salaried white academics. It does not seem to have even occurred to any submission exponent to question whether the calculus of costs and benefits of resisting might be different for [others who live in crime prone areas]...Regrettably, for most victims crime is not the isolated happenstance it is for white male academics.[359]

The point to be taken from both arguments is that guns can have different costs and benefits to individuals depending on the circumstance. It is neither advisable nor wise to advocate that everyone be armed. Neither should one argue that guns never serve as a form of self-defense. As previously stated, all factors should be considered in different areas, in order to better evaluate the advantages and disadvantages of bearing arms.

6.5 Model

The deterrent possibilities of firearms are continually disputed in criminology literature and in the press. An intriguing question is whether or not this deterrence may be demonstrated theoretically. In an attempt to examine this question, I use a very simple model from economics, where crime is depicted as a business-like activity. In a crime, a criminal faces some average reward, R, minus the cost, C, of his action. If law-abiding citizens are unarmed with certainty, then the situation facing the criminal is

$$R-C$$

the income minus the cost. He will commit the crime if R is larger than C, in other words, if he can gain more than the cost of his "labor".

In a world with open handguns, then a criminal facing potential victims knows that a handgun owner can inflict damage D, D>R, so to rob or assault a handgun owner would give the outcome

$$-D$$

---

[359] Kates, 1991, 14.

which is less than zero. Because the losses exceed the gains, most criminals would avoid handgun owners and, instead, choose a victim who does not posses a gun.[360]

In a world with concealed handguns, the problem facing the criminal becomes more complicated. Now the criminal is unaware as to whether or not his potential victim has a gun. It could be that he will take his reward without a struggle or it could be that he will suffer damages. So, let p be the probability that the victim is armed. This leads to the expression:

$$(1-p)[R-C] + p[-D]$$

In other words, with probability p, the criminal will attack an armed citizen, and will suffer a loss, -D, and the rest of the time, the criminal will attack an unarmed citizen and will reap the rewards, R-C.

It can be shown that as p gets large, then the criminal will be unwilling to risk committing his crime, for fear of suffering larger damages than he could gain.[361] As an analogy, if the media reports the number of people in a community who have registered for and purchased guns, then the criminal becomes aware that a certain percentage of the people are armed and potentially dangerous. If, out of a community of 100 people, 65 purchase handguns, then the criminal learns that the probability of encountering an armed victim is roughly 65%.

This very simple model allows us to address both the question regarding the possibility of deterrent effects of firearms and also the relative effects of concealed versus open weapons on deterrent properties. The results suggest that firearms can serve as a deterrent to criminal activity. The model also indicates how some people's possession of handguns can provide benefits to others. If a criminal knows that some people own guns, but is unsure as to who owns them and who does not, then he or she can become less likely to risk an encounter with any potential victim for fear that that person may have a gun and be able to defend himself. Thus, the model offers support for the idea that concealed weapons may offer greater deterrent benefits than the simple use of open weapons.

The above model assumed that criminals are unarmed. If we relax this assumption, the results change only slightly. Assume instead, that criminals are armed, and that they know that with a probability p, as above, some victims are armed as well. If a criminal meets an unarmed victim, then she will take her reward with certainty. If she meets an armed victim, then in only half of the cases will she successfully complete her crime.[362] Now the situation facing the criminal is:

$$(1-p)[R-C] + p[1/2(R-C) + 1/2(-D)]$$

---

[360] Kates, 1991, refers to this phenomena as "displacement" and claims that it does not add to the social good, because crime has not been deterred, rather it has just been moved to other victims.
[361] The probability would be $p=[R-C]/[R-C+D]$.
[362] This assumption is made for simplicity and does not significantly change results.

Now the probability necessary to deter the criminal will be twice as large as in the case when the criminal was unarmed.[363] In this model, the victim's potential possession of a weapon still serves as some sort of deterrent. A weakness of this model is that it does not allow for an escalation in violence. This possibility, among other issues, is developed in the next section.

6.5.1 Reputation: The Chain Store Paradox

Another model that can be used to analyze this problem is based on the "Chain Store Paradox", a reputation model. The basic idea of this model is to show how to use uncertainty to our advantage. If a criminal is uncertain as to whether or not a person is armed and willing to fight, she may be deterred from attempting the crime. The difference between this model and the one above is that the exact probability need not be known to be a deterrent. Criminals form beliefs about the probability, based on their own or others' experiences. If potential victims develop a "reputation" for fighting crime, then deterrence can be effected with a lower level of probability than is required by the above model.

Applying the model to fit this situation, a potential victim will decide whether or not to defend himself, subject to a certain cost, and a criminal will decide whether or not to rob that person and take her reward.

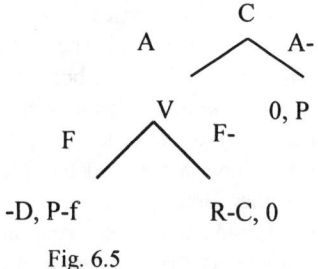

Fig. 6.5

To explain this graph, the criminal's payoffs are to the left of the victim's. Using the same notation as before, a criminal can gain nothing, 0, if she does not assault (A-) the victim, and the victim keeps his possessions, P. If the criminal assaults, (A), and the victim fights, (F), then the criminal receives -D, and the victim keeps possessions, P, minus the cost of fighting, f. If the victim does not fight, (F-), then the criminal receives R-C and the victim has nothing, 0.[364]

---

[363] The new probability is p=2[R-C]/[R-C+D]. Note that if the probability of success in armed conflict were different, it would change only the magnitude of probability of armed victims necessary.

[364] Note that this model does not include the criminal's additional strategy of fighting in response to a victim's actions. The model follows Kreps and Wilson (1982) and Selten's (1975) CSP model. Additional strategies for the criminal will be taken up later in the chapter.

If the cost of fighting, f, is large enough that P-F< 0, then it can be shown that the victim will not fight and that the criminal will always assault. However, if there exists some doubt regarding the victim's cost of fighting, then the criminal is unsure as to whether or not the victim will fight. As the doubt increases, then it can be shown that the criminal will be deterred from assault.[365]

If we examine these results in terms of concealed handguns, we see that if a victim does not possess a gun, then the cost of fighting an armed criminal is arguably larger than the gain of holding onto possessions. Knowing this fact, a criminal will be able to assault an unarmed victim with a level of impunity. If there is some chance that the victim is armed, however, then the cost of fighting decreases, and it can become in the victim's best interest to fight. In this case, it is no longer in the criminal's best interest to assault, because she stands to lose. As evidence mounts that the costs of fighting are low (if the criminal hears of armed victims from the newspaper or from criminal friends) then criminals will form beliefs that a large percentage of potential victims are armed. Thus, criminals will be less likely to risk assault.

As seen in the examples above, as well as in other cases, the results of this model are supported by empirical evidence. Research indicates that many crimes that could be deterred by guns (such as robbery, rape, burglary, or murder) have tended to decline following highly publicized incidents involving victims' gun use. These incidents include gun-training programs, cases of defensive gun use, and laws regarding household gun ownership.[366]

These models above have rest heavily on the assumption that criminals fear injury from an armed victim and would choose to avoid it. Support for the validity of this assumption comes from surveys where many inmates responded that they worry about confronting an armed victim and that they have sometimes chosen non-confrontational crimes in order to avoid this situation. Responses have also indicated that if a criminal, or a criminal's friend, has come into contact with an armed victim, then the deterrence effect can be even larger.[367]

> 56% of the felons agreed that "A criminal is not going to mess around with a victim he knows is armed with a gun" and 57% that "Most criminals are more worried about meeting an armed victim than they are about running into the police." Over 80% of the felons felt that a criminal should always try to determine whether his victim was armed, while 39% said they personally had aborted at least one crime because of the belief that the intended victim was armed and 8% said they had done so 'many' times.[368]

However, the assumption that armed victims will deter criminals need not always hold. A very legitimate worry is that if a victim draws a weapon, instead of

---

[365] For proof, see Kreps and Wilson, 1982.
[366] Kleck, 1991, 6.
[367] Kates, 1991, 19-21.
[368] Kates, 1991, 21.

deterring the criminal, an escalation in violence may ensue. As a source for further concern, surveys of felons report that almost one-quarter of the felons claimed that the possibility of an armed victim was "an exciting challenge" rather than a deterrent.[369] Furthermore, a significant number of criminals use drugs or other intoxicants while committing their crimes. A pertinent fear is that the effects of these drugs may make the criminal indifferent to the dangers of potentially armed victims.[370] If this is the case, then the above model is insufficient in that it does not account for these possibilities. Another, more sophisticated model becomes necessary.

Again, a potential victim will decide whether or not to defend himself, subject to a certain cost, and an armed criminal will decide whether or not to rob that person and take her reward. In addition, however, if the victim fights the criminal, the criminal would have to decide whether or not to fight back, and escalate the violence, E. The criminal may also choose to escalate the violence if the criminal does not fight.[371]

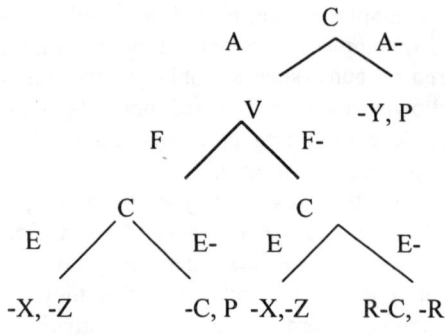

Fig. 6.6

In this case, (depending on the values given to the variables C, R, Y and X) the criminal may fear conflict or may either be indifferent to or prefer the situation in which the victim is armed and fights. If the latter is the case, we can make no theoretical judgments about the deterrent value of firearms. Here, the criminal will always attack, so whether or not it is wise for the individual victim to fight depends on the payoffs to that person, (-Z, or possible death or injury, compared to 0),. If the victim does better (has a higher payoff) by fighting, then he will fight. Otherwise he will not.

The two models suggest a situation in which criminals try to develop a reputation for having a low cost of escalating, or, in other words, they enjoy the challenge of an armed victim. This altered strategy introduces the setting of

---

[369] Kates, 1991, 21.

[370] Ibid.

[371] This occurs frequently enough to be a problem, see Kates, 1991. Some criminals harm their victims before their victims resist to prevent them from resisting later.

uncertainty both as to whether or not the victim is armed and as to whether or not the criminal enjoys confronting an armed victim. In this case, the criminal may act differently, depending on her type. The model in this case does not provide a strong argument about the deterrent nature of armed victims.

Interestingly, however, the model does not make a theoretical basis for an argument *against* armed victims either.[372] Although an armed victim would be better off facing a criminal who fears him, he may do no worse being armed, compared to unarmed, against one who enjoys a challenge.[373]

In contrast, drawing from the analysis in the Gangs chapter, it is easy to imagine a gang rule that specifies that all armed resistors must be killed, whereas unarmed resistors would be treated less harshly. In terms of the above models, the effect of this rule could create an equilibrium in which potential victims would be better-off remaining unarmed whenever they ventured into territory controlled by that particular gang. If this tactic were successful in disarming victims, then other gangs would have an incentive to adopt a similar rule. Following this pattern, it is easy to envision a situation in which victims, as a rule, would prefer to be unarmed.

The results of this model have interesting implications for the argument regarding the deterrent nature of an armed citizenry. The extreme sides of the argument do not correspond to the results found in the model. Anti-gun people would claim that a firearm will never protect a victim. Pro-gun people will assert that an armed victim will always be able to deter a criminal from committing her crime. The model suggests that the more moderate stance appears to be correct. In some cases the presence or possibility of a weapon may be a deterrent, in others, it may not be. In both cases, the presence of uncertainty - as seen in using concealed weapons - provides a larger deterrent effect than does certainty.

6.5.2 Massacres

The results of the models have interesting implications for the use of gun control when applied to massacres, such as the unfortunate 1999 Columbine, Colorado incident. Calls for more stringent gun control are usually increased following an unfortunate incident in which one person uses a firearm to kill or injure a large group of people. An example of this type of massacre can be seen in the highly publicized case in 1994, in which Colin Ferguson shot 19 people on the Long Island Railroad train. The man was so merciless that he actually stopped and reloaded his gun and then continued to shoot, before finally being stopped by some daring passengers. Although calls for gun control were understandable in this case,

---

[372] As the probability, ε, increases that a criminal prefers, or will fight an armed victim, then if the payoffs to the victim are very low (in this case, death or injury) for armed conflict, then it can be shown that, for a time, some victims will be deterred from arming themselves. Eventually, beliefs may change and victims may arm themselves again, causing the beliefs of the criminals to change, leading many to avoid attack.

[373] This claim comes from the fact that we can further extend the model to account for the possibility that the criminal will escalate violence even if the victim does not fight. If this possibility is included in the model, then the victim will be better off fighting.

the results of the model indicate that gun control might not have been the best response.

Ferguson purchased his gun legally, but he could also have purchased it illegally. Had guns been illegal, the passengers on the train would have been unarmed. (The passengers were, in fact, unarmed.) The results of the models indicate that the only time when a victim would be better off being unarmed facing a criminal is when the criminal would not escalate violence facing an unarmed target, but would escalate facing an armed one. This was clearly not the case in our example. Despite the fact that the passengers were not armed, Ferguson opened fire on them. Had at least one person been armed, he or she might have been able to shoot him and save the others. (That person would have had ample time to do so while Ferguson reloaded his gun.)

In the case of massacres, therefore, the model would indicate that instead of gun control, it would be better for potential victims to be armed. A victim would do at least as well, if not better, by being armed. This result is supported by some additional evidence. In March, 1984, in a Jerusalem cafe, three terrorists attempted to machine-gun a crowd. They were able to kill only one victim before being shot down by handgun armed Israelis.[374]

6.6 Statistics

Theoretically, the models suggest that by allowing concealed weapons, we may see a decrease in violent crimes because some criminals fear armed citizens. The notion is similar to decisions made in a business. If a business tries to determine which line of products to sell, and one line has high expected costs relative to the expected sales, then the business might be expected to dump the product in favor of one that appears favorable. Similarly, if a significant number of people are armed, then the expected cost of committing a crime will increase until it is larger than the expected benefit or gain from the crime. When this is the case, we can expect that would-be criminals will be more inclined to switch from crimes involving conflict with a potentially armed victim to either non criminal behavior or to crimes which entail a low likelihood of encountering the victim, such as property crimes.

The question is, is this theory supported by evidence? John Lott and David Mustard, among others, claim that recent data does support the idea that the use of concealed handguns can introduce a deterrent effect upon violent crime. In their "Crime, Deterrence, and the Right-To-Carry Concealed Handguns," the authors ran regressions on state and county level data to test the impact of allowing concealed handguns on all types of crime. If their results are correct, they do appear to support their claim.

In testing to see how the presence of concealed weapons laws affects the natural log of the crime rate for nine different categories of crime, the authors

---

[374] Kates, 1991, 16. "When presented to the press the next day the surviving terrorist bitterly complained that his group had not realized that Israeli civilians were armed."

found that the laws coincide with fewer murders, rapes, and aggravated assaults, but that auto theft and larceny rates increase.[375] These results appear to support the idea that concealed handgun laws coincide with a criminal's choosing to switch from conflict related crime to those with which the likelihood of conflict is lower.

According to the data, "[w]hen state concealed handgun laws went into effect in a county, murders fell by 7.65 percent, and rapes and aggravated assaults fell by 5 and 7 percent."[376] The results indicate that if all counties had had concealed handgun laws, murders in the US would have declined by 1,414.[377] The authors claim that the results also indicate that if states without concealed gun laws had instituted these laws, the number of rapes there would have declined by 4,177, the number of aggravated assaults would have declined by 60,363, and the number of robberies would have declined by 11,898.[378] However, they claim that if the states had instituted the laws, according to the results, they would have experienced an increase of approximately 247,165 property crimes.[379] It is not obvious whether the projections hold, but the data make both sides of the issue pause to examine it.

Because most economists have used state level data in statistical analysis of crime, the authors also ran the regressions using state level instead of county level data, in order to compare their results to previous ones and to their county level results. The only changes they found from the county level data were that the results showed a negative and almost always significant relationship between allowing concealed handguns and the level of crime; and that allowing concealed handguns appeared to have more of an effect on the crime rate than did the arrest rates.[380] In other words, in testing their results by using state level data, the authors found even stronger support for the claim that allowing handguns can help to reduce crime.

The authors tested their results in various ways. They checked for differential effects in high versus low crime counties and found little difference.[381] They checked to see if the handgun law affects all counties equally and found, as they had expected, that the laws have a larger effect for more populous counties. They had believed that this would be the case, because more populous counties were more likely to have restricted people's ability to carry concealed firearms prior to the laws.[382] However, by aggregating the two types of counties, in which, as argued previously, different factors may affect the level of crime, Lott and Mustard may have introduced methodological errors into the analysis.

---

[375] Lott and Mustard, 1997, 18.
[376] Ibid, 19.
[377] Ibid
[378] Ibid, 19-24.
[379] Ibid, 19.
[380] Ibid, 26. It should be noted here that, in reference to what I have argued earlier in the paper, some of these results arrive from aggregating data from rural and urban areas. Thus, the results could have errors.
[381] Ibid, 29.
[382] Ibid, 31.

The authors also tested to determine the short and long term effects of the passage of concealed handgun laws. They found that the "regression results provide consistent strong evidence that the deterrent impact of concealed handguns increases with time."[383] To provide an indication of this effect, they provide a graph similar to the following, which shows a marked decline in violent crime in the years after concealed handguns were allowed.

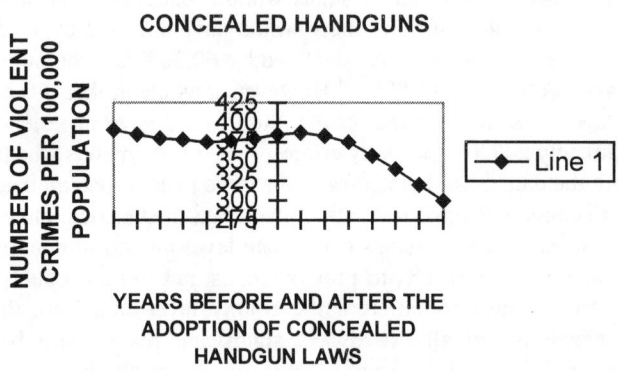

Fig. 6.7[384]

The authors also tested the effects of issues such as measurement errors, political influences, and the question of why states adopted concealed handgun laws (possibly either because crime was rising or falling in the state) among other issues. The results did not affect their conclusions.[385]

An important test to determine whether or not the reputation model above may be appropriate would be to determine whether or not the crime rate falls with an increase in the number of gun permits issued. In other words, if the criminal is reacting to the possibility/probability of encountering an armed victim, then an increase in the number of permits issued should indicate an increase in that probability. The authors were only able to obtain this type of information from three states, Arizona, Oregon, and Pennsylvania. The results from Oregon and Pennsylvania do indicate a relationship between a change in handgun permits and a

---

[383] Lott and Mustard, 1997, 35.

[384] Graph found in Lott and Mustard, 1997, 35. I am grateful to John Lott for calling it to my attention.

[385] Ibid, 39-43. Please refer to the paper for more detail and for other tests run by the authors.

change in crime. The results from Arizona imply no consistent pattern and show only a weak indication of the deterrent effect of handguns.[386]

Kates provides some evidence regarding the self defense properties of guns by citing data which claims that handgun armed individual succeeded in repelling criminals (however armed) in 83-4% of the cases.[387] Based on a survey sponsored by anti-gun groups, he states that handguns are used in defense against approximately 645,000 crimes per year.[388] These figures do have an impact upon felons. Responding to a survey conducted by the National Institute of Justice in state prisons across the United States, 34% of the convicts admitted to having been shot at, "scared off, wounded, or captured by an armed victim, and 69% knew of at least one person who had had this experience.[389]

6.6.1 Accidental Deaths

Another important concern regarding the use of handguns is whether the number of accidental deaths resulting from their use rises with the passage of concealed handgun laws or is large enough to overcome the potential benefits of owning guns. Lott and Mustard note that in 1988, the latest year for which a breakdown in accidental gun deaths is available, there were 200 accidental deaths due to handguns. Of this number, 22 accidental deaths were in states that allowed concealed handguns, and 178 were in states without these laws.[390] They claim that, given the above results regarding the numbers of murders prevented, if their results are accurate, "the net effect of allowing concealed handguns is clearly to save lives."[391] While this statement might go too far, we may be comfortable asserting that the net effect of allowing handguns is not necessarily to lose more lives.

The authors further tested to determine how the passage of concealed handgun laws affected the number of accidental deaths. The results imply that accidental deaths rose by approximately .5 percent when concealed handgun laws were passed. The results imply that passage of the laws in states that do not have them would produce less than one more death.[392] A more rigorous test, which was not attempted by the authors would have been to test the effects of the passage of concealed handgun laws on the numbers of accidental deaths over time, to see if they revealed an increase over time. Another test would be to determine whether or not the number of accidental deaths rose with an increase in permits issued.

---

[386] Ibid, 51-62. The results from Arizona may have been affected by the fact that because the change in the law was recent, the authors were unable to control for all of the variables that they controlled for in other regressions.

[387] Kates, 1991, 12.

[388] Ibid.

[389] Ibid.

[390] Lott and Mustard, 1997, 19.

[391] Ibid, 19.

[392] Ibid, 62-64.

6.6.2 Gun Control

Another appropriate test would be to determine whether or not gun control laws had any deterrent effect on various crime rates. Several groups of researchers have tried to address this question. The results are mixed, but a majority of tests arrive at the result that gun control laws have no net effect in reducing violent crime rates.[393] If these results are accurate, then this is an empirical counterexample for the idea that gun control laws prevent more crime than they allow (through the growth of the black market, lack of deterrence, etc.). Perhaps allowing weapons does have a deterrent effect on the crime rate. According to Kleck, "If gun possession among prospective victims tends to reduce violence, then reducing such gun possession is not, in and of itself, a social good."[394]

6.6.3 Summary and Problems

Despite potential problems, the results provide at least some support for the notion that allowing concealed handguns can have a deterrent effect upon violent crime. According to Lott and Mustard, the results imply that criminals are less willing to risk an encounter with a potential victim if they believe that he or she may be armed. Combining this result with their results regarding accidental deaths from handguns, the conclusion could be reached that concealed handgun laws have a net beneficial effect.

Other issues must, however, be taken into account before the above argument is embraced. The decrease in crime observed coincides with a decrease observed at the national level. Crime rates have been falling impressively, especially in America's bigger cities, such as New York and Chicago, which were previously infamous for their high rates. Throughout the U.S., serious crime has been reduced. In the cities with a population of more than one million, violent crime fell 8% in 1994. Murders fell 12% nationally in the first half of 1995, and serious crimes fell 1% to 2%. In the suburbs, felonies dropped between 4% and 5% in 1995.[395]

If crime fell nationally, and not only in counties that had passed concealed handgun laws, then perhaps other factors were involved. Some factors attributed to the decrease in crime include the hard line policies that have been adopted recently. President Clinton's program, which increases the number of policemen on the streets has been claimed to have a positive effect on the decrease in crime. Other factors include demographics, as there are fewer people in the crime prone category - males from the ages of 15-29.[396] Another potential cause in crime's decrease is the tendency of policemen to underreport crimes. (Because job security

---

[393] Please refer to Kleck, 1991, for more details about the relative strengths and weaknesses of the tests, and for the results.
[394] Kleck, 1991, 6.
[395] Lacayo, 1/15/96, 50.
[396] Ibid.

and potential promotions may be tied to the reduction of crime rates, there can be a built-in incentive to underreport.)[397]

Drugs and drug use can have a significant influence on the crime rate. Drugs are generally less expensive than they were a decade earlier. Therefore, fewer robberies need be committed to support drug habits.[398] A decrease in the use of crack cocaine could also influence the crime rate. Crack cocaine has been responsible for a large percentage of crime and violence, either through drug wars over territory or through crimes committed in order to obtain money to purchase crack.[399] Crack cocaine is extremely psychologically addictive. Crack is not as physically addictive as is heroin, but its "highs" are so intense that the user's behavior deteriorates rapidly and he or she will often resort to violence to obtain the drug.[400] A decrease in the use of this drug should have beneficial effects on the violent crime rate.

If the passage of concealed handgun laws does, in fact, result in a decrease in violent crimes, then the results must control for the above factors. Lott and Mustard do control for arrest and conviction rates, increased sentencing penalties, demographics, police employment and payroll, measures of income, unemployment insurance payments, and the price of drugs. The results, using these controls, either do not change or are improved.[401]

Finally, as noted earlier, because the dataset contained both rural and urban data, it is possible that the results suffer some methodological errors. If this is indeed the case, then some of the results found in this study would be misleading.

6.7 Implications and Suggestions

If the results are to be believed, they provide at least partial support for an argument in favor of allowing concealed handguns in order to reap the potential benefits of deterrence. As with all dangerous equipment, however, certain restrictions should be placed upon the ownership and use of firearms.

6.7.1 Training

If concealed handguns are to be allowed, training in their use should be essential. Just as people must demonstrate that they are capable of driving a car before they are issued a license, potential handgun owners must demonstrate their ability to use a handgun with skill and responsibility. The reason behind this necessity follows the same logic as that for a driver's license. Like a motor vehicle, a handgun is a potentially dangerous piece of equipment, which can greatly harm the user and others if not used correctly. Guns should be allowed to responsible individuals and owners must be trained.

---

[397] Pooley, 1/15/96, 55.
[398] *The Economist*, 1/6/96, 19.
[399] *The Economist*, 8/3/94.
[400] Ibid
[401] Lott and Mustard, 1997, 18-62.

The requirement of training is consistent with the idea behind the reputation model. If a person owns a gun, but cannot use it properly, then the likelihood of his capably defending himself against an armed and trained criminal may decrease. If, however, the potential victim is trained, then the likelihood of his defending himself will increase.

Training requirements would give law-abiding citizens an advantage over many criminals. A large number of criminals are untrained in the use of firearms. Children are given guns when they join gangs and are instructed to carry them at all times and are forbidden from losing them, but they are not trained in their use. Consequently, many are unskilled.

> Where once gangbangers could squeeze off only a handful of shots, one at a time, now they are able to take out literally dozens of enemies in a single spray. And not just the enemies: innocent bystanders too. For Curtis, the young Gangster Disciple, this is the unfortunate part. "You try to just hit your mark," he says, "but with these guns, you never know who you gonna get."[402]

If the criminals were untrained and unsure of hitting their mark, whereas the victims were trained, then the victims would have a better chance of stopping the crime. Not only would this training provide better protection, but it would also be a bigger deterrent to untrained criminals.

The above point negates the claim that training requirements are detrimental to the deterrent effect of handguns. It could be claimed that if training is required, then some people will seek black market guns, in order to avoid the requirement. If avoiding training results in a lower level of skill in firearm use, then a person is not making himself better off, in terms of a deterrent against crime, by obtaining a gun illegally.[403]

A good test of the beneficial effects of training would be to determine if there is an indication of how training can affect crime rates. If crime rates decrease to a greater extent in states that require training, then there would be some evidence that training does have some effect on the criminal's decision. Somewhat surprisingly, Lott finds that an increase in training requirements leads to an increase in crime.[404] Lott attributes this effect to the fact that an increase in requirements reduces the number of available guns either because people must wait to purchase their weapons or because they refuse to fill the requirement.

Another good test regarding a potential benefit of training would be to determine whether or not training requirements had any effect on the number of accidental deaths. Because training increases skill and ability, it appears likely that

---

[402] *The Economist*, 12/17/94, 23.

[403] In a conversation, February, 1997, John Lott mentioned that training requirements can have a beneficial effect, but if they are too long or cost too much, they can decease the benefits of deterrence by provoking some people to decide not to obtain a weapon. I am grateful to him for the conversation and for the information.

[404] Lott, 2000.

accidental deaths would decrease if training were required. If we could find supporting data for both tests, then we would have a strong argument that training requirements offer the benefits of deterrence while reducing the possibilities of accidents.

6.7.2 Waiting Periods

There are several arguments for and against mandatory waiting periods. Opponents cite cases such as the Los Angeles Riots of 1992, in which the police were unable to defend people from the rioters, and people were unable to purchase weapons on short notice to defend themselves.[405] Supporters of the laws argue that waiting periods can deter "heat of the moment" crimes, providing a necessary cooling off period. They also cite the fact that mandatory background checks of applicants, which are done during the waiting period, have blocked more than 40,000 people, criminals or others who were considered unfit, from purchasing guns.[406]

Polsby and Brennen believe that "[i]t is entirely possible that waiting period laws could result in increased numbers of *killings and non-lethal woundings*"[407] This idea rests on the assumption that every day that a person must wait to purchase a weapon is equivalent to a risk of that person being attacked and wounded or killed by a criminal. Although possible, given the falling crime rates, it does not seem likely that most people are in daily danger that requires such immediate action.

Lott and Mustard do not find that this idea is supported statistically. Using state level data, they find no statistically significant nor economically consistent relationship between the presence or length of waiting periods and crime rates. They state that the length of waiting periods does have some effect. Longer periods first lower and then raise the murder and rape rates, with the reverse being true for aggravated assaults. Although the authors give no indication why this effect might occur, the assumption that they seem to make is that an increase in crime is due to the lack of available weapons for deterrent purposes, while the decrease is due to the fact that criminals must wait for or can be denied access to firearms. Based on the results, the authors make only the statement that it would be difficult to argue that longer waiting periods have an overall beneficial effect on crime.[408]

Following the logic above, those who were aware that a background check would bar them from a legal handgun purchase, would seek alternative access to a gun. Thus, in principle, the law only applies to law-abiding citizens. One could claim that a long waiting period serves as a deterrent to some who might purchase a gun for protection, leading to a loss in the positive externalities handguns offer. That person has two options then. He could buy a gun illegally, which, if he still intends to use the gun only for protection, should result in the same amount of

---

[405] Polsby and Brennen, 1995, 6.
[406] Herbert, 4/1/95.
[407] Polsby and Brennen, 1995, 7.
[408] Lott and Mustard, 1997, 36-37.

deterrence to criminals. He could, otherwise, choose not to buy a gun at all, or to wait until the waiting period law is dropped, which entails a personal waiting period of longer than the official period.

A good means of checking the impact of waiting periods would be to determine the effect of waiting period laws on the number of handgun deaths in which people knew each other. If this rate were to fall with the implementation of waiting periods, then there would be strong grounds to argue that these laws have a beneficial impact upon "fit of rage" crime rates. The number of people saved from these laws could be compared to the numbers lost due to inabilities to purchase weapons immediately during riots or other public disturbances. Because riots are generally rare,[409] it is likely that the net effect of the laws will be beneficial.

6.7.3 Safeguards

Children all too frequently fall victim to firearms, often accidentally, through their own use or through use by friends. Recent efforts have been made by politicians both to establish a legal age at which a person can use and own a handgun and to make safety locks mandatory so that children in a home with a gun cannot accidentally shoot the gun and hurt themselves or others.[410]

Current research shows that a large proportion of gun owners do not take safety precautions. In a 1995 survey, half of all gun owners admitted that they keep their weapon in an unlocked area, and a fourth keep these unlocked guns loaded. 59% of parents who had a gun in the home admitted that they did not lock the gun away from their children.[411] This neglect leaves the weapons open to theft, accidental shootings, suicide and homicide.

Concerns arising from this neglect are not unwarranted. In 1991, 5,356 children aged 19 and under died from firearm homicide, suicide, and other firearm related deaths. Of these, unintentional deaths due to firearms totaled 551.[412] In recent years, the presence of armed children in the schools has become a problem. Security experts and law enforcement officials estimate that, of the firearms brought to schools, 80% come from the children's homes.[413] If more safety precautions were taken in the home, some of this problem could be reduced.

Although some individuals protest the intrusion of the government in this manner, these measures can help protect children and others from the dangers of weapons, and can also be an incentive for people to follow rules that they neglect, despite beliefs that they are necessary. This idea reflects the logic inherent in the collective action problem.[414] Although people may recognize that it is desirable for everyone to take steps to make firearms more safe from children or others, they themselves may be unwilling to take the extra time or expense that such action

---

[409] Polsby and Brennen, 1995, 5.
[410] Melcer, 3/4/97, 2.
[411] U.S Department of Justice, [E], 1/5/97.
[412] U.S Department of Justice, [C], 1/5/97.
[413] U.S Department of Justice[A], 1/5/97.
[414] See Olson, 1965, for more detail on the collective action problem.

entails.⁴¹⁵ Unilateral action, then, should not always be expected. Certain measures could make the problem more easy to overcome. Safety mechanisms could be mandatory with the purchase of any firearm - so that buyers do not have an incentive to avoid the expense.⁴¹⁶

6.7.4 Penalties

Kleck finds empirical support for moderate gun control, restricting access to "high risk" groups. These groups generally include: convicted criminals, mentally ill people, drug addicts, alcoholics, and minors.[417] These individuals are also those targeted by the current Brady Law. This finding is also consistent with results of the models. These people are least likely to be deterred by armed victims, nor to differentiate between resisting and non-resisting victims. They represent the most dangerous individuals when armed.

Allowing concealed handguns by law-abiding citizens does not mean that crimes committed with handguns should go unpunished. Kleck finds empirical support for the claim that some crimes are deterred by adding penalties (mandatory or discretionary) to punishments for crimes committed with a gun.[418] Lott and Mustard find, in their data, that probability of arrest can have a deterrent effect on crime.[419] There is also anecdotal evidence in support of the deterrent effect of increased penalties for crimes committed with guns. New York city police found a decrease in armed criminals following these rules.[420] Chicago police have also found that the risk of higher penalties can persuade criminals to leave their guns at home.

> "We'll arrest a whole crew and still find no guns," says Paul Jenkins, the Chicago police department's director of news affairs.[421]

Because of the dangers inherent in firearms possession, and because of the intimidating properties these weapons have, it is very important to impose strict penalties to deter gun owners from using their weapons in a negative fashion. If the penalties are imposed correctly, then it is possible for them to serve as some

---

[415] A simple analogy could be seen in pollution reduction. I may dislike pollution and may believe that we should take steps to reduce pollution, but may be resistant to the idea of purchasing a converter for, or discontinuing use of, my smog-producing car. If everyone has the same reaction, then pollution will continue or even grow.

[416] Obviously, authorities are not going to perform daily checks to ensure that these rules are obeyed. Penalties could be applied, however, to those who do not conform to the rules. If, for instance, a person is accidentally shot due to the fact that the safety measures were not used, then the gun owner could be guilty of murder. This risk could serve to provide incentives to take precautions.

[417] Kleck, 1991, 14-19.
[418] Kleck, 1991, 18-19.
[419] Lott and Mustard, 1997, 36.
[420] Pooley, 1/15/96, 56.
[421] Lacayo, 1/15/96, 53.

deterrent for the violent use of firearms.[422] If this effect is combined with the crime reducing effect of handguns in the hands of potential victims, then perhaps the net effect of guns possession by law abiding citizens can be to reduce crime.

6.7.5 Caveat

Two points should be noted. The above models provide an understanding of how concealed handguns can serve as a deterrent force against crime. If the models and the statistical evidence are correct, then we can agree that guns do indeed provide a deterrent to crime. It would be a mistake to conclude, however, that by increasing the number of guns to law-abiding citizens, we would continually decrease the level of crime. Even without the consideration of the dangers and costs of an armed citizenry, economics suggests that this plan will not succeed. The Law of Diminishing Marginal Returns claims that inputs to any particular problem contribute to a certain point, and then their contribution begins to decrease in effectiveness. If we recall the graph used by Lott and Mustard to demonstrate the deterrent effect of handguns, we may imagine that, following the law, over time this effectiveness will decline. Thus, the deterrent effects of firearms should not be overstated.

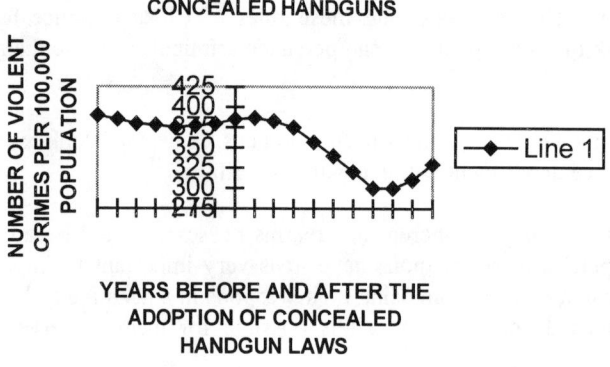

Fig. 6.8

The second point is more serious than the first. The models should not be interpreted as the final word in the issue of gun control. The models have an important drawback in that they allow the criminal only two strategies: rob the victim or not. While this model may be applicable in the short term; in the long term, it is possible that criminals can develop other strategies.

By using concealed weapons as a deterrent, we effectively increase the expected cost of crime for the criminal. We can compare this strategy to increasing

---

[422] See Chapter 1 for more detail.

the costs, for a firm, of production, or of doing business.[423] In the short run, an increase in costs can cause a firm to suspend production or to switch to another product. In the long run, the firm will invest in research and development in order to lower its costs of production for the desired product. In the same way, the criminal can be expected to find some way of reducing his or her costs in the long run. Evidence of this strategy can be seen in many criminal activities. For instance in the case of auto theft, if people lock their cars, then criminals break into the cars by picking the locks or breaking a window. To counter these actions, people have installed car alarms. These alarms slowed car theft for a while. Some criminals reacted, however, by towing the car to another location so that they could dismantle the alarm without being seen or heard.

Transferring this tendency to adjust to new settings to the handgun model, the possible conclusions can be grim. If a criminal wishes to rob an individual and fears that he or she may be armed, then he may not risk that possibility, but may choose to shoot the victim in the back to avoid the encounter and yet be able to rob the victim. This is only one potential strategy, but it should be a sobering one for handgun enthusiasts. It is unclear whether, in the long run, the net effect of concealed handguns will be deterrence or more deaths.

6.8 Conclusion

The literature regarding firearms possession is vast. The above arguments merely scratch the surface of the gun control debate. The intent in this chapter was not as much to provide an answer to the dilemma of gun control, but rather to give an example of how economic theory and game theory can be used to illustrate, and provide a mechanism for, the arguments of either side of the debate.

Based on the results of the models, the argument here tends to support the notion that the possession of firearms by law-abiding people can serve as a deterrent to crime in some cases. In making this assessment, the chapter supports gun control - i.e. the right of law-abiding individuals to own guns, provided they follow certain requirements, including waiting periods, training, and safeguards.

The chapter also argues that while guns may certainly serve as a deterrent, other crime deterrent factors must not be overlooked. These factors include, among others, the effect of social control. In their efforts to discredit each other, both sides to the gun control argument focus on extremes and overlook important aspects of crime deterrence. It may be the case that the deterrent effect of firearms is small or negligible in some areas, while very important in others. A careful consideration of all potential factors could help determine when and where firearms can serve as a deterrent to crime. In this way, the use of theoretical analysis can make a large contribution to a very emotional subject, because it allows the reader to take an

---

[423] See Chapter 1 for more detail.

abstract look at the situation and to consider compromises which might otherwise be impossible.

Chapter 7   Bibliography

Abraham, M.D., P.D.A. Cohen, R-J van Til, & M.P.S. Langemeijer. (1998): "Licit and illicit drug use in Amsterdam III. Developments in drug use 1987-1997." Amsterdam: CEDRO.

Alba, R.D., and S.F. Messner. (1995): "*Point Blank* Against Itself: Evidence and Inference About Guns, Crime, and Gun Control," *Journal of Quantitative Criminology*, 11, No. 4, December, 391-410.

Anonymous. (1997): "Working Girls: Lila: The Danger Zone," <http://slt.pobox.com/working.4.html>.

ARF Marketing Services. (1992): "Facts About: Alcohol, Other Drugs, and Driving," <http://www.arf.org/isd/pim/alc_othr.html.>

ARF Marketing Services. (1992): "Facts About: Cocaine," <http://www.arf.org/isd/pim/cocaine.html.>

ARF Marketing Services. (1992): "Facts About: LSD," <http://www.arf.org/isd/pim/facts1.html.>

Associated Press. (199?) "Charges Filed Against 5 Men In Drug Squad," *New York Times*, March 2, A18.

Associated Press. (1995): [A], "Stepdaughter dead after 'tragic' error," *Chicago Tribune*, December 13.

Associated Press. (1995): [B], "Drug use by Teen-Agers Increasing, a Study Finds," *New York Times*, December 17, A1.

Associated Press. (1996): [A], "Private prisons shackle Texas with confusion," *Chicago Tribune*, November 7, 34.

Associated Press. (1996): [B], "High court to review sexual predator law," *Chicago Tribune*, December 9, 17.

Associated Press. (1997): "4th arrest is made in California bombings," *Chicago Tribune*, February 4, 11.

Ayres, B.D. (1995): "Border War Against Drugs Is Stepped Up," *New York Times*, February 26, 26.

Bagley, B.M. (1992): "After San Antonio," *Journal of Interamerican Studies and World Affairs*, 34, Fall, 1-12.

Bayer, H. (1995): "Voice of the people: Private prisons don't measure up," *Chicago Tribune*, April 15.

Beck, A.J. (1997): "Special Report," Recidivism, U.S. Department of Justice, Office of Justice Programs, Bureau of Justice Statistics.

Becker, G.S. (1968): "Crime and Punishment: An Economics Approach," *Journal of Political Economy*, March/April, 73, 169-217.

Becker, G.S., and W.M. Landes, (Eds.) (1974): *Essays in the Economics of Crime and Punishment*, National Bureau of Economic Research, Columbia University Press, New York.

Becker, R. and A. Martin. (1996): "Gang leader found guilty of ordering rivals' killings," *Chicago Tribune*, November 15, 5.

Belluck, P. (1996): "The Youngest Ex-Cons: Facing A Difficult Road Out of Crime," *New York Times*, November 17, 1&17.

Berger, J. (1995): "Accused Serial Killer And 92 Days of Freedom," *New York Times*, April 4, B1&B2.

Berger, J. (1995): "Paroled Killer Is Suspected In 3 Deaths," *New York Times*, March 28, B1&B6.

Berger, J. (1995): "Suspect in Murders Traces Troubled Past," *New York Times*, March 29, B1&B5.

Browne, J. and V. Minichiello. (1996): "Research Directions in Male Sex Work," *Journal of Homosexuality*, 31, No. 4, 29-56.

Butterfield, F. (1995): "Crime Continues to Decline, but Experts Warn of Coming 'Storm' of Juvenile Violence," *New York Times*, November 19, 12.

Butterfield, F. (1996): "Experts on Crime Warn of a 'Ticking Time Bomb'," *New York Times*, January 6, 6.

Byrne, J. and M. Brewster. (1993) "Choosing the Future of American Corrections: Punishment or Reform?" *Federal Probation*, 57, No. 4, December, 3-9.

Califano, J.A. Jr. (1995): "It's Drugs, Stupid," *New York Times Magazine*, January 29, 40-1.

Centrum voor drugsonderzoek, CEDRO, 1997. "Drug Use Statistics," <http://www.frw.uva.nl/cedro/>

Chapman, S. (1996). "A better solution for sexual predators," *Chicago Tribune*, December 22, 19.

Chanoff, D. (1994): "Street Redeemer: James Galipeau," *The New York Times Magazine*, November 13, 44-47.

Chiem, P.X. (1996): "Calumet City cops put dent in prostitution," *Chicago Tribune*, October 28, Sec. 2, 1-2.

Clines, F.X. (1994): "A Futuristic Prison Awaits the Hard-Core 400", *New York Times*, October 17, A1&B10.

Coalition on Prostitution, (1997):"Advocating for Prostitutes' Rights Within Criminalization," Excerpted from: Recommendations Regarding Police Abuse for Commission on the Status of Women: Joint Hearing on Violence in the Workplace. <http://www.bayswan.org/COSW.html.>

Collins, J.J., R.L. Hubbard, and J.V. Rachel. (1985): "Expensive Drug Use and Illegal Income: A Test of Explanatory Hypotheses," *Criminology*, 23, November, 743-64.

Cook, P.J. (1986): "The Relationship Between Victim Resistance and Injury in Non-Commercial Robbery," *Journal of Legal Studies*, 405&407.

Cowell, A. (1995): "Zurich's Open Drug Policy Goes Into Withdrawal," *New York Times*, March 12.

Davis, N. J., (Ed.) (1993):, *Prostitution, An International Handbook on Trends, Problems, and Policies*, Greenwood Press, Westport.

Davis, S. and M. Shaffer. (1997): "Prostitution in Canada: The Invisible Menace or the Menace of Invisibility?" Sex Workers Alliance of Vancouver, Commercial Sex Information Service, Vancouver.

De Witt, K. (1995): "Crowded Jails Spur New Look At Punishment," *New York Times*, December 25, 1&8.

Dell'Angela, T. (1995): "A lesson from clearing: No area safe from gangs," *Chicago Tribune*, December 27, 1& Back page.

DiIulio, J.J. Jr. (1995): "Moral Poverty: The coming of the super-predators should Scare us into wanting to get to the root causes of crime a lot faster," *Chicago Tribune*, December 15, Sec. 1, 31.

Dillon, S. (1995): "Speed Carries Mexican Drug Dealer to the Top," *New York Times*, December 27, A6.

Downe, P.J. (1997): "Constructing a Complex of Contagion: The Perceptions of AIDS Among Working Prostitutes in Costa Rica," *Social Science and Medicine*, 44, No. 10, May, 1575-83.

Duke, S.B. (1993): "Perspective On Drugs: How Legalization Would Cut Crime," *Los Angeles Times*, December 21.

The Economist. (1994): "Drugs and crime: The wages of crack," September 3, 29-32.

The Economist. (1994): "Prostitution: Green-light areas," November 12, 73-4.

The Economist. (1994): "American Gangs: There are no children here," December 17, 21-3.

The Economist. (1994): "Columbia's Drugs Business: The Wages of Prohibition," December 24th, 1994 -January 6th, 1995, 21-4.

The Economist. (1995): "Columbia: Drug test," February 25, 46-8.

The Economist (1995): "Sentencing: Perception and reality," March 18, 58.

The Economist. (1995): "The right to carry guns: Totin' again," April 15, 26-7.

The Economist. (1996): "Will crime wave goodbye?", January 6, 19-20.

The Economist. (1996): "Prisons: The turn of the screw," January 20, 55.

The Economist. (1996): "Crime: And punishment," January 27, 25-28.

The Economist. (1997): "Young Offenders: Misunderstood," March 8, 64-5.

The Economist. (1996): "Columbia: Coca clashes," August 17, 35-6.

The Economist. (1996): "Drug dealers? What drug dealers?" October 12, 58.

The Economist. (1997): "Drugs: Addictive Justice?", March 29, 26-7.

The Economist. (1997): "Organised Crime: Streamlined for success," October 11, 29-30.

Falco, M. (1989): *Winning the Drug War. A National Strategy*, Priority Press Publications, New York.

Farley, D. (1998): "Benefit Vs. Risk: How FDA Approves New Drugs," Food and Drug Administration.

Federal Bureau of Prisons. (1997) "Quick Facts," May.

Fisher, I. (1995): "Pataki is Pressing to Ease Sentences in Some Drug Laws," *New York Times*, January 30, A1&B4.

Florida Corrections Commission. (1996): *1996 Annual Report*, "An Assessment of Florida's Privatization of State Prisons."
<http://www.dos.state.fl.us/fgils/agencies/fcc/reports/final96/private.html.>

Florida Legislature Office of Program Policy Analysis & Government Accountability. (1995): Report No. 95-12 *Review of Correctional Privatization (November)*. <http://www.state.fl.us/oppaga/corr/R95-12S.html.>

Forer, L. (1994): *A Rage to Punish: The Unintended Consequences of Mandatory Sentencing*, W. W. Norton & Company, New York.

Foucault, M. (1975): *Discipline and Punish: The Birth of the Prison*, Translated by Alan Sheridan Vintage Books, Random House, New York.

Freeman, R.B. (1996): "Why Do So Many Young American Men Commit Crimes and What Might We Do About It?", *Journal of Economic Perspectives*, 10, No. 1, Winter, 25-42.

Gavzer, B. (1995): "Life Behind Bars," *The News & Observer, Parade Magazine*, August 13, 4-7.

Gibbs, N.R. (1994): "Murder in Miniature," *Time*, September 19, 26-31.

Glass, C. (1996): "What this country needs is...Sex and drugs," *New Statesman* London; England, 4 April, 126, 24.

Greenhouse, Linda, (1997): "Likely Repeater May Stay Confined," *New York Times*, June 24, A10.

Greenwood, P.W., C. P. Rydell, A.F. Abrahamse, J.P. Caulkins, J. Chiesa, K.E. Model, and S.P. Klein, (1994): "Three Strikes and You're Out: Estimated benefits and Costs of California's New Mandatory-Sentencing Law," RAND.

Gregory, T. and A. Barnum (1996): "Aurora's gang violence fails to fade," *Chicago Tribune*, November 12, Sec. 2, 3.

Hahn, B. (1996): "U.S. study: Teens more tolerant of marijuana," *Chicago Tribune*, December 20, 18.

Hay, J. (1994): "Police Abuse of Prostitutes in San Francisco," *Gauntlet Magazine*, Issue #7, Vol. 1.

Heard, J. (1997): "Gun law heading for City Council showdown," *Chicago Tribune*, February 7, Sec. 2, 1&4.

Heineke, J.M. (1978): *Economic Models of Criminal Behavior*, North-Holland, Amsterdam.

Herbert, B. (1995): "Guns For Everyone!" *New York Times*, April 1.

Hevesi, D. (1995): "Gang Leader Details Crimes of Drug Ring," *New York Times*, March 1, Sec. 2, B1&B4.

Heymann, P.B. (1994): "Billions for New Prisons? Wait a Minute," *New York Times*, July 9.

Holmes, S.A. (1994): "The Boom in Jails is Locking Up Lots of Loot," *New York Times*, November 6, 3.

Horowitz, C. (1994): "The Dirty Secret of Cellblock 6," *New York*, October 10, 28-37.

Janofsky, M. (1995): "Baltimore Grapples With Idea of Legalizing Drugs," *New York Times*, April 20, A16.

Janofsky, M. (1995): "In Drug Fight, Police Now Take to the Highway," *New York Times*, March 5.

Johnston, L.D., P.M. O'Malley, and J.G. Bachman. (2000): "'Ecstasy' use rises sharply among teens in 2000; use of many other drugs steady, but significant declines are reported for some." University of Michigan News and Information Services: Ann Arbor, MI.

Jolin, A. (1993): "Germany," in N. J. Davis, (Ed.), *Prostitution, An International Handbook on Trends, Problems, and Policies*, Greenwood Press, Westport.

Jones, C. (1995): "Crack and Punishment: Is Race the Issue?" *New York Times*, October 25, 1&9.

Kates, D.B. Jr. (1991): "The Value of Civilian Arms Possession As Deterrent To Crime Or Defense Against Crime," *American Journal of Criminal Law*, 18.

Kiernan, L. (1997): "Children on Trial," *Chicago Tribune Magazine*, January 19, 10-18.

Kleck, G. (1986): "Crime Control Through the Use of Force in the Private Sector," draft manuscript, Florida State University School of Criminology.

Kleck, G. (1991): "Guns and Violence: A Summary of the Field," Summary of Point Blank: Guns and Violence in America, Aldine de Gruyter.

Krauss, C. (1997): "Flaw in Enforcement Allows Foreigner to Buy Gun Illegally in Florida," *New York Times*, February 25, A14.

Krauthammer, C. (1996): "What are we to do with pedophiles?" *Chicago Tribune*, December 16, 21.

Kreps, D.M. and R. Wilson. (1982): "Sequential Equilibria," *Econometrica*, 50, 863-94.

Kuntz, T. (1994): "Stone Walls Do Not a Prison Make, Shoppers," *New York Times*, November 6, 3.

Landers, A. (1997): "Sexual abuse damage can last a lifetime," *Chicago Tribune*, June 25, Sec. 5, 3.

Laycayo, R. (1994): "When Kids Go Bad," *Time*, September 19, 32-5.

Laycayo, R. (1996): "Crime: Law and Order," *Time*, January 15, 48-54.

Leigh, C. (1995): "Bad Luck at Lucky's or Caught Between the Rapists and the Police," Prostitute's Education Network. <http://www.bayswan.org/rape.html.>

Levitt, S.D. and S.A. Venkatesh. (1998): "An Economic Analysis of a Drug-Selling Gang's Finances," Working Paper 6592, National Bureau of Economic Research, June. Copyright by authors.

Logan, C.H. (1992): "Well Kept: Comparing Quality of Confinement in a Public and a Private Prison," *Journal of Criminal Law and Criminology*, 83, 577-613.

Lott, J.R. Jr. (2000): *More Guns, Less Crime*, 2nd Edition, University of Chicago Press, Chicago.

Lott, J.R. Jr., and D.B. Mustard. (1996): Editorial, *The Cincinnati Enquirer*, January 23, A8.

Lott, J.R. Jr., and D.B. Mustard. (1997): "Crime, Deterrence, and Right-to-Carry Concealed Handguns," *Journal of Legal Studies*, XXVI, January.

Madigan, C.M. (1996): "Drugs and Politics: Supply vs. Demand," *Chicago Tribune*, Perspective, Sec. 2, September 22, 1&10.

Maggies. (1997): The Toronto Prostitutes' Community Service Project. <http://www.walnet.org/csis/groups/magggies/index.html. >

Martin, A. and R. Becker (1996): "Gangbanger trials have their own rules," *Chicago Tribune*, November 17, 1&6.

Martin, A. and M. O'Connor. (1997): "Gang 'prince' stakes claim to the throne," *Chicago Tribune*, September 21, 1&12.

Marvell, and C. Moody. (2001): "The Lethal Effects of Three-Strikes Laws," *Journal of Legal Studies*, 30, 89-106.

Marx, G. (1995): "State keeps eye on track record of private firms that run prisons," *Chicago Tribune*, March 19, Sec. 2, 1&4.

McKinley, J.C. Jr. (1995): "Accounts of Calculated Cruelty in a Bronx Gang," *New York Times*, April 10, B3.

Melcer, R. (1997): "Blagojevich bill aims at handgun violence," *Chicago Tribune*, March 4, Sec. 2, 2.

Mendes, S. and M. McDonald. (1999): "Putting Severity of punishment Back in the Deterrence Package," Presented at the Sentencing and Society: An International Conference, Scotland.

Mendes, S. and M. McDonald. (2000): "Certainty, Severity and their Relative Deterrent Effects: Questioning the Role of Risk," Presented at the American Society of Criminology meeting, November, San Francisco.

Milgrom, P., D.C. North, and B.R. Weingast. (1990): "The Role of Institutions in the Revival of Trade. Part I: The Medieval Law Merchant," *Economics and Politics*.

Millett, K. (1975): *The Prostitution Papers*, Paladin Books, Herts, England, (Original, 1971.)

Miron, J.A. and J. Zwiebel. (1991): "Alcohol Consumption During Prohibition," *American Economic Review*, May, 81, 242-47.

Miron, J.A. and J. Zwiebel. (1995): "The Economic Case Against Drug Consumption," *Journal of Economic Perspectives*, Fall, 9, No. 4, 175-92.

Moffett, M. (1995): "Attention Shoppers! Paraguay's Bargains May Be Going Fast," *The Wall Street Journal*, May, 30, A1&A9.

Mydans, S. (1995): "Hispanic Gang Members Keep Strong Family Ties," *New York Times*, September 11, A1&A8.

Mydans, S. (1995) "Wheelchair Offers No Respite for Gang Member," *New York Times*, March 9, 12.

Myers, L. (1995): "Decade of Destruction: Losing a generation of youths to crack," *Chicago Tribune*, December 31, 1&6.

Myerson, R.B. (1991): *Game Theory: Analysis of Conflict*, Harvard University Press, Cambridge, Massachusetts.

National Center for Policy Analysis. (1995): "Private Prisons Succeed," Analysis based on testimony of Charles W. Thomas, Director of the Private Corrections Project, before the Subcommittee on crime of the U.S. House Committee on the Judiciary, June 8, 1995.

Navarro, M. (1995): "Columbia's Heroin Couriers: Swallowing and Smuggling," *New York Times*, November 2, A1&A12.

Navarro, M. (1996): "Marijuana Farms Are Flourishing Indoors, Producing a More Potent Drug," *New York Times*, November 24, 12.

New York Times. (1995): "Gang Members are Migrating Across the Country, a Survey Finds," *New York Times*, December 18.

Nieves, E. (1994): "A Moral Code to Live By, to Fight By and to Die By," *New York Times*, December 25, 13.

Nieves, E. (1994): "Hartford Becomes Test Case in Fighting Menace of Gangs," *New York Times*, December 26, 1&11.

Nossiter, A. (1994): "Making Hard Time Harder, States Cut Jail TV and Sports," *New York Times*, September 17, 1&11.

O'Brien, J. (1996): "Apathy on drugs is decried," *Chicago Tribune*, December 25, Sec. 2, 1&4.

O'Brien, J., M. O'Connor, and G. Papajohn. (1995): "U.S. goes behind bars to indict 39 gang leaders," *Chicago Tribune*, September 1, 1&12.

O'Connor, M. (1995): "West Side drug king 'punished'," *Chicago Tribune*, December 21, 1-2.

O'Connor, M. (1996): "Hoover files to be used against him," *Chicago Tribune*, January 4, 1&17.

O'Connor, M. (1997): "Son of Rukn leader facing prison term," *Chicago Tribune*, March 11,Sec. 2, 3.

Olson, E. (1997): "Swiss Weigh Fate of Clinics Offering Legal Heroin," *New York Times*, September 28, 3.

Olson, M. (1965): *The Logic of Collective Action: Public Goods and the Theory of Groups*, Harvard University Press, Cambridge, Massachusetts.

Olson, M. (1995): "The Devolution of Power and the Societies in Transition: Therapies for Corruption, Fragmentation, and Economic Retardation," Presented at the conference on Russian Reforms: Established Interests and Practical Alternatives, April 13-15, Moscow.

Ordeshook, P.C. (1986): *Game theory and political theory: An introduction*, Cambridge University Press, Cambridge.

Ottawa: Department of Supply and Services, (1985): "Pornography and Prostitution in Canada."

Papajohn, G. (1995): "Gang chief's new image in jeopardy," *Chicago Tribune*, September 1, 1&12.

Papajohn, G. and T. Dell'Angela. (1995): "Indictments open door for next gang," *Chicago Tribune*, September 3, 1&16.

Petersilia, J. (1999): "Alternative Sanctions: Diverting nonviolent Prisoners to Intermediate Sanctions: The Impact on Prisons Admissions and Corrections Costs," *Minimizing Harm A New Crime Policy for Modern America*, E. Rubin, (Ed.) Westview Press.

Plate, T. (1975): *Crime Pays*, Simon and Schuster, New York.

Poe, J. (1996): "New day for youngest drug offenders," *Chicago Tribune*, October 21, 1& 12.

Pollan, M. (1995): "How Pot has Grown," *The New York Times Magazine*, February 19, 31-57.

Polsby, D.D. (1995): "The False Promise of Gun Control," *Issues in Public Policy* No. 4, Northwestern University.

Polsby, D.D., and D. Brennen. (1995): "Taking Aim at Gun Control," Heartland Policy Study, Heartland Policy Institute, October 30.

Pooley, E. (1996): "One Good Apple," *Time*, January 15, 54-56.

Porter, B. (1995): "The Toughest Job In America Is Getting Tougher," *The New York Times Magazine*, November 26, Sec. 6, 42-82.

Possley, M. (1995): "Chicago gang sets up shop in Missouri town," *Chicago Tribune*, December 17, 1&12.

Possley, M. (1996): "Jury hears: 'Yummy' knew too much," *Chicago Tribune*, November 1, 1&24.

Possley, M. (1996): "Last, violent days of boy's life detailed," *Chicago Tribune*, October 30, 1&14.

Possley, M. (1997): "New law convicts a killer," *Chicago Tribune*, January 23, 1& Back page.

Prostitutes' Education Network. (1995): Statistics, "Prostitution in The United States- The Statistics," <http://www.bayswan.org/stats.html>

Prostitutes' Education Network. (1997): Statistics, "Prostitution Law Reform: Defining Terms," <http://www.bayswan.org/defining.html>

Purdy, M. (1995): "Drug Turf Is Safer as Dealers Avoid Streets," *New York Times*, January 2, 1&10.

Ramirez, A. (1994): "Privatizing America's Prisons, Slowly," *The New York Times*, August 14, Sec. 3, 1&6.

Reuter, P. (1995): "Myanmar's Heroin Habit," *New York Times,* Op-Ed, January 4, Sec. A.

Reuters. (1997): "Guns kill U.S. kids at highest rate in industrialized world," *Chicago Tribune*, February 7, 12.

Report to the Subcommittee on Crime. (1996): Committee on the Judiciary, House of Representatives, August, "Private and Public Prisons - Studies Comparing Operational Costs and/or Quality of Service," GAO/GGD-96-158.

Riddel, M. (1996): "There has been a flurry of calls this week to clear unsavoury types, such as the homeless and prostitutes, off the streets. Crass! Hypocritical!" *New Statesman,* London; England, 2 August, 125, 7.

Riordan, T. (1994): "Patents: A prison that looks like a suburb enclosed in barbed wire," *New York Times,* Business, October 3, 2.

Rubin, E. (Ed.) (1999): *Minimizing Harm: A New Crime Policy for Modern America*, Westview Press.

Rushford, Hirsch, Ford, and Adelson. (1975): "Accidental Firearm Fatalities in a Metropolitan County (1958-73)," *American Journal of Epidemiology.*

Saari-Sieberg, K. (1998): "Rational Violence: An Analysis of Corruption," Ph.D. Dissertation.

Sack, K. (1995): "Pataki Prohibits Violent Criminals From Outside Jobs," *New York Times,* January 25, A1&B5.

Sampson, R.J., S.W. Raudenbush, and F. Earls. (1997): "Neighborhoods and Violent Crime: A Multilevel Study of Collective Efficacy," *Science*, 277, August 15, 918-24.

San Francisco Task Force on Prostitution. (1996): Final Report 1996, <http://www.bayswan.org/3sumrec.html>

San Francisco Task Force on Prostitution. (1996): "A million children a year forced into prostitution," Final Report.

Schaffer, C.A. (1999): "Basic Facts About the War on Drugs," *Schaffer Online Library of Drug Policy*, <http://206.61.184.43/schaffer/library/basicfax.htm#q6.>

Schelling, T.C. (1966): *Arms and Influence*, Yale University Press, New Haven, CT.

Secter, B. and F. McRoberts. (1996): "Salvi, Durbin take no prisoners in gun-control battle," *Chicago Tribune*, October 1, Sec. 2, 6.

Seelye, K. (1995): "Two Sides in the Gun Debate Duel With Personal Stories," *New York Times*, April 1, 1&26.

Selten, R. (1975): "Reexamination of the Perfectness Concept for Equilibrium Points in Extensive Games," *International Journal of Game Theory*, 4, 25-55.

Shrage, L. (1996): "Prostitution and the Case for Decriminalization," *Dissent*, 43, Spring, 41-5.

Simon, C.P, and A.D. Witte. (1982): *Beating the System: The Underground Economy*, Auburn House Publishing Company, Boston, Massachusetts.

Smith, P. (1993): "Private Prisons: Profits of Crime," *Covert Action Quarterly*, Fall.

Special Committee on Pornography and Prostitution. (1985): (The Fraser Committee), "Pornography and Prostitution in Canada," Ottawa: Department of Supply and Services.

Steffensmeier, D. and M.D. Harer. (1993): "Bulging Prisons, and Aging U.S. Population, and the Nation's Violent Crime Rate," *Federal Probation*, 57, No. 2, June, 3-10.

Stevenson, R. (1994): "Harm Reduction, Rational Addiction, and the Optimal Prescribing of Illegal Drugs," *Contemporary Economic Policy*, 12, July, 101-8.

Stigler, G.J. (1988): *Chicago Studies in Political Economy*, University of Chicago Press, Chicago.

Stocking, B. (1995): "Crack stranglehold tightens in rural counties," *The News and Observer*, August 13, 1, 10A,&11A.

Stout, D. (1995): "Body Is Found After 6 Months And Paroled Murderer Is Suspect," *New York Times*, March 13, B5.

Sullivan, K.M. (1996): "Why the Brady Law is Constitutional," *New York Times*, December 6.

Supreme Court of the United States. (1997): "Kansas v. Hendricks," No. 95-1649. Argued December 10, 1996 -- Decided June 23, 1997, Legal Information Institute.
Terry, D. (1994): "Gangs: Machiavelli's Descendants," *New York Times*, September 18, 26.

Terry, D. (1995): "Detroit Family in the Jaws of a Monster," *New York Times*, December 4, A8.

Terry, D. (1997): "Chicago trial Could End Long Reach of Man Said to Run Gang From Jail," *New York Times*, March 23, 12

Thomas, J. and A. Martin. (1996): "Drugs turn a street upside down," *Chicago Tribune*, November 24, 1&19.

Thoumi, F. (1992): "Why the Illegal Psychoactive Drugs Industry Grew In Columbia," *Journal of Interamerican Studies and World Affairs*, 34, Fall, 37-63.

Treaster, J.B. (1994): "Beyond Probation: Breaking The Cycle of Juvenile Arrests," *New York Times*, December 29, A1&A11.

Treaster, J.B. (1995): "Minor Players, Major Penalties: The Rockefeller Drugs Laws Took Prisoners - for Life," *New York Times*, March 5, 29-30.

U.S. Department of Justice. (1996): "Crime in the United States," Federal Bureau of Investigation, Uniform Crime Reporting Press Release, October 13.

U.S. Department of Justice. (1997): [A] "Basic Facts: Guns in Our Schools," Federal Bureau of Investigation, Uniform Crime Report, January 5.

U.S. Department of Justice. (1997): [B] "Basic Facts: Homicide," Federal Bureau of Investigation, Uniform Crime Report, January 5.

U.S. Department of Justice. (1997): [C] "Basic Facts: Kids and Guns," Federal Bureau of Investigation, Uniform Crime Report, January 5.

U.S. Department of Justice. (1997): [D] "Basic Facts: The Extent of Gun Violence," Federal Bureau of Investigation, Uniform Crime Report, January 5.

U.S. Department of Justice. (1997): [E] "Basic Facts: Unintentional Shootings," Federal Bureau of Investigation, Uniform Crime Report, January 5.

U.S. Department of Justice. (1997): [F] "Three Myths Used Against Gun Control," Federal Bureau of Investigation, Uniform Crime Report, January 5.

U.S. Department of Justice. (1997): [G] "Total Number of Handgun Murders In 1994."Federal Bureau of Investigation, Uniform Crime Report, January 5.

U.S. Department of Justice. (2000): "Crime Index Trends, January through June 2000." Federal Bureau of Investigation, Uniform Crime Report, December 18

Vaksberg, A. (1991): *The Soviet Mafia: A shocking expose of organized crime in the USSR*, Translation by J. and E. Roberts, St. Martins Press, New York.

Verhovek, S. (1995): "Why Not Unconcealed Guns?" *New York Times*, September 3, 1&4.

Wackenhut Corrections Corporation Home Page. (1997): "Integrated Solutions for Corrections Challenges," <http://www.wackenhut.com.>

Wackenhut Corrections Corporation Home Page, (1997): "Staffing," <http://www.wackenhut.com.>

Walmsley, R. (2000): "World Prison Populations: an attempt at a complete list," Imprisonment today and tomorrow, 2nd Edition, D. van Zyl Smit and F. Dünkel, (Eds.) Deventer and Boston, Kluwer.

West, D. (1995): "Rape Victim Takes Spotlight And Aims It at Parole System," *New York Times*, August 25, A1&A10.

Weisheit, R.A., and L.E. Wells. (1996): "Rural Crime and Justice: Implications for Theory and Research," *Crime and Delinquency*, 42, No. 3, July, 379-97.

Wilkerson, I. (1994): [A] "Crack's Legacy of Guns and Deaths Lives On," *New York Times,* December 13, A1&B12.

Wilkerson, I. (1994): [B] "Crack Means Power and Death, to Soldiers in Street Wars," *New York Times,* December 13, B12.

Wilkerson, I. (1994): "Doing Whatever it Takes to Save a Child," *New York Times*, December 30, A1&A10.

Wolf, E., and M. Weissman. (1996): "Revising Federal Sentencing Policy: Some Consequences of Expanding Eligibility for Alternative Sanctions," *Crime and Delinquency*, No. 2, April, 192-205.

World Sex Guide. (2001): <http://www. worldsexguide.org/nv_legal.txt.html>

World Sex Guide. (1996): "The Legal Situation in Nevada," <http://www.worldsexguide.org/nv_legal.txt.html>

Wren, C.S. (1996): "Adolescent Drug Use Rose In Latest Survey From 1995," *New York Times*, December 20, A8.

Wren, C.S. (1997): "Keeping Cocaine Resilient: Low Cost and High Profit," *New York Times*, March 4, A1&A10

Zoglin, R. (1996): "Now for the Bad News: A Teenage Time Bomb," *Time,* January 15, 52-53.

Chapter 8

Index

addictive, 73, 74, 78, 97, 98, 99, 103
AIDS, 48, 50, 51, 53, 96, 166
alcohol, 53, 75, 82, 83, 84, 97, 98, 99, 100, 102, 105, 138
alliances, 107, 110, 111, 112, 123
anarchy, x, 92, 107
anonymous, 94, 102, 139
Becker, viii, 3, 6, 26, 55, 164, 170
black market, 62, 67, 68, 76, 79, 83, 85, 96, 97, 100, 101, 102, 105, 135, 136, 138, 154, 156
Brady Law, 126, 159, 175
Chain Store Paradox, xix, 146
cocaine, 32, 74, 78, 79, 81, 93, 96, 97, 98, 100, 155, 163
contracts, 42, 44, 63, 65, 66, 67, 69, 93, 94, 116, 117, 118, 119
Corrections Corporation of America, 39, 177
cost/benefit, xi, 2, 44, 95, 101, 111, 112, 113
criminalization, 47, 52, 53, 68, 72, 75, 85
Davis and Shaffer, 47, 48, 50, 53, 54, 60, 61, 63, 70, 71, 101, 165, 168
deterrent, 2, 3, 8, 18, 19, 20, 25, 29, 33, 42, 43, 59, 89, 129, 138, 141, 142, 143, 144, 146, 147, 154, 155, 156, 157, 158, 161
DiIulio, viii, 1, 165
expected cost, 6, 23, 39, 54, 55, 56, 57, 88, 89
extortionist, xiv, 21, 63, 67, 108, 118, 119, 122
Freeman, 85, 167
Holland, 54, 96, 102, 103, 104
Hoover, Larry, 13, 92, 122, 172
incapacitation, 18, 19, 21, 33
inelastic, 85, 137
institution, 18, 19, 31, 42, 67, 109, 118, 119

Kates, 126, 131, 132, 133, 134, 137, 138, 143, 144, 145, 147, 148, 150, 153, 169
Kleck, 127, 130, 131, 132, 133, 134, 142, 147, 154, 159, 169
lobbies, 44, 45
Lott and Mustard, 125, 141, 143, 150, 151, 152, 153, 154, 155, 156, 157, 159, 160, 169, 170
marijuana, 17, 75, 77, 85, 168
monopoly, 62, 67, 69, 88, 90, 92, 115
Olson, 62, 82, 83, 114, 135, 158, 172
organized crime, 61, 62, 74, 78, 89, 103, 109, 122, 176
parole, 15, 16, 19, 21
Petersilia, 4, 172
pimps, 63, 65, 66, 67, 68
Plate, 13, 172
power, x, xiv, 21, 30, 43, 48, 52, 84, 90, 91, 92, 93, 94, 109, 112, 113, 115, 123, 137
probation, 4, 11, 12, 16, 25, 42, 80
profit, 13, 35, 39, 41, 45, 59, 63, 76, 82, 86, 87, 89, 99, 104, 107, 119
prohibition, 75, 82
rational choice, ix, xii, 2, 11, 62, 82, 94, 99, 107, 108, 115, 119, 121, 138
recidivist, 10, 12, 38
rehabilitation, 1, 8, 10, 11, 12, 17, 25, 33, 37, 42, 74, 78, 79, 98, 99, 100, 101, 102, 105
retribution, 8, 9, 10, 18, 19, 25, 26, 29, 30, 31, 33, 83
self defense, 130, 131, 132, 153
Simon and Witte, 48, 49, 78, 84, 98, 172, 175
social loss, xv, 9, 10, 15, 33
Supreme Court, 18, 19, 20, 125, 131, 175

three strikes, 22
victim compensation, 26, 28, 29, 30, 31, 32
voting with one's feet, 103

Wackenhut Corporation, 37, 39, 177
Wolf and Weissman, 1, 7, 12, 21, 32, 177

Druck: Strauss Offsetdruck, Mörlenbach
Verarbeitung: Schäffer, Grünstadt